PERFORMANCE MANAGEMENT

Creating
The Conditions
For Results

by
Michael D. McMaster

Metamorphous Press
Portland, Oregon

Published by

Metamorphous Press
P.O. Box 10616
Portland, Oregon 97210

Copyright © 1986 by Michael D. McMaster
Copyright © 1994 by Michael D. Master (Foreword)
Editorial and Art Direction by Lori Stephens
Printed in the United States of America

McMaster, Michael D., 1943—
    Performance Management : creating the conditions for results / by
Michael D. McMaster.
        p.   cm.
    Includes bibliographical references
    ISBN 1-55552-041-3 (pbk.) : $18.95
    1. Management by objectives. 2. Performance. I. Title.
HD30.65.M387   1994
658.4'012—dc20   94-2566

To Charles D'Arcy Fox and his commitment to training integrity, personal value, and results.

Acknowledgements

This book would not have been possible without the support and assistance of Charles D'Arcy Fox. He was able to see the potential at times when I was wavering and has kept me on track. He took the risk of supporting someone who was virtually unknown and championed my work. His personal respect and caring for people showed up in this book. When I needed inspiration, he was there and his active participation was invaluable. This acknowledgement would not be complete without mentioning the dedication of A. G. Edwards & Sons, Inc. to training, to their employees, and to the possibilities of organization.

Two other people were instrumental in my development. The first, John Grinder, provided the communication basis for the book and worked extensively with me in my early stages of development. As co-developer of Neuro Linguistic Programming and a brilliant communicator, his influence is obvious here. The second, Werner Erhard, has been less direct but equally powerful. I discovered his work after the manuscript was written and had to go back and revise parts which were in conflict with ideas of responsibility and commitment. The application of this material has been transformed out of my relationship to Werner's work.

Up until now, I had viewed the task of editing and layout a rather ordinary job. Linda Barton and Eric Friedman of The Works in St. Louis have caused me to realize that it can be a work of art. They brought their own dedication to ensuring clarity, as well as the beauty of the books' design. Any remaining unclarity is due to my own stubborness.

Finally, I acknowledge the contribution of my wife, Marion, who supported me through the difficult parts of developing my work as well as the writing of the books. There were many times when her solid belief in me was all I had to go on.

Creating this work has deepened my relationship with everyone who was involved in it from direct collaborators to workshop participants to companies. I thank them all and wish that all of you use the material to deepen your own relationships.

Contents

Preface

Creating the Conditions for Results/Performance Management is a book about the art of achieving results. Books on management, on communication and on training abound as though these were separate subjects that could be learned, somehow, independently of each other. Actually, the word *management* derives its original meaning from the art of training horses. If you are willing to agree that management is the art of training and that communication is the art of sharing, then you would look for a book that combined these concepts into a unified approach to achieve results.

Management in fact is training through communication. "Performance Management" is a way of thinking about management as a training-communication process.

Take a moment and ask yourself, how often have the results of my plans matched the outcomes I had in mind? If you want to see your employees' results match or exceed your intentions, now's the time for you to start Mike McMaster's prescription for results, *Performance Management*.

Charles D'Arcy Fox
Corporate Vice President
A. G. Edwards and Sons, Inc.

Foreword

As I review this book from the perspective of current thinking, of work with clients over ten years, and in the context of the times, I find myself pleased that it has not become obsolete nor even particularly outdated. It is intended to be a book about management and human performance and both of these areas have, surprisingly, become even more important. Surprisingly because they always seemed important and I didn't expect them to become more so. But the business environment has become more competitive than ever and the pace of change is accelerating.

Looking backward, we can now see that the era was already beginning to change when this book was written. I did not see it then, and the few voices raised to point the way were not being listened to. The Japanese were already proving successful, but the West was taking little serious notice. Microprocessors were making old relationships to information and knowledge obsolete, but we were still using old machine age thinking to deal with the new challenges.

The management and human issues raised in this book, however, appear to be universal enough to still be applicable. What has changed, more than the content and skills, is the context in which to apply them. I wrote the book to begin to move toward a more communicative and flexible approach to managing for continually increasing performance and to get away from the consequences of the more hierarchically based MBO.

The issue is no longer MBO. The context today is, in the words of Konosuke Matsushita, "the day to day mobilization of every ounce of intelligence of all employees in the service of the firm. Only by drawing on the combined brainpower of all its employees can a firm face up to the turbulence and constraints of today's environment."

We live in an environment of a change in era. It is an evolutionary shift as large as the change from agriculture to machine or from scribe to printing press. These eras require new languages, new thinking, new structures to take advantage of them. And the old structures which used to work and support productivity now create obstacles and destroy productivity. But being both successful in the past and familiar, we do not see them as the source of our current problems. That is because we have not seen that the context has changed.

My friend, Michael Rothschild, has likened this era change to the introduction of electric motors to replace steam. The efficiencies of electric were supposed to be dramatic but in fact they were not generally realized. Factories had been designed to take advantage of large, central steam power. When electric was introduced, it was put in place of the steam but the factory design was not changed. It wasn't until about twenty years later that new factories for new industries began to realize the benefits by building flat factories with clusters of mobile machines with many small sources of power. The new power in the old house (structures) produced little of the possibility gain. We now find ourselves in similar positions with our physical organization, with our reporting and information systems, and with our communication and relationships.

To realize the gains possible from pursuing the matters in this book, your thinking and language need to take account in ways they never have before of the following:

- people have freedom of choice and do not need the job they currently have to survive
- people have higher levels of education and more access to new information than ever before
- commitment and responsibility are rising social values and organizational necessities
- information can now be made available broadly without interpretation and is required for speed
- knowledge is the new capital and those who win in the future will focus on its continual increase
- invention is a function of teams and communities more than individuals
- it is the coordination of action based on a common intention that is the engine of production.

The last shift in context that I want to mention is the most difficult. In a machine age of hierarchical structure, large groups of people at work, and an impersonal society where work has been designed to be done with only a limited amount of participation and thinking, we have dealt with the problem of individuality in ways which won't work in the microprocessor age. Management has absorbed, without being aware of it, a psychology based in a Newtonian model that has separated mind and body and left us with a core of manipulation. (There are other psychologies available, but they are not broadly known.) Our management is based in a model of "getting people to do something" so deeply that we have trouble thinking in other ways. But this model will not get us firmly into the microprocessor age.

What will replace this psychological context—and therefore the psychological language—is to begin to work with intention, commitment, and individual responsibility. If you can find a dictionary from the late 1800's, you will find a way of using words which is intentional and responsible and not concerned with internal states. It is a language which can be used in management to produce respect and results. It is a language appropriate to the concerns of organization and management. It is a language of public speaking and action.

As you might see from the preceding, the change in my own thinking has been dramatic. That is why I was pleased on reviewing my work of ten years ago to find that the seeds of my current work are obvious in the earlier work. The practices, the skills, and the intentions behind this book are still alive for me. What is missing in the book, but takes another book to put forward, is the development of a language and structure to think with that is created from the demands of organization in a new era of technology. As Joel Barker says in *The Business of Paradigms*, "When the paradigm changes, we all go back to zero."

Given that the era is just beginning, the challenge is to invent a language and way of thinking that brings commitment and individual responsibility in our public language to an organizational framework. The challenge is to create that language according to your own culture.

Our productive organizations are our greatest inventions. I continue to acknowledge all of those who are engaged in the continual process of improving them. These will be the largely unsung contributors to the future of the planet. May your years in management reap the rewards of contributing to the lives of those for whom you are responsible.

M.D.M.

Introduction

Performance Management Systems have been around for a long time under one name or another. Management by Objectives (MBO) was probably the first organized presentation of the idea. There have been dramatic advances in the fields of systems theory and communications theory since these previous works were completed. This work begins where these previous efforts left off. It is the first complete representation which incorporates these advances. The benefits of this present work have been demonstrated in the practical world at an organizational and individual level.

The first unique feature of the books in this series is that they present a complete system. That is, they meet the requirements of systems theory. They provide for all of the processes to insure continued functioning to meet the specified design needs of an organization. The nature of a complete system is that all of its part are required and depend on the operation of the others for success. Extracting and using only a part, say the Evaluation process, particularly at the behavioral level, may enhance your existing methods or results, but the power of this representation will be severely diminished if taken outside of the complete system.

"Systems" of the past have failed due to a combination of two major errors. The first is that what has been labelled a system has been merely a collection of activities and not really a system at all. The second is the lack of adequate communicators—managers—to actually accomplish what has been designed into the system. A working human system must take into account the nature of the people who compose it.

The second unique feature of this series is that the specific behaviors required to make a human system work are presented with explicit models and extensive examples. Each part of any system must function in ways which support that system. Until now, we have largely depended on the native talents of the individuals selected as managers for our results. The *system* requirements, however, are often different from the naturally occurring response of the individual manager. The required responses can be learned by managers with a minimum of time and effort by organizing behavior according to the material presented in this series.

The purpose of Book 1 is to support those who must actually make any system of management work. It provides the explicit tools for getting the job done. Many times we are left with lofty ideals and good intentions to achieve a goal without knowing how we are going to do it. The realities of our organizations fall short of our intentions due to the pain involved in getting to its realization through other people.

Communication lags behind intentions to such an extent that the cost of realization is usually higher than individuals are willing to pay. It's not that we can't get there without these communication skills. It's just that the confrontation, the effort, and struggle, the frustration and slowness which attend these efforts without a high degree of effective communication usually defeat those of us who set out on such a path. The satisfaction available in participating in creating a vision can be achieved with attention to the process of communication required to get there.

Book 1 is applicable to company presidents and first-line supervisors. Creating the conditions for growth happens primarily through face-to-face communication at all levels of an organization. This book includes dialogue, examples, and stories which can be used in any communication between people. It is a practical guide which provides the tools which are needed to make a Performance Management System functional in an organization.

The tools, however, will not be enough on their own. To hand a non-mechanical person like myself a set of plumbing tools and expect me to produce a trouble-free plumbing system would be folly. I might actually accomplish the job, but it would take an exorbitant amount of time—and the result might never be achieved. Some brief training or instruction in the particular use of each tool and an example of its application will go a long way to insuring a competent use of time and the desired end-results.

The models which have been presented as a framework in Book 3 are outlined explicitly in Book 2. This book provides a framework which achieves results. It also provides the structure and conditions to consider in developing a Performance Management System of your own. There are a minimum number of steps which must be accomplished to achieve any goal. Occam's Razor—or simple economy—suggests that the maximum requirements be the same as the minimum. You will discover that every model which actually works in producing the result covers the same basics. After considering the models presented and their development, you will be in a position to accept them as your own or begin the development of unique ones for your situation.

The third book presents the use of the communication techniques within explicit models for Planning, Coaching, and Evaluation. The models used have been presented in detail in Book 2. In Book 3, they are presented as a way of organizing behavior and sequencing events which will achieve a result. They are used as the framework for introducing the use of the communication tools. Every executive and every supervisor will find examples of how to deal with problem situations and how to create the conditions of growth in this section. They will apply whether or not you use a formal Performance Management System.

Book 4 of this series contains the theory of communication, of people, or organizations, of action which supports the rest of the material. It will interest trainers, executives, and anyone who wants to actively create the context for an organization. It provides a basis for acceptance or revision of the material in the rest of this series. It is my hope that it will assist you in the clear communication of your vision, in your ability to create a context for growth and participation which will realize the potential of all the people in your organization.

1.

The Required Communications

The Required Communications

The management process is mainly one of communication between people who can see and hear each other. Some of the communication is by telephone, computer terminal, or written memo, but the majority is face to face and verbal. The others are unique only in that they require more care over clarity and limit the non-verbal information available for use.

All effective communicators have three things in common. The first is that they *know their intended outcome.* They are clear on the results they intend to accomplish by the particular communication and what those results would look, sound, or feel like. Part of the clarity results from having no conflicting desired outcomes. The second is they have *adequate flexibility to vary their communication.* That is, if what they are doing is not moving in the desired direction, they can change what they are doing. They have different styles and techniques for approaching the same goal with different people at different times. You have all experienced the salesperson who goes through the same tape loop with every customer no matter what the response. That model is inadequate for sales and inappropriate for management. The third is an *awareness of the responses to their communication.* Being able to see and hear are major abilities of effective communicators. They can notice subtle shifts and use these as signals for varying their method of presentation or switching to eliciting verbal responses. They are responsive to the reactions of the person receiving the communication.

The material in this book is the practical "how to" for the particular

3

communication techniques which will be referenced throughout the other three books. As communication techniques, they have particular places within the management process where they are necessities for consistently positive results. They are not, however, limited by any such usage. They may be employed at any time, in any communication. The only limit to their usefulness is restrictions that you put on yourself or in areas where you don't think to use them. In sales, in personal relationships, in handling strangers' children in airports, these techniques can be used for positive results.

There is no substitute for finely tuned, sensory acuity. Each of the techniques referred to will require an ability to see and hear what is presented to you by others. We are presented with more information than we can possibly use (at a conscious level) in every face-to-face communication. Each message is given to us in a variety of ways. The power of any technique is greatest when used as responses to another person's internal states.

We are usually so concerned with our own internal states and conscious operation that we leave little of our attention for awareness of the outside world. Studies indicate that only a small fraction of the communication we receive is from the verbal portion, yet we cannot consciously notice or recall the rest of the communication we receive. Awareness of our own *responses* to a communication is not an adequate standard of meaning. We must be able to sort responses to the current words and gestures from responses to past or irrelevant situations.

Awareness of the effects of our own communication on others is the single most important part of success. Each communication is a unique experience and requires a sensitive feedback mechanism. This requires being able to see and hear what is available without putting interpretations on it before it is registered. Many of us store and have available only our interpretation of what was seen or heard and fail to discover that we are reacting to ourselves and not to other people as they are actually presenting themselves.

Really Seeing and Hearing Response Is A Great Tool

The greatest communication ability is to take in all of the communication offered by another person and to respond in an appropriate manner — appropriate by *that person's understanding of the world.* Failure to be able to respond in this way seriously reduces the ability of the recipient to actually receive our communication.

4

Intention

Before we develop the specific techniques, we should consider the organizing element of communication, the purpose of a communication — intention. Any set of techniques can be used for good purposes or bad; they can be used in appropriate places or inappropriate ones. The techniques themselves are independent of intention or value. Their effectiveness in communication, however, will be directly related to intention. For example, if I create a "double bind" for you — say, request you to say No to me when you have told me you can't say No — it will depend on my intention how you respond to me during and after that request. If I am trapping you into saying No for my benefit, you may do it, but you'll resent me later and it will affect our future dealings adversely. If I am creating a situation which provides a new learning for you in a useful context for you, then you will have a continued positive relationship with me. The techniques presented are extremely powerful when used consistently. Their long-term positive effect will be realized only with a clear intention to use them for mutually satisfactory relationships.

Management requires positive long-term relationships for its continued effectiveness. Fortunately this is in harmony with our desires as human beings. This provides the overriding intention which determines what specific techniques are appropriate at any given time. Intention has many levels. Within the framework of a positive relationship, I may decide that a certain job has to be done, that it has to be done by you, that you may need to change your responses to certain situations in order to do the job, and that I will provide the conditions for you to initiate that change. I may decide that I want your creative input, that I simply want you to receive what I say, or that no decision will be made until you have agreed to it. Any of these may describe my intention and the appropriate words and actions for me to use in the context of a communication will be determined by that intention.

The clarity of your intention will strongly influence the effectiveness of your communication. If you want to make a democratic decision *and* you want a particular result, chances are that your actions and subtle communications will produce confusion or resentment. If you want to believe that a mutually beneficial result is possible *and* think that in a particular case only one side can win, chances are the other person will feel like fighting or will feel

Having Clear Intentions Results in Effective Communication

5

manipulated. The most common example may be those meetings you attend which do not have clearly defined outcomes and the official leader does not have clear intentions. These meetings invariably end up being run by the person there who has "a bone to pick" or some other strong intention.

At the level of application of specific techniques, a strong and unambiguous intention will provide the unconscious selection mechanism. Whether to use specific or non-specific language, whether to pace or lead, whether to present or question, all these will be determined by the response of the other person in the context of your intention. Getting stuck, not knowing what to do, are generally results of internal conflicts of intention. How many times has being concerned about looking/feeling foolish kept you from doing what you later knew to be the appropriate thing? That is a conflict of intention. It doesn't happen when the original intention is clear and strong.

Framing

When you initiate a communication, particularly if you have taken the time to be clear about your intention, the other person has the disadvantage of not sharing the context which you have set for this interaction. If you are in a position of authority or have a history of unsatisfactory communication with someone, that person is likely to experience significant discomfort until he or she knows your intentions and has been satisfied regarding the context. *Framing* is the verbal process for making these intentions explicit. It allows the participants to determine what behavior is appropriate and what internal resources they are going to need for the particular interaction.

Each of us has an internal representation of what various words and situations imply. A Planning session, a meeting to solve a problem, a negotiation, an evaluation, or an informal meeting with a boss — each has a different meaning and significance for each of us. It is not apparent that these representations are different until we actually encounter a situation where the other person's behavior doesn't make sense to us. Even then, we often assume that there is "something wrong" with the other person rather than simply suspect that there is some piece of information or experience which is not shared in common.

Framing is the process of making our internal representations external. By providing some background rather than merely a label such

as "Evaluation Session," we share more of a common
Framing Is the   understanding. We can give our intention, the
Way To Make   company's intention, our feelings, the expected form
Internal Meanings   of the result, and the process we intend to use to
External   get there. Often, time constraints are important
                       considerations. Willing participation is easy to get
when it is clear what is expected. Most of us want to reduce the potential
risk by knowing the expectations and boundaries, particularly when
those who can provide rewards and punishment are involved. At any
rate, a reduction in caution and defensive behavior can be expected even
in the worst of cases.

Congruent non-verbal behavior supporting the stated intention will
go a long way toward producing the desired participation. Congruence
can be counted on when your intentions are aligned. Incongruent
behavior is a reflection of internal conflict at the level of intention. While
some of us have not learned the appropriate social gestures, voice tones,
etc. to go with particular situations, most managers have these within
the range of their normal behavior and can count on them when their
intentions are congruent.

The ultimate test for congruence will be the behavior which follows
the framing. Many intentions are stated clearly and then violated by the
behavior of the manager who had conflicting outcomes or who simply
stated what was "supposed to be said" without any true belief or
understanding. Having an explicit process for arriving at an intention
will ensure that results match intentions, that intentions are perceived
as sincere and provide the other participant with the means to assist in
arriving at the stated goal. We become equal participants in a process
which leads to a mutually understood result. (For explicit examples of
framing, see Book 2, *Planning.*)

Rapport

We all have different backgrounds, different experiences, different
abilities, and different views of the world. These differences mean that
we each see and experience the world uniquely. We operate in the
world from our own understanding — our maps of the world — and not
from what is real.

We communicate effectively only when we share some portion of our
personal, internal representations of the world. A common under-

Understanding Is Based on Real Shared Information Not Assumptions standing or agreement about the world is required as a base for further understanding. This is obvious at the level of the meaning of particular words. Dictionaries provide us with a general enough base so that if we share the English-language cultural experience we can share an approximation of meaning of words.

Being human provides some commonality; being from the same culture widens the shared areas; being from the same family widens it greatly. However, even twins have significant differences and will have unshared areas which cause disagreement and misunderstanding. As managers, we share very little with those we deal with. That poses a significant challenge to develop the awareness and flexibility to communicate with, make sense to, or get agreement in many other world views.

The first requirement of effective communication is that rapport be established. This word, virtually missing from the management vocabulary, represents an experience of a common base from which communication can begin. It is the feeling that we share some part of a map or world view or experience of living in a common world. Rapport is generally defined by descriptions of the feelings which result from it, such as trust, comfort, openness. Rapport is a relation between people, where at least one has such confidence in the other that he or she is willing to cooperate. This level of willingness stems from a feeling that that person's world is well understood.

It is not necessary to be able to identify positive feelings about another person to be in rapport. While this is the most common state in rapport, it is possible to resent or feel uncomfortable in a relationship and still be in rapport. It is possible that what makes sense in our world at a particular moment is that someone be authoritarian; and rapport would be created by that behavior. In one situation, I established a profound rapport only after saying, "I don't like the way you are acting. You make statements and then withdraw. In fact, I don't like you the way you are. And I know that there is someone inside you who is much better than that."

All of the elements which create rapport with another person are related by the fact that they are responsive to that other person. They are responses which the other person can make sense of in relation to that person's view of the world and his or her place in it. Praise and compliments will not work where the recipient doesn't experience that it is deserved. In this instance, the person may tend to feel pressured and begin to question your judgment or sincerity. Matching another's world to establish rapport may require factual "negative" comments and statements which match that person's negative internal dialogue.

Rapport is generally thought to be established by using words which indicate agreement and understanding. This normally involves the content of a conversation. That is, you need to talk "conservatively" to a conservative and "liberally" to a liberal. Or you should learn about a favorite hobby or interest so that you can "share" it. It is true that these may establish a certain commonality of world view. This is most likely to have the affect of rapport if you do, in fact, understand and have sympathy with the interest or way of being.

Consider for a moment the number of times you have been with someone who agreed with your views or had similar interests. Haven't there been times when you couldn't get away from that person fast enough? When you didn't want to cooperate with that person? Even in an event where you shared a common interest? Agreement at the level of content is the least effective level for establishing and maintaining rapport. It often imposes the choice of compromising your integrity or of losing rapport. It has the further disadvantage of requiring that you be in, and stay in, agreement, which doesn't allow for leading or change.

Rapport can be established and maintained at the level of the process of living much more easily and powerfully without requiring any compromise of integrity. Verbally this means speaking in a way which matches the way the other person understands the world. Non-verbally it means being in the world in a way that matches another's way of being. This includes posture, breathing, gesture, movement, voice tone. The ways of being in and understanding the world are the most profound aspect of our experience of the world and therefore create the maximum potential for rapport.

• Rapport Through Responsive Listening

The content of verbal communication, while the least important part of that communication in terms of rapport, can be used to increase the speed with which rapport is established. Our culture and our educational system have spent considerable time teaching us the importance of the content of our words and we are consciously aware of this area. Content, however, needs only to be received — not agreed or argued with. When I speak to you, I make

Show that the Content Is Received, Not Agreed To

9

the noises called words so that you will get a particular message. What I require as a response is an indication that you did, in fact, receive those words.

The first response to a verbal communication which will contribute to rapport is a reflection of the content. The simplest way to do that is to repeat the words that were just said. Some of the obvious complications of that technique can be reduced by prefacing the repeat with a phrase, say, "Let me see if I got this right. You just said that you think it would sound silly if you simply repeat the words that someone just said."

The next level of using content is to paraphrase what was just said. To retain its effectiveness this requires that your paraphrase in fact match the important content, contain some of the words or phrases of the original, and give an indication of the reason for repetition: "So what you're saying is that another level of sophistication is to paraphrase what was just said, making sure to match the important facts and use some of the same words." Another way of using content is to state that you understand and then expand the content in such a way that you demonstrate your receiving the original message: "Then I might say 'I see' and follow that with something like, 'When the other person hears me expand on the content, then they'll also know that I understood the message.' "

The most powerful effect will be when you can immediately demonstrate by your response that you received the message and have processed it in a way that makes sense to the sender.

To Have Rapport We Must Know that Our Messages Are Received As Sent
The risk here is that if you are wrong, it will give the opposite message. The sender will know that you didn't receive the message and will often assume that you are simply ignoring what was just said. Compare these two responses — "I don't need to consider this other stuff you just presented; I can go ahead and simply respond the way I feel." "I can respond with what seems an appropriate application and demonstrate my understanding, but I won't know for sure if I'm getting it unless I pay careful attention to the response to my statement. If I'm not sure of that response, I can fall back on some of the other techniques and maintain or even increase rapport." The first attempt misses the main points and makes me feel like I wasn't heard (read). The second response demonstrates that you got the preceding words in the way I intended them and I feel received and appropriately responded to — the optimum combination.

• *Rapport Through Vocal Matching*

All verbal communication is accompanied by at least one other expressive element: the voice. Different voice tones and inflection can
create many different meanings to the same word. "Yes," for instance,
can mean anything from an enthusiastic commitment to grudging agreement, to "Maybe," to "No." On a similar level, emphasis on different parts
of a sentence indicate different meanings. In most cases, the voice quality will be determined by unconscious factors and the verbal content will
match the conscious intention.

Verbal content refers here to the combined meaning of the words
used. The individual words selected are generally selected from the
unconscious as well. In that event, they also indicate
more than the meaning and conscious intention of
the speaker. Compare the following sentences: "I can
see we'll be in a mess if I don't get this report done
on time. I should start on it." "I sure hope this report
gets done on time or I'll hear about it from the boss.
I'd better get started." "I'll have the report done by Tuesday at two."
Which one is most likely to result in getting the report done? Which one
of those sentences would you like to hear? In what tone of voice would
you like to hear it? The fact is, we don't know, from the words, which
one will get it done. "I'd better get started," for instance, may mean,
"...but there's not much hope," or "I'm determined to get it done no matter what it takes." The choice of words does indicate approaches and attitudes which will provide clues to the internal processes of the speaker.
The last sentence, for instance, indicates someone whose intention is
focused on the job rather than internal factors or irrelevant external
pressure.

The Verbal
Content Gives
Clues to the
Meaning

Another major vocal element is the stress we put on particular
words, phrases, or sentences to highlight them from the rest of what we
are saying. In answer to a question, we will often
provide a complete answer in the form that is
expected of us but we will stress the part which is of
particular interest to us. For example, if a salesperson asks me what I like in a car, I might respond
with something like: "I look for fuel economy, a
sporty look, and safety. I also want to know that repairs will be minimal.
I like to drive a car that handles well. I need to be able to take three or
four passengers." If my voice tone was significantly different when I said

Vocal Stress
Is Another
Indication of
Intention

11

"fuel economy" and "repairs will be minimal," you may want to sell me by concentrating on those features. Don't do it without checking, though. At the time, I was shopping with my father-in-law and may have said those items for his benefit! What really turns *me* on is a car that handles well. I also used a special tone of voice for that part.

Now let's tie all of these vocal elements into rapport. Each difference in my voice and my total selection of words were generated from unconscious sources to match my intention — which may or may not have been conscious and congruent. If rapport requires an indication that the message is received and then an appropriate response, we must respond without guessing wrong about the intention. Notice that I said "without guessing wrong." We don't need to be right, we simply need to be close enough or general enough to give the experience of appropriate receiving. The words and their vocal emphasis provide the primary source for this match. Each stressed word or phrase had special significance to the speaker. By repeating those words and phrases in similar tonality or vocal style, you will indicate to the speaker that you received the message in an appropriately meaningful way.

Let's return to being the car salesperson. Had you responded by attempting to sell me a car with emphasis on the economy features, you would have failed — and never known why. Had

It's Safe To Respond to Both the Words and Vocal Emphasis

you simply responded to my tonality, you might have said, "Most of our cars are *economical* and certainly *repairs will be minimal.* We also have one which *handles especially well* and would meet your other requirements. Shall we try out the one that *handles best* (pause) or would you like to start with the *economy* models?" (All italicized words are said in the prospect's tonality and require no guesses about the meaning of that tonality.) This communication will elicit a choice from me as the prospect which matches my unconscious as well as conscious intentions. More than that, it will establish a significant state of rapport. The prospect will have the feeling that the salesperson understands the situation exactly and has responded in an appropriate manner, that is, by using terms which respond specifically to the message being sent. The salesperson has, in fact, fully respected the prospect's communication.

In reviewing the agreed goals in a Planning session, a manager can use the employee's tonality to indicate that the employee's full communication has been received. Knowing the meaning of each tonality will help in future relations, but simply responding with the same tonality will be all that is needed to significantly increase rapport. Notice that this can be done even when there is disagreement about the content or the relative importance or value of an item.

Other vocal elements include the basic patterns which are unrelated to the content but reflect the way of being of the speaker. These include phrasing, rate of speaking, pauses, type of words (slang, academic, etc.), accents, and patterns of rising or falling. Choice of words will also indicate whether the person is using visual, auditory, or kinesthetic representation internally. (See *Representational Systems* on page 22.) Being in tune with someone can literally be assisted by tuning your voice to theirs. Loudness, tightness, and source of voice (breathing) are also factors in vocally matching another person.

Matching is intended to indicate a direction rather than an absolute state. There are many times when an absolute match is impossible, too uncomfortable, or socially unacceptable. The primary goal will be met by shifting your verbal and vocal components toward the other person. This will indicate your attention, acceptance, and willingness to make an adjustment.

• Rapport Through Physical Body Matching

In any face-to-face communication, the above patterns apply to everything that can be seen as well as heard. Each gesture, posture shift, and facial expression reflect something about the being, the internal state, of a person. As with the vocal elements, each of these physical elements has a meaning which is seldom obvious. Matching them, with the accompanying words, will indicate that you received and can respond to the total communication of another human being.

We'll review here the major areas one at a time. There are far too many individual components to deal with them all. On the other hand, once you get the idea, you can discover which are most effective for you and discover new areas continuously. These are things to be aware of whenever there is another person within sight or sound.

The two major body areas are breathing and posture. Each is a significant part of our existence as living human beings. Each has developed into a normal pattern based on our way of being in the world. They are related to our physical and psychological history and have been formed and developed throughout our growth. They are also directly related to emotional states and internal changes. When you get angry, for instance, your breathing and muscle tone both change.

Anything coming from the physical and psychological history of a

human being must be unique to that human being. Although these were
developed in contact with others in the culture and
Matching so are likely to have similarity, the power of obser-
Recognizes the vation and matching lies in responding to the
Unique Quality unique, that is, to the individual. You will be re-
of Each Person sponding from your shared experience as a human
being to the uniqueness of the particular individual
at a particular time. Failing to notice these distinctions is the largest
obstacle to building rapport.

The regular breathing pattern of someone you meet is the combination of the one developed over that person's total personal history plus
the changes due to the effects of the immediate situation. A response to
this breathing rate will have immediate impact for rapport. An important part of this breathing is where and how it is taking place in the
body. The extremes are breathing deep in the belly to breathing high in
the chest.

Matching breathing rate and posture with another human being will
establish a significant level of rapport without any other elements being
added. This is a natural level of rapport which can readily be observed
in lovers and intimate friends when they are in accord. Two old friends
on a park bench will look like they are engaged in a gentle dance or, in
repose, like a mirror is between them. This is often referred to as
mirroring.

Each time the internal state of a person shifts, breathing and posture
will shift as well. By noticing and matching such a shift, you give that
person a profound message that you are responding
Responding to to each of his or her internal shifts. Your response
Another's Shifts also respects the confidential nature of another's
Recognizes Their internal processes by matching at the same level as
Internal States opposed to being, say, an intrusive mind-reader.
That person will simply get the message that you are
communicating with the intention of receiving and responding.

Another major area is the mobility of the body. Each of us has distinct
patterns to our movement. Rate, amount, area of the body, and timing
are major elements which can be matched and responded to. Extremes
are useful for considering their effect on communication. Recall two
people you have seen in conversation (one of them might have been you)
who had very different patterns of movement. One, for instance, might
have been very military in bearing. Sitting or standing with a very
straight back, gesturing only occasionally and in all other ways keeping

the body very still. The other was constantly in motion, with constant posture changes, continual gesturing with hands and head and seeming to be unable to remain in one place. In the majority of cases, at least one of the parties will seem uncomfortable and few of their conversations will last any significant amount of time. Many people report discomfort under such circumstances. Others are less aware of the difference — but you seldom see two such people in regular contact.

The major elements of posture, which is a reflection of personal physical adjustments to a way of being in the world, are the shape of the spine and resulting head position and the balance of the body related to its center line. A body which is leaning to one side presents a significantly different adjustment to a situation than one which is evenly balanced on both feet. These two elements provide powerful and immediate unconscious messages at initial contact with another person.

Another major area involved in rapport is the face. The amount, frequency, and type of expression are all reflections of the person behind the face. We continually use the individual changes and expressions to provide meaning related to words and experience. The patterns of these changes, however, indicate many things about the total experience of a person as a living being. People who smile in reaction to many things, who frown and reveal their feelings openly are not likely to be perceived favorably by ones who seldom change expression in obvious manners.

Recall someone you have seen who comes from a "tough" background. This is a person who seldom reveals any emotion by the expression on his face. Most find this individual hard

Matching Also to "read." We can assume that it made sense *to that*
Involves Changes *person,* say to be safe in the world, not to readily
in Facial reveal emotions. Or maybe you have met executives
Expression or professional people who exhibit a similar, nonexpressive style only with a different general appearance. An individual who can be "read like a book" will seldom have an easy time establishing rapport with such a person. After all, one is acting in a way which demonstrates that he or she doesn't understand the world of the more expressionless person. The way to match such a person will be to demonstrate that you have control over your expressions, most obviously by similarly controlling your expression when talking to or looking at that particular person.

The need for rapport arises from the element of relationship which is involved in all human interaction. Many management theories separate task behavior from relationship behavior. While this may have useful functions, there is never a complete separation in successful human interaction. The process level of rapport, that is, the actions which take place outside of the content of the situation, can be maintained throughout the most task-oriented activity. Further, the ability to establish rapport provides the basis for a task-oriented relationship to function. There is never too much relationship behavior going on — there is often too much of the wrong kind of relationship behavior.

With an understanding of rapport and how to establish it, we are ready to proceed to specific behaviors aimed more directly at specific results. The communications aimed at specific results will all get better results more consistently when occurring from a base of rapport. Making requests, giving orders, gathering information, accessing creativity, all use specific techniques which are far more powerful when combined with rapport.

Problem Description Statements

One of the major problems of management — and many other human relations — is one of expressing dissatisfaction with the behavior of another and obtaining a change in that behavior. This problem is frequently connected to rapport, fear of losing it, or fear of longer term negative repercussions. It is common to shy away from these confrontations — and common not to get the desired results. The other common solution to this problem is to reduce the element of relationship and aggressively demand particular behaviors. Many of us tend to fluctuate between the two extremes. The net effect of all this is far from optimal in terms of relationships or operating results.

We have just discovered how rapport can be established and maintained outside of the content of the situation. With an effective way to communicate problems, we can combine these techniques and get behavior changes without the generally anticipated catastrophes. We will consider later how to deal with the emotional flare-ups that most of us fear (and which may still take place despite our best use of the techniques presented). When you are prepared to deal with the worst, it seldom arises.

Now let's consider a method of making statements which tells another that we don't like his or her behavior and leads to changes rather than argument. (Remember that all verbal techniques assume attention to rapport as well.) A Problem Description Statement* takes a

*Early development of this concept was done with Tim Boone who supplied the name.

recurring behavior and states in it a way which indicates appropriate responses and leaves no room for counter-attack.

The statement has three parts. The first is a factual report of the performance or lack of performance of a behavior. The second is a factual report on the results of that behavior. The third is a report on the effect of that behavior on the speaker. All three parts are important elements which contribute to the total effect of the statement.

The format can be used for single occurrences of a behavior but it is generally best suited to repeated occurrences. Single occurrences can more readily be approached with an attitude of clarifying the instructions, the results expected, and the importance of the actions. Having done the above and still not improved the results, it is time for a Problem Description Statement.

Let's assume that an employee gets the monthly statements and reports into my hands later than the deadline for the third time in six months.

I might say:

> When you give the reports to me later than the deadline, I don't have time to prepare my report to the board and I don't feel confident that I can explain what's happened satisfactorily.
> *or maybe:*
> When you don't get the reports to me on time and haven't given the warning that we agreed on, I don't have time to change my managers' meeting and I can't keep the agreement I have with them to supply accurate information.

Let's look at these statements in some detail. The first part of each names a behavior which can be agreed to or not. That is, was there a specific deadline? Did you deliver on time? Did you give the adequate warning or not? These questions refer to elements which were previously made explicit and are readily verifiable and can be agreed to. There is no room for opinion or argument. The second part of the statement is an external result which can be understood by the other person and which is totally within my experience. It can contain the factual details or the affect on others. This part assumes that an employee is committed to producing the results intended by the manager. The final part puts me into the statement. The results have an impact on me and, being in a relationship with me, you care about those results. This part will often include feel-

*Making Clear
Statements
Avoids Blame
or Evaluating
Behavior*

17

ings and will always be expressions about myself — never disguised comments about you.

Many managers disguise their thoughts behind a statement which starts with "I feel." There is an assumption behind such a statement which prevents attack. That is, feelings are internal states which cannot be challenged. I cannot tell you that you don't feel something. If you say that you think it, we can make the assumption that you are using logic or being reasonable and challenge what you say. So when you say, "I feel that you didn't keep your agreement," you are expressing an opinion or asserting a fact and shielding it from potential argument.

The Problem Description Statement is worded in such a way that there is no opening for excuses or questioning the value of the behavior desired or other forms of "being reasonable." Any particular time that a behavior or result is not obtained, a reasonable explanation may be accepted. After a repeated number of times, no reasonable explanation is appropriate. Agreements to perform in specific ways, once fully understood, are commitments around which an employee may be expected to organize circumstances so that results are obtained. Excuses, reasonable or not, are statements that such commitments are not being taken seriously.

The Problem Description Statement treats excuses and reasons as irrelevant and returns to the original statement whenever such responses are received. Once acceptance of the statement is obtained, then problem-solving or other appropriate action towards behavior change may be done.

Precision Model Questions

In most interactions regarding a work situation, the manager is in the position of knowing less about the specific situation than the employee. Certainly, the manager can expect not to know some particulars which the person actually performing the work does know. In most instances, then, the manager will want to gather some information before getting very far into solving problems or making suggestions.

This process often causes the employee to feel maneuvered into a corner by the manager or seems to waste a great deal of the manager's time by letting employees tell their story in their own *Precision Model* way. Neither of these approaches produces satis- *Questions Give* factory results. The manager's questions often do not *You High-Quality* have a frame or context for the employee, and *Answers* employees listen to questions with an attitude of, "Where is this going?" or "What is the manager

18

after?" The approach of saying, "Tell me about it," also leaves the employee not knowing what information to give or how to give it and the manager's resulting impatience often results in suspicion or other negative feelings.

Framing can be used as the first step in asking questions to overcome much of this problem. The frame consists of telling the employee the purpose of the questions and any reasons for the form of the questions. *A manager might say:*

> You've mentioned the problem with the new machines. I've heard about it before but sitting in my office here, I don't have the full information. To be able to decide how to proceed, there are a few things I need to know about what has been happening. I'll have to ask you a few questions so that we can move into making a decision with some shared information.

The full questioning model and its applications to problem-solving can be found in *Precision: A New Approach to Communication.* Briefly, the set of questions to be asked follow. Notice that each question uses the words that were presented by an information source and do not guess at any content. The basis for asking a particular question is:

> Could the word be referring to something I am not aware of?
> Might it make a difference if I knew what it was?

Two Yes answers provide the indication that a question is appropriate. In any initial communication, there are bound to be some words which demand questioning based on this test. The advantage of the questioning model is that it provides short questions which demand short answers. Information is cheap with this model. A few questions can save a lot of time and trouble.

These are the specific questions:

Noun Blockbuster:	Whenever a noun might be naming more than one thing or the referrent is unknown in some way.
	(*Question:* Which *noun* specifically? "Which *disks* specifically?")
Action Blockbuster:	Whenever a verb might be referring to an action in which it is not certainly known how it is performed or what result is intended.
	(*Question:* *Verb* how specifically? "*Ruined* how specifically?")
Universal Blockbuster:	Whenever a pronoun or adjective sug-

19

gests that a whole group or class is the same or included in a situation. Common words are *all, everyone, none, only.* (*Question:* "Are there *any* exceptions?")

Comparator Blockbuster: Whenever an adjective compares one item or group to another without stating what it is compared to. Common words are *better, higher, smarter, up, increase,* and percentages are also included in this category. (*Question: Adjective* compared to what? "*Better,* compared to what?")

Boundary Crossing: Whenever a word or phrase indicates that something is impossible or something is necessary. Common words are *can't, must, have to, no way.* (*Question*: "What will happen if we do?" *or* "What stops us from doing it?")

The Precision Model Questions all require a statement to work with. Once any kind of response to a question or direct statement has been obtained, the full information which it represents can be obtained. Before the above specific questions are asked, however, the first step is usually to obtain a complete verbal thought. That is, who did what to whom? Subject, verb, object. The first question will be:

Who did that?
What did they do?
Who/what was it done to?

If a statement is made and you don't know what an appropriate response is, look for a basic missing piece of the thought which has been left out. Let's look at a problem statement and discover how the Precision Model Questions function.

A dialogue between employer and manager might go like this:

E: The trucks need repairing.
M: Need repairing how, specifically?
E: The transmissions need an overhaul.
M: Which trucks need repairing?
E: All but two of the delivery trucks are having problems.

M: What problems are they having?

E: They are getting hard to shift and they jump out of gear.

M: Do both of those happen with all of them?

E: No, only two of them jump of out gear.

M: What will happen if they aren't repaired?

E: The ones that jump out of gear are dangerous and might get into accidents. They all are annoying the drivers and making their jobs harder.

From here, the manager has high-quality information on which to base a decision, suggest some action, or request more information. By high-quality I mean that using the Precision Model Questions has provided the most specific, least ambiguous information. The response in this case might be to fix the two which jump out of gear immediately, plan a schedule for repair of the others, and direct an investigation into the significant differences between the trucks which didn't need repair and the rest.

Notice that the information-gathering took very little time and got a great deal of information. The use of the model is meant to get potentially significant answers quickly and easily in a directed manner. If you're feeling that employees might resent or otherwise resist such questioning, remember that they are done with framing and the basic rapport techniques. In this context, they will appear to be simply in the normal course of conversation around work.

A side benefit of this type of questioning when used consistently by a manager is that it will begin to train employees how to question and how to present information. Regular use will increase the quality of information which is brought to you.

Accessing Creativity

There is more to successful managing than getting the information you need and directing people in what to do. Many of us would be happy if these were done consistently well. However, most of us also seek more than that. We may be unable to get much involvement, much creativity, or much real commitment from our employees, but we never lose the realization that more of all of these ought to be possible. We also know that work would be a rewarding experience for all concerned if our people brought these qualities to their work.

Rapport and framing are needed more than ever in this area. Gathering information with a controlled model is much safer for all concerned

Rapport and Framing Are Two Ways to Engender Trust than asking for input without knowing the result beforehand — and creativity always falls into this category. To be creative, involved, and committed all involve risk. Without trust and an idea of direction, not too many people, managers or employees, are willing to engage in the desired activity. One of the most important features will be the behavior of the person requesting this type of participation. Modeling the appropriate behavior for a situation calling for creativity will be as important as any techniques used to assist the process.

The first move for creativity is away from the known. It requires creation of an expectation of the unexpected. The words you choose to elicit creative resources from others will have a major impact on the result. One of the assumptions behind such attempts is that each individual contains a rich personal history which can be re-sorted in many different ways to produce new results. Another is that there are many possible paths to a desired result and that the best will not be immediately obvious. These suggest that words should be appropriate to many possibilities and that ideas shouldn't be judged until after all that can be obtained is heard.

For accessing creativity directed at a particular result, a good job of framing is probably the most powerful technique available. Creativity

Framing Is A Powerful Way To Access Creativity requires a particular mental set or attitude which is different from the normal operating mental set. We want to expand the possibilities of thought and, at the same time, keep them within certain bounds. We also want to remove the perceived threats of stepping outside the normal boundaries which have been determined by organizational and social rules of behavior and penalties for error. The first sessions are always the hardest. After a few sessions have established a feeling of safety and success around the procedures, there will be a safer environment in which to be creative.

The language of framing should contain many words which are general and which invite multiple responses. These words access the unique individual experience of each person.

Here is an example:

> I've called this meeting to explore all of the possible ways we might solve the problem of employee motivation. When we do this kind of thing, many of the answers won't work in practice and some will seem

outrageous. Yet we want all of those suggestions too. Often some of them can be combined to produce useful answers, often an impossible idea will spark a really unique and practical solution later. In one meeting to solve a problem of paint scratches on our product, someone suggested that we stop painting it all together. This unlikely suggestion led to changing the time in manufacturing when we painted it and solved the problem.

Sometimes a particular idea will spring to your mind which you'd be embarrassed to suggest — suggest it anyway. At other times, you'll think you have the best answer and we don't need to continue — give your idea and then think of another one. Sometimes you'll want to criticize an idea that has been suggested — don't, even if it's your own. When it seems like you've run out of ideas, look over what's been suggested and see what else pops into your mind. Good, let's start with all the ideas you already have and create new ones as we go.

Another technique which can assist the flow of ideas is using the Action Blockbuster to get more possibilities by continually asking, "How else might we solve the problem?" The technique for directing creative flow without stopping it involves using this question in a structured manner. (See *Precision: A New Approach to Communication* for detailed application of this and the following idea.)

Our experiences and understandings are represented in a particular set of words once we have spoken them. These sets of words, once said, often prevent us from considering new alternatives. *Creative* For that period of time, they have a certain meaning *Problem-Solving* which prevents us from thinking about the same *Depends On* situation in new ways. One of the techniques for *Flexible Thinking* accessing creativity is to talk about problems and solutions in new words. One way is to restate a problem in a new way before trying to solve it. The problem of "How can we stop getting scratches on our plated sheets?" might be redefined as, "How can we produce plates without scratches?" Or, "How can we keep all scratches on the unplated side?"

New ways of talking about potential solutions can also produce creative ideas. A question to trigger new ways of talking and thinking about solutions is to ask, "How will that (suggestion) lead to a solution to (problem)?" In one workshop, participants were attempting to solve a problem of a liquid leaking from a jar of their product which was causing many returns and unhappy merchants. Suggestions revolved around buying new sealing equipment and changing the material or process of

23

sealing. I asked, "How would changing the lid glue solve the problem of leaking?" The answer, "It would produce a better way of sealing," led to the question, "How else might we produce a better seal?" Which led to the simple solution of wrapping cello tape around the jar lid. This temporary solution led to a turnaround in merchant and customer acceptance and lasted for over two years as an economical answer.

Representational Systems

Our experiences, our ideas, and all of our thinking is represented in our minds in particular ways. We don't have the real world inside our heads, we have maps or symbols or representations of that world. These representations include all of the experiences we have and all of the thoughts we have — and our thoughts are possible only because of our previous experiences. The information we obtain from these experiences comes through our senses. That is, we see, hear, and feel events and things from the external world. We represent or store these events in the same manner. We have the ability to recall sounds, sights, and feelings just as we experienced them and we have the ability to use these representations to store, sort, and retrieve information. The words that we use are derived from these representations.

The significance of all this is that our thinking and our communication is affected by which of the three basic representational systems we are using — visual, auditory, or kinesthetic (feeling). Although we all use all of these systems, most of us have developed a favored or most common system of representation. In this case, we can consider the particular system or combination of systems used as being the way that people think.

Our Representational Systems Give Clues to Our Internal Maps

Knowing how a person is thinking is a powerful piece of information. Matching your communication to the way a person is thinking will dramatically improve rapport and increase the ability of that person to understand what you are communicating.

There are two relatively easy ways to detect which representations a person is using. The first is by noticing the words they use, which refer to particular systems. The second is by noticing the person's eye movements. Some of the words which identify a particular system follow.

Visual	Auditory	Kinesthetic
see	hear	feel
look	listen	touch

picture	tune	rough
bright	loud	cold
imagine	say	grasp
clear	harmony	handle
color	repeat	load
focus	sound	gut reaction

It is particularly useful to notice patterns of these words and to be able to respond to them in kind. A repeated use of one group will indicate that the other person communicates best in a particular system. That person will understand and be affected most by thoughts expressed in the same system — his or her own language.

Every person has a consistent pattern of eye movements which matches the particular system he or she is thinking with. The following diagram represents the predominant pattern. A very large majority of the people you meet will follow this pattern.

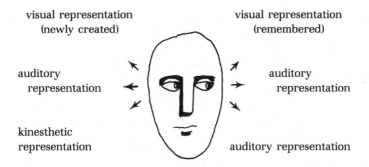

visual representation (newly created)

visual representation (remembered)

auditory representation

auditory representation

kinesthetic representation

auditory representation

This is a reference pattern which serves as a good starting place. Any individual may be different from this diagram. For instance, a left-handed person may have the sides reversed. Each person, however, will have a consistent pattern — visual, auditory, and kinesthetic will always be in the same particular places for each person.

This predominant pattern in the diagram provides an opportunity to realize the unique nature of each individual communication. We first encounter another person with a set of expectations or beliefs about what responses we should get and what they should look, sound, and act like. The other person will never totally match the previous experiences we have had with other people. Each person will provide us with a unique pattern which we can respond to in a way which discovers the individual

Learn to Respond to the Unique Meanings of Each Individual

25

meaning, or we can treat people within our existing beliefs. The most successful interaction will occur when we respond to the particular meaning and response of the unique individual we are communicating with. The diagram, like all "body language," is not a language but merely a point of reference which can provide a starting place for discovery.

The easiest use of representational systems is simply to match, in word and look, the systems that another person is using. This will be a powerful tool in establishing rapport. Another which requires more practice is to respond with appropriate sequences based on the observed patterns of an individual. Many interdepartmental disputes and instances of lack of required communication can be traced to the basic differences in the representational systems that two people use who are supposed to be in regular communication. The importance can best be demonstrated by an example of mismatched representational systems. *For instance, consider this exchange in a job interview between manager and prospect:*

> M: Let me tell you what this job is about.
> P: Good. I've been looking forward to this.
> M: Sounds like you're really interested.
> P: Yes. I can already picture myself in this position.
> M: OK. Let me tell you exactly what your responsibilities will be. (proceeds to read out a job description) Well, what do you say to that?
> P: Um. It looks all right ... um ... but I can't really see myself doing it.
> M: Listen, we both probably need to talk it over before we decide. I'll give you a call next week and let you know.
> P: OK. Let's see how it works out.

By this point, the prospective employee doesn't want the job and the manager wonders why the prospect even bothered to come for the interview. They have very little rapport and the prospect couldn't really understand what the job was about because it was presented in auditory terms while the prospect was primarily visual. How many of your own communications have followed a similar pattern?

Pacing and Leading

The techniques so far have provided a basis for establishing rapport and increasing the understanding between individuals. By themselves and used as described, they will go a long way towards improving communication and positive feeling between people in a work setting, or any other situation for that matter. In a social context, the techniques provide the basis for increased contact and rewarding interaction.

Pacing and leading refers to the technique of matching, or establishing rapport *(pacing),* and then moving in a desired direction so that the other person follows *(leading).* It is an extension of the techniques of rapport into a context of intentionality — into situations where results are valued.

Most communication in the working environment is more outcome-oriented than in personal or social relationships. The intention is to produce specific results with, or through the efforts of, others. In this setting, there often exists the power of the system within which the communication takes place and which is relied on to produce the desired results. This reliance seldom produces the quality and degree of results desired. An outcome which is made the personal outcome of all involved will produce dramatically better results than one which is merely imposed by the system.

Pacing and Leading Use Rapport With An Intention

The other major required communications besides those designed to get results are those which involve strong emotions. Many times, even when intentions have been explicitly agreed to, individuals will get into emotional states where they cease to perform the required functions. Any relationships can be expected to contain these situations and working relationships are no exception. We want to be able to deal with these situations in a way which brings the relationship and the individual back to a state which is useful for our agreed intentions.

Rapport is not enough. We all know too many managers who have good rapport with everyone who works for them but they seldom get the job done in an effective manner. We are dealing with relationships which have a common and specific purpose as their reason for being. We must be able to keep those relationships on purpose.

Individuals in highly emotional states generally do not have access to all of their normal resources. Frightened people often freeze, anxious people often are suspicious, excited people often forget important details, depressed people can't remember positive things, angry people don't see or hear very well. These states and many others need to be changed before productive relationships can proceed. Common to all of these states is that individuals who are in it can seldom produce the resources to get out of it on their own.

As indicated above, the first step is to establish rapport by pacing, or

27

matching, the other person. This requires pacing another's emotional
state without falling into it. Say the state is anger. If

Pacing Is we were to get angry too, we would end up in a
the First fight where neither of us had access to our full
Step in resources. How can you pace an angry person
Dealing With without getting angry or getting into a fight? Recall
Emotion that earlier in this book we considered matching
posture, facial expression, muscle tension, breathing
rate, and voice tone as elements of rapport. With an angry person, all
of these can be matched without getting angry oneself. An angry person's words can also be matched by saying something like, "You're really
angry at those people. You think they're really stupid. Right now, you'd
like to get even with them." Notice that the language doesn't imply agreement — only that you heard and understood. Your posture and tone of
voice will let the person know that you really understand.

The leading will occur when you move out of that match by gradually
changing your voice, posture, breathing, etc., and also introducing a new
idea or approach. For example, you might continue the above with, "I
bet you'd like to find *some* way to fix what happened. *(pause)* And we
could probably begin to do that right now. With a little thought we might
come up with a solution that will satisfy everybody." As this is being said,
the "angry" components of your voice and body will be released and
finally some of the intensity with which you are talking until you finish
the last statement in a "normal" manner. In the worst of cases, it will
take very little time if the pacing is done well. The pause will give the
other person an opportunity to continue the outburst and indicate to
you that more pacing is needed.

People at workshops regularly make comments like, "You can't yell
at employees or customers." Or, "You can't get depressed with depressed
people." You don't yell *at* people and you don't get depressed with them.
You yell with them and you match behaviors without affecting your own
internal states. Pacing is a match to communicate a message, not a state
of empathy.

Consider the earlier case of intentional communication — that is,
communication towards an outcome. Our working relationships are
such that the employees have agreed to perform a specific function
which contributes to the outcome. Any specific task, however, may produce resistance or other responses antagonistic to the desired outcome.
Pacing and leading will produce effective results in this case as well. Let's
say a particular supervisor's crew produces more than the other crews

on a regular basis. However, this supervisor also fails to hold Performance Evaluation sessions and few promotions are made from this crew, even though his manager has stated that he must have evaluations with his people.

The conversation might go like this:

S: I think those evaluation sessions are a waste of time. I talk to my people all the time and they always know where they stand. Besides, you can see by my production records that I'm doing the best job in the plant.

M: Your production records are great — no doubt about it. And I see you on the floor talking to your people more than most of the others. That's probably part of the reason your crews always do so well. They have good spirit and lots of contact with you. After working with you for a while, some of those people ought to make good supervisors.

S: Yeah, a couple of them would be pretty good. Most are just content to do what they're doing.

M: Those few can't become supervisors without getting good evaluations from you and showing that they've been developed by you to get there. Your own ratings are less than they ought to be compared to your production records. You think Evaluation sessions are a waste of time. Some of them are. And some of them help you and your employees. The company requires that each employee have an evaluation once a year — even if it's a waste of time — and you'll have to start doing it.

S: If you want me to waste my time, I guess I don't have a choice.

M: You're right. You don't have a choice about doing the evaluations and you'll probably always feel that you could be doing more productive things. *(pause)* You might be surprised to find, as you start doing them, that some of the sessions can actually be productive. It might provide an opportunity to check your assumptions about some of your employees, to let some of them know how they are appreciated, and to boost your production even further.

S: I doubt it, but I'll give it a try.

M: Good. It'll meet the company requirements and you can get the kind of results there that you get on the rest of your work. Are you willing for that to happen?

S: Yeah. As long as I'm doing it, I might as well put it to good use.

The printed dialogue here cannot convey the subtle shifts of posture and voice tone which add considerable power to the words. These shifts are

simply matched to the supervisor's voice and body
Subtle Shifts on those words which match his experience. What
Facilitate the the dialogue reveals is the way that the manager
Matching Process paces first, demonstrates understanding of the
supervisor's world, and accepts the supervisor's
experience. At no time does the manager attempt to change the supervisor's feelings or opinions — the individual experience is never denied.
The strongest suggestion is one of the possibility of change, not even the
necessity of change, except in actual behaviors.

The technique of pacing and leading is based on an approach which
suggests that you are not likely to consider my world (idea, emotion,
judgment) unless I am first willing to consider yours. I must do this by
actually modeling or demonstrating that I can be open to yours by
words, voice, and action. Once I have demonstrated my ability and
willingness to operate in your world, you are much more likely to be
open to participating in mine. Pacing and leading will create the willingness in another person to at least consider your world.

The principle involved is to accept the experience of another person
even when denying the generalizations of that person. Our opinions,
judgments, and feelings derive from our experience. When they are at-
tacked, we feel that our experience is being denied, which is an attack
on our world and being. When I maintain a position which validates
your experience, you will be willing to consider different interpretations
and generalizations.

Pacing occurs at the level of experience. Matching at this level allows
each individual to maintain personal integrity. Leading is done at the
level of generalizations from experience. There are many possible
abstractions to be made from a particular combination of experiences
and each new combination adds many more. New and different
generalizations can include experiences which previously seemed
incompatible.

Reframing

In a particular context, events appear to have a particular meaning.
From our immediate point of view, the feelings we have in response to
circumstances seem the only appropriate ones. At any moment in time,
our opinions, feelings, and beliefs can be experienced as the only sensible ones to have. Yet years, days, or even hours later they may change
and we will feel the same way about the changed opinions, feelings,
beliefs.

We are complex beings with minds which can create contexts or frameworks for understanding; in fact, which *must* create contexts to make sense of events. We change our experience by changing the context in which it occurs. Imagine being in an elevator with only one other person and that person treads squarely on your toe. Without a word to you or any indication that it matters, the person simply proceeds off the elevator. What are your thoughts and feelings? Now imagine a crowded elevator and one of the people trying to get off before the doors close treads squarely on your toe, mumbles "excuse me" and leaps past the closing doors. What are your thoughts and feelings? You think and feel differently about the event, do you not? Now imagine in the first case that you are moving toward the door at the same time but weren't paying attention to the other person who was old and moving slowly. Or in the second instance, the person who stepped on your toe is the one who was just promoted into the position you wanted. The events change again, do they not? Yet the impact on your toe and the physical pain are identical in all cases.

It is often difficult to realize, when presented in the real world with situations like the above, that we don't know much of the context and have only made it up from what seemed apparent.

We Have to Create Contexts Based on Knowledge, Not Internal States Simple reframing can often be done by making explicit more of the information surrounding events. Employees who are made aware of intentions, beliefs, external circumstances can more easily create appropriate contexts for understanding and operating in their working environments. Difficult as it often is to change the context for evaluation of events based on knowledge of the external world, we have a much harder time changing the context when it is created by our internal emotional states. In this case, most of us need help in getting out of problem situations or negative emotional states so that we can behave in appropriate ways.

As stated earlier, each behavior — and feeling and thought — is the one which makes the most sense to the "owner" in the particular context. I seldom experience myself as being wrong or my feelings as inappropriate at the moment of my reaction. Moments, or even days, later I may change that opinion. The change comes not merely from time but from the context being different. (Especially since when I'm looking back on a situation, the context is not the same as when I'm in it.)

How is it that a behavior or reaction which makes total "sense" to one person can appear so inappropriate or "unreasonable" to another? The

*Our Personal
View Changes
the World, Not
the Events*

acts, events, and objects of the external worlds are the same. We can both see and hear the same things and still have this wide split in our reactions. The only difference is our individual, private viewpoints, contexts, frameworks. This suggests the course of action to recover from such situations. As long as I can see the situation from a different perspective, I can assist you in getting out of your present reactions. In the classic scene, Tom Sawyer is whitewashing the fence and Ben and the others come by on their way to swimming and end up paying for the privilege of whitewashing the fence. When the others call it work, Tom says, "Well, I don't see why I oughtn't to like it. Does a boy get a chance to whitewash a fence every day?" *That put the thing in a whole new light.* He changed the entire personal significance of the event.

Let's consider a few more examples before we consider how to master the technique. One situation that is common is where someone who has to deal with the public regularly gets annoyed at the "stupid" things people say and do or the "unrealistic" things they ask for. Telephone operators, airline attendants, waitresses, sales clerks, customer-service departments — all are famous for behaviors which are contrary to their supposed function. Customers are afraid to approach them or leave feeling worse than when they arrived. In the context of the customer service person, the customer is stupid or unreasonable. The employee, who deals day in and day out with the events in question, knows all of the rules, considerations, and possibilities. They quickly forget that the customer may have never flown before, may not know that an operator has only a few seconds to handle each call, that company policy prohibits certain actions, that most of the rules have a sound basis in experience.

Managers of these departments know how hard it is for employees to remain pleasantly in contact with customers consistently. Yet the situation persists. Telling employees what their job requires, say, courtesy, or pointing out that "the customer is always right" seldom has a lasting impact. How can the situation be reframed? One method is by pointing out the above differences and then restating that part of the job is to "provide an introductory course on being a customer." You see, this poor customer, lacking the experience or inside knowledge of the employee, doesn't yet know how to be a good customer. They must be trained with the respect due to any voluntary, beginning student!

Any "problem" can be "an opportunity for change." Any job can be "a boring task" or "part of a grand project." The person who changes tires at Indianapolis doesn't experience it as "a menial task." The hod carrier can say he is "carrying bricks" or he can say "I'm building a church." A manager can "make sure people do what they're supposed to" or can "support them in reaching their goals."

A manager who can't handle other people's anger or "negative" emotion is unlikely to do a good job in her one-to-one communications — particularly in Evaluation sessions. One such manager had an employee from a family background where everyone yelled at each other. The manager would always withdraw in these encouters and "win" through silence and superior position. The situation has turned around by having the manager treat each session as a training situation to try out various techniques related to rapport and pacing and leading and simply to discover what happened. Some sessions worked better than others but all worked immensely better than the earlier ones had. Both are now much more effective with each other and have a good working relationship, if with more volume than most.

The technique involves stepping outside of the context which is limiting the potential responses. This is easiest to do if the limits are not
Reframing Is the   your own. If an employee's behavior appears inap-
Verbal Way to   propriate, ask yourself, "In what context does that
Pace and Lead   behavior make sense?" and then, "What is the
                                      context which would make sense to that person and
produce an appropriate response?" You may have noticed the similarities to pacing and leading in this discussion. Reframing is a verbal technique of pacing and leading.

Metaphor

One of the difficulties of changing the context for someone else is that it requires adequate pacing before it is likely to be accepted. Simply suggesting that a situation be viewed differently will seldom produce the desired results. Remember, at the time, your reaction seems the best possible response to you no matter how inappropriate it seems to me.

That reminds me of a story. A sales trainer needed to be "harder" on the trainees. In particular, she had to be willing to raise her voice and be rude to trainees in the role-plays. She was a quiet and polite person and previous advice along this line had produced no noticeable change in behavior. One day at a break, I told her about a friend of mine who had grown up in a very strict home where people never raised their voices. He told me that he had been determined that his own child would have a different kind of upbringing and so he was very permissive and often even allowed the "rules" he made to be broken.

When the child got older, however, she had no friends because she didn't know how to make the required adjustments to other people. My friend also noticed that as time went on, both he and his wife were getting less pleasure from her existence and were expressing their love for her less frequently and less sincerely. The little girl was also becoming less happy and lively and increasingly harder to get along with. After talking with a wise friend, they both decided that the little girl needed some rules and, even more, would have to learn to respond better to other people.

Knowing that *"you can't explain things like this* to a little girl — usually you can't even explain to adults how to change their reaction to people — so you help her in *the only possible way,"* they made a short list of rules and enforced them very strictly. They also began to notice their own reactions to certain unpleasant behaviors and to give the child an immediate response which was a short, blunt expression of dislike. They also allowed their annoyance, anger, and frustration to show on their faces and sound in their voices. (Of course, they also let their love and appreciation show, in the same way.) As my friend put it, "You show real reactions so they can learn."

After a few initial reactions of surprise and unhappiness, the little girl quickly adjusted her behavior to the new circumstances. My friend reported to me that in a few weeks she had a number of new friends and the last time I saw her she was a delight to be with. We talked for a while about other children we knew and then went back to our offices.

The actual story was a bit longer and there were a few more bits like those in quotes which were said with a special emphasis, but that was essentially it. The sales trainer began to give trainees more realistic situations to respond to on training calls and is now doing a job which the trainees appreciate.

A metaphor is any story, from a true episode to a fairy tale, which captures the interest of the listener and makes a point about a particular situation. It is a teaching tale which relates to the *Metaphors* listener's life and suggests a new way of looking at or *Present a New* thinking about an event or condition. It provides a *Way of Thinking* gentle and respectful vehicle for allowing people to *and Seeing* look at situations, ideas, and other people freshly without seriously disturbing their conscious beliefs. I once worked with a man who seldom told me how to do a job. He would

34

tell me when my results weren't satisfactory and tell me when they exceeded the standards — not an easy job in a management position. While I can't remember any specific instruction being given by him, I remember the many times he would tell me about different bosses he had had and the different difficulties he had overcome during his career. As I look back at that time, I realize that I formed most of my current business philosophy then and it has served me well. It was also learned in a form which allowed for reconsideration and change as I found myself in different circumstances.

A metaphor, or a series if required, are best told as stories or remembrances and then moved on from. The great temptation to explain a metaphor will usually reduce its impact. Whenever we hear a story which holds our interest at all, we are actively engaged in making sense of it within the context of our own lives. By the time the metaphor is finished, we are just beginning to relate it in some way to ourselves. To have it "explained" right at that moment is an insult to our intelligence and intrusive in the process which is going on. We will frequently start to react to the advice or "explanation," often negatively, and cease to work on the relevance of the metaphor.

For some, metaphor is a common way of communicating. For those who don't find it a natural part of their conversation, particularly in a work setting, a little homework will go a long way. Time spent thinking about a metaphor which might reframe a situation for another will produce a story which can be effective and will be told in a way which gets the message across. Metaphors require patience in preparation, telling, and waiting for the response. But, while you're waiting, you can always be thinking of, or even telling, the next one. I once knew a psychiatrist whose clients made wonderful lasting progress when all he ever did with them was tell stories.

The best metaphors are usually real-life stories adjusted to fit the circumstances. These tend to have more reality for us and more emotional impact. The art of using metaphors can be refined for the rest of your life to your great benefit. The simplest and most basic will be very useful indeed.

Anchoring

A metaphor sometimes seems to have the desired effect and then the results seem to fade. In fact, the impact of effective communication often seems to diminish over time until the changed behavior reverts to its original position. Much of our communication is attempting to change a complex system — a human being — and any single communication will seldom take care of all of the needs of that system. This makes it seem like even immediately effective communication is not worth the effort: It needs to be continually repeated.

Much of our communication is sent and received outside of our conscious awareness. This is particularly true of metaphors. They are designed to bypass the normal critical facilities of the listener. A metaphor which is obvious to conscious awareness will generally be rejected without effect unless the listener is already receptive to the idea.

Let's consider our own responses to communication for a moment. There are people, situations, words, and objects which cause shifts in our emotions and thoughts regularly. Some of these seem to be automatic. Think for a moment about which ones of these make you feel good; which people, situations, words, and objects just automatically bring on a good feeling. Which ones can give you a lift without any particular effort?

You may have noticed that just thinking about these things gave you a little lift. Your own words can provide changes in mood as effectively as any of these things or people. Many of you have *We All Keep* some person or situation which you have arranged *Objects Which* to be available to give you that positive feeling. *Trigger Good* A picture on your desk or wall, an object which *Feelings* reminds you of a success or pleasure, a room where you can go, a person to call, a particular chair to sit in — even a set of words you repeat to yourself or a gesture you make — any of these can serve to bring back positive feelings and thoughts when you are feeling the need for them.

Some of you may have noticed how the routines you used to go through to feel better have been abbreviated. Once you may have gone to a special room or place and looked at pictures on the wall and remembered certain events. Now you just need to think of going to that room and your mood changes. Maybe you used to call a certain person and now you just picture that person's face. Maybe you said a set of words, now, as soon as you set yourself to do that, you feel better already.

The power of all of these relates to our mind's way of associating. Every event is stored in our minds in full detail. That means that when you look at a picture, it reminds you of all of the feelings, sounds, and surroundings of when it was taken, or of when you received it. And the next time you look at it it also reminds you of all of the feelings and surroundings of the last time you looked at it. After a time, if all of the strong emotions around an object, person, situation, words, gesture, etc. are positive, any recall or reminder will also bring forth those positive feelings.

Often we are more aware of the negative feelings in these kind of things. There are few people who can't think of an object, situation, person, or even words which automatically produce negative feelings. From anger to fear to depression, most of us have triggers which will seem to set us off uncontrollably in ways that we would rather not happen. The same principle is operating. The negative is stronger in the automatic mode because the mechanism is one of survival — it tells us we had better react a certain way to ensure our survival. And it doesn't give us a choice of thinking about it. When we are aware of this mechanism, we can also use it for positive feelings and controlled effects.

The specific object, person, word, or situation, which can recall the specific internal state, we call an *anchor.* It is the hook which is attached

Anchors Will Bring Back Positive, or Negative, Responses
to a string of feelings and thoughts. Each recall of an anchor, whether conscious or not, will recall the internal states associated with it. The anchor may be a gesture which goes unnoticed but has the same effect as if done on purpose. The anchor may be an object which you unconsciously look at when you begin to feel angry and which you aren't aware of

seeing — but it has the desired effect.

In fact, we are surrounded by anchors and continually use them in our speech and gestures. A group of managers from the same company reported on how they each knew the moment they saw their boss whether he was angry or not by his characteristic look and posture in that mood. As they thought about it, they began to remember the last few times they had reacted even though it had not been directed at them. It was apparent just in watching them recall that they were again feeling those same feelings they had as the recipients of that anger. Then we set it in a context where we could laugh at the reactions they displayed to an anger which wasn't directed at them and wasn't even present at the time — and anchored that to the look of their boss. They went back to work and didn't have to respond to the angry looks of their boss in the same old ways. (Don't worry, when this particular boss got angry at them, they had plenty of time to react in an "appropriate" manner.)

37

The consistent use of anchors will produce powerful results. We have our own in existence and can create all of the new ones we care to. Everyone around us has his or her own particular set and we can create new ones in them as well. In fact, we can't avoid it. The only thing we can do is be aware of these anchors and choose them purposely; otherwise, they will be merely random influences. Most of us, being unaware of their existence, operate so that we continually confuse them. One manager, for instance, toyed with a pen when he was annoyed or impatient. He also toyed with the pen when he was excited and interested. In Planning sessions with his employees, at some point he would be likely to start toying with the pen. The employees interpreted the gesture as negative and would cease to take an active part in the planning. Some employees were aware of the gesture and some were not, but it affected the behavior of all of them. Rather than trying to get rid of the gesture of annoyance, I simply got the manager to use another gesture, toying with his glasses, when annoyed, and the employees could use the signal appropriately.

The anchor can be meaningful or totally unrelated to the purpose. It might be a sound which means something, like gears grinding or an angry tone of voice. It might be a gesture of impatience or simply two fingers pressing together. It might be the look on a face or a glance to a corner of the room. Anything can be associated to anything else and serve as an anchor, if it is consistently used.

In a meeting, the specific outcomes of the meeting can be posted on a flip chart. When the meeting begins to drift off topic, reminding participants of the purpose and pointing to the flip chart will bring them back to the purpose. After a time or two, it will be unnecessary to verbally correct participants. Merely pointing to the flip chart will bring the meeting back to the purpose. After some consistent use, pointing to the chart, even when the outcomes are no longer visible on it, will serve the same function as the first verbal correction did.

Anchors Can Still Work in Abbreviated Form

One manager who walked with a cane for a while used to pick the cane up and let it drop on the desk as he directed the meeting back to its purpose. Soon other employees would simply lift the cane and drop it if the meeting was getting off topic. Although the manager has recovered and no longer walks with the cane, it can still be found on the desk in group meetings and serves its purpose simply by being there.

One thing you might notice about these anchors is how respectful

38

they are. Instead of an overt message of correction, they supply a more subtle cue for individuals to reorganize their own resources in a way appropriate for the circumstances. They don't demand obedience, merely a timely response within their own framework.

These anchors can be particularly useful in dealing with situations where the other person is likely to get emotional. In customer service areas, employees often react negatively to hearing anger or frustration in the customer's voice. In one case, an employee learned to anchor an angry voice on the phone to an immediate rapport response, which was to say in a tense voice, "Boy, I bet you think this store doesn't care about you when you ...(fill in customer's complaint)." After this response to an angry voice, the employee was past responding with her own negative emotion and could continue most effectively. Later, she created positive anchors for the customer by using a particular voice tone in talking about the desire for customer satisfaction.

Kinesthetic anchors are extremely powerful. To anchor a confident feeling before a presentation — or to be used during it — a specific posture and way of touching your hands together can produce remarkable results. To produce the *Kinesthetic* original self-anchor, think of times when you have *Anchors Work* been confident and as you access each experience, *on Others* assume the particular posture and touch your *and Ourselves* fingertips together (or whatever gesture you like). Continue this process until you can produce the confident feeling merely by assuming the posture and repeating the gesture. Now, whenever you desire that same feeling, simply repeat the posture and gesture. Touching other people will anchor whatever they were feeling when you touched them. To get them to re-access that same state, simply touch them in the same way. This can be done in Planning and Coaching sessions to recall creative states or other resources which are appropriate to the circumstances. A "meaningless" brief touch is all that is required.

The most powerful anchors are combinations of the three systems — visual, auditory, and kinesthetic. The least powerful, yet not to be ignored, are words where the specific meaning is intended to elicit the response. These are generally consciously processed and any resistance to changing states will be directed against them. The non-verbal means of communication is the most powerful in this particular area.

It may be apparent by now that the more effective your ability to communicate, the greater the requirement for integrity. It would seem that these techniques are powerful enough to manipulate people in ways which are contrary to their self-interest. There is some truth to that. However, there is very little long-term danger to the other person when used without integrity. The effects are generally indirect and associational; that means that you can't make people do things which aren't in their own interest. The real danger is to yourself and your relationships. You may be experienced as being a manipulator and generate suspicion and ill will around you. If these techniques are used without regard for the interest of others, they will begin to dislike and resent you.

Integrity also is what gives the techniques their power. First, in the sense that integrity means "working in harmony," the techniques and their content must be coordinated with the objectives in a consistent manner. This is extremely difficult to do if you have multiple goals or are trying to take advantage of someone. Second, integrity means "within the context of the situation which includes another person." If the goals are compatible and agreed to, then any technique which leads to them is appropriate. I will be delighted if you "manipulate" me toward a goal which I have expressed my desire to attain. Used without integrity, these techniques will produce short-term results, at best, with longer term negative consequences *for the user.* Used with integrity, they will produce short-term results and long-term committed relationships of mutual benefit.

To Work, Techniques Have To Be Linked to Integrity

Awareness

All of the techniques for communication which we have considered require the ability to know when to use them. It is not merely a list to try, one at a time, until something works. Each communication is in response to something and each has a particular reaction. The factor determining the next appropriate communication is the response to the last one. With the ability to detect responses well developed, the ability to select the most appropriate next step becomes virtually automatic.

There is no substitute for finely tuned, sensory acuity. We are provided with more information than we can possibly be aware of in every face-to-face communication. Each message is given to us in a variety of ways. When there is more than one message, when intentions are not clear or when they conflict, all of the information will be communicated in various ways at the same time. When the verbal portion says Yes and the non-verbal portion says No, both must be respected — responded to — for complete and successful communication.

Each shift in an internal state produces changes in the external presentation of a person. We have already acknowledged that we cannot not respond to another human being or to the internal changes in ourselves. Each change in external presentation is a response to a change in internal state. In other words, any change internally can be seen, heard, and felt by another person with well-developed sensory distinctions.

Rapport is attained by matching another person. Matching at the level of that person's internal changes before it becomes conscious to that person or explicit in his or her verbal communication is incredibly powerful. This is what people who are known as "sensitive" do regularly — usually outside of their own awareness. They simply respond to the minimal cues which are available to us all with some practice.

All of the areas we considered in discussing body and voice matching for rapport are elements for communication which will register changes of internal states. Posture, breathing, voice tone, muscle tonus, rate of movement, and many more subtle cues all reflect the internal states of a person. Changes in them each indicate a shift in internal state. Notice, then, that by matching these changes or responding to them in some way, you will be changing your own state in some way to match the other person and will increase your ability to be aware of someone else.

Being Sensitive Means Having Awareness of Subtle Changes

More subtle cues include skin color changes, eye movements, pupil size changes, lip size changes, minor muscle tonus shifts. These may seem outside of the normal range of awareness or attention and even intrusive. Each, however, is already being received by your sensory apparatus. The shift to make that sense data useful is to allow it to register and to be willing to utilize it. Most of your vague feelings about people come from this sensory information which has gotten by your conscious screening processes and registered an impression in spite of your unwillingness to receive it — unwillingness in the sense that you have trained yourself some time in the past not to notice such things. Remember how we were taught not to stare and not to copy? We learned to reduce our sensory input to fit the social norms as we understood them at the time. We simply need to redevelop some muscles we've always had.

So far we have been concerned with the internal states of others. What about our own? What is their place in communication? How do they help us and how do they hinder us? Most of us are usually so con-

41

cerned with our own internal states and conscious operation that we leave little of our attention for awareness of the outside world. Some of us spend a great deal of time flipping from one emotional response to another with little regard for the requirements of the surrounding world and people. Others have rigid patterns which hide their internal responses from most other people and even from themselves. Both of these extremes suggest an over-developed concern for our own internal states.

Each shift in our internal state and the accompanying bodily shifts represents some new data being received or a new response being generated from the total possibilities of our experience. The bodily shifts are often the only signals available to us that we have just shifted. We need to be in contact with these shifts to know when the world around us has changed, when the people we communication with shift, or when our own evaluations change.

The importance of our internal shifts and the bodily changes which accompany them is the signals they provide. That is, the actual content is not the center of attention. The value does not *Our Internal* lie in being able to analyze yourself. The usefulness *Shifts Are* is simply as a signal. A signal is something which *Important Signals* gets your attention and points it in the appropriate direction. It tells you that something may need attending to and in what area. After it has gotten your attention and been identified, it no longer is useful — it has done its job.

For instance, in giving a presentation you may notice before you start that you are nervous. This is probably related to other experiences, often from childhood, and after noting the feeling, you can move on to the actual presentation. As the presentation proceeds, you will get various signals indicating confidence and relaxation; or you might notice that, even though you are performing well, the same nervous feeling is still there. After a time, you notice that you are feeling anxious and the nervous feeling has increased. That signals that something has changed. Minimal cues are being received from the listeners that they are not receptive or that your message is not getting across. This will serve as a signal to observe what is actually happening and make an adjustment if possible. You may find you skipped a major point. You may find that it is only one or two people who are sending the messages. You may find that you haven't lost anything but that a particular activity from the audience was being misinterpreted. By using your changed state to notice the world around you, you are increasing your ability to function in it — to respond appropriately. Remaining focused on a persistent internal state usually causes us to miss the signals the world is providing and become more and more inappropriate to our surroundings.

How many times have you had a planning session or just given instruction and later, when the job was not followed through, known that you didn't expect it to be done *at the time* of the original communication? What stopped you from acting to correct the situation or verify it then? Generally it will be because you were ignoring the importance of your own internal signals.

Sensory Grounding

Your internal signals are the result of events in the external world. These events may have been totally outside of conscious awareness. They may have been obvious but their significance was missed. Or they were registered for later response. In any case, the events comprise sights, sounds, and feelings. These are the building blocks of our experience, these are the material we have to work with.

Language which is sensory-grounded, thinking which is sensory-grounded, is the most reliable we have. Language which is grounded in the senses is the closest to our actual experience that we can get. We share a basic nervous structure with other human beings and generally can communicate effectively at the level of what is seen, heard, or externally felt. We share no internal feeling or experience directly with another person and therefore this is the hardest area to communicate effectively in. Tracing, or being able to trace, these feelings to their external sensory source provides the means to share even our internal "private" feelings.

Using sensory-grounded language, we can describe and refine the external events until we know that the other person has a recreation of the same event — or at least a close enough approximation. We can point, draw pictures, act out — until the other has been provided with adequate sensory-based information. The ability to do this consistently reduces the amount of time which must be spent in actually doing it. The solution to any disagreement usually lies in becoming familar with each other's sensory-grounded information. Evaluations are usually carried out at a much higher level of abstraction and this is the source of most of the tension which characterizes these sessions. Some of the common words which indicate this trouble include "poor" job,

Using Sensory-Grounded Language Is the Best Way to Communicate Clearly

"courteous service," "not ambitious enough," lack of flexibility, don't "get along" with fellow workers, need to "communicate" effectively. None of these and the hundreds of other such words which appear in evaluations tell the listener anything about what might be seen, heard, or felt in the actual situation or a better one. I've known people to give up in disgust after changing their behavior a number of times trying to match a supervisor's idea of being courteous and never even finding out what it would look or sound like to that supervisor.

Sensory-grounded language provides the distinctions for sorting behavior from abstractions. "Provide good customer service" is an abstraction about which everyone has an idea and which may be different for every person. In fact, you can count on it being different for every person and that the difference will be significant in enough cases to require resolution. Each higher level of an organization deals in higher abstractions. The protection from confused interpretation lies in the ability to reduce these abstractions to their sensory base.

Sensory-grounded language also provides the distinctions for sorting behavior from evaluations — from your response to it. When you see or hear a poor job being done or people reacting to each other in non-productive ways and you emotionally burst into speech, you can count on the words you use being evaluations. You will characterize the job as being bad and the person as being wrong far beyond the level of the immediate and specific action. The solution to this situation is to describe what you saw and heard along with your evaluation of the event.

Thinking and speaking at the level of sensory-grounded language will have another positive effect. It will separate what it is — actual experience — from your evaluations of it. This allows the meaning of an event to be separated instantly in time from the actual event and provides the opportunity for retaining both. Particularly in emotional situations we only retain our reaction to an event and not the experience of the event itself. This process will also tend to provide a buffer from the emotional explosions which we feel, and either act on inappropriately or suppress at a cost to our bodies.

Separate Actual Experience from Evaluation of It

Naming

Separating experience, by thinking in sensory-grounded terms, provides a powerful tool for communication. You are able to recall events in detail, you are able to separate your emotional response from external events and you are able to notice the source of your evaluations. For in-

44

stance, if someone's voice begins to go up in a conversation, you can recall at which point the voice began to increase in volume and accompanying bodily changes, you can recall when you began to respond with feelings of defensiveness and you can remember your evaluation of that person getting angry *and the source* of that evaluation. With all of that information available to you, you can choose the best response — and select another if the first proves inadequate.

There are times when your own emotional reactions to a situation or person get in the way of responding appropriately. You are less effective at your work because these reactions get in the way of doing what needs to be done. There are times when a group is unclear about what is happening and no one seems to be able to sort out how it got there or where to go next. There are particular people around whom we seem to be in a state of confusion. One executive I know of has an incredibly high turnover of both staff and connecting department managers, a high percentage of whom actually leave with physical illness. He has everyone around him guessing about his intentions and motives. These people never know what is expected and feel confusion whenever they deal with him.

All of these situations have in common an inability to clearly see external events and use what is seen productively. Often what was clearly seen becomes obscured and no longer available for conscious use. The technique which clears situations up fastest is called *naming*. It is as simple as naming what is.

In a state of confusion, it is as easy to name what is as in a state of clarity. The first step is to name the state you are in and then the particulars of the confusion. Naming is not to be confused with blaming or with statements about the past. It is a technique for making clear what is — not what was. It requires the ability to access and express information in sensory-grounded terms.

Naming Is a Special Way to Define the Present

What is heard, seen, and felt are all elements of naming. Statements about external events must be so clear as to be recognizable by other people with certainty. Statements about internal events (say, confusion) should be as expressive as possible. These events cannot be shared with certainty but, since they are internal, neither can they be argued with if stated as what is. One of the powers of naming is that it leaves no room for dispute. You may be evaluated based on what you name or you may be asked to be more specific, but you can't be argued with.

For example, the executive referred to above can be told by an employee, "What is happening right now is that I'm uncertain of what you really want me to do. I've asked you to clarify which program has priority and haven't understood your answer. I would usually go by what I read in your expression but I can't read your expression at all. I'm feeling nervous that I'll make a choice which will turn out to be the wrong one unless I understand your priorities." This is with an executive whom employees say they can't read, whose people regularly burn themselves out, around whom none of the employees know where they stand. A clear statement of the current event will accomplish all that is required — simply naming what is.

The major requirement besides clarity around sensory-grounded information is the willingness to name what is so. Much more than specific abilities, it is that willingness which is usually missing. You may appear naive, foolish, etc. and you may get a reaction, real or imagined, which you won't like. What you will get, however, is clarity. In my experience, that is a worthwhile condition. There is a saying which is relevant: "You can't con an honest man." What honesty means is that a person is willing to see and hear what is so and is willing to speak it as well. If I name what is happening and my feelings about it, the clarity produced will keep us from getting lost or fooled.

It is necessary to be able to clearly distinguish between what is external and what is internal. In doing so, you will also be able to speak "for yourself." Statements about the internal experience of other people cannot be expressed in sensory-grounded terms. Statements about your guesses, named as such, supported by the external evidence you have used can be part of naming only where they are clearly labelled as such. They are appropriate only for expressing what is so *for you* with no implication that they have any more reality than that. In groups which are confused, unproductive, or generally lost, the person willing and able to name what is so will soon have control of that meeting. There is a tremendous power in simply "telling the truth." Not as opposed to lying. Not as opposed to covert manipulation. Just in the sense of knowing the difference between what is external and what is internal and being able to express both separately and clearly.

Naming Has to Be Based on What Is Sensory-Grounded

Contrast the following two statements:

You are confusing me. Every time we get into this discussion you get mad. Make up your mind which one you want. How do you expect me to do the job if I can't be sure what it is?

I am confused. You said you wanted me to do both of those things and that this was the one to start on first. You sound like you're angry at me for getting it wrong. I don't know what to ask to make sure I get it right and I get embarrassed if I have to keep asking the same question. How can we make sure I get the priorities right in the future?

In a meeting, naming might go something like this:

I'm lost. The agenda item we agreed to work on is to arrive at a decision about firing Jones. We seem to have gotten into an argument about company policy and whether it is right or not. We agreed to get an opinion from each person and then decide by vote. Some of you are expressing strong emotions about the situation and disputing the ideas of others. I suggest that each person has a say and that reactions be limited to questions for clarification.

Naming is always presented with the possibility held open that the external facts are incorrect and correction would be welcome. It also holds open no possibility for one's own experience to be denied. This will be realized by others if opinions are clearly stated as opinions and feelings clearly stated as feelings. Events can be named only for oneself. Even external "facts" are what I saw and heard, not what actually happened and what was actually said. This way of thinking and expressing allows us to fully respect the experience of others without denying our own.

There is a great power in being willing and able to name what is so. People who manipulate others to suit their own ends, generally use the unwillingness of those others to directly confront what is happening. They use a lot of implication and subtle messages. Naming the implications or its affect on you removes all of the power of the situation.

Calibration

One of the refinements of awareness which will assist you in all of your communications is the ability to distinguish small cues and to recognize their individual significance. The previous section referred to an executive who nobody could read, who could so effectively hide the "normal" reactions in his face, body, and voice that those around him didn't have any idea what he was thinking. This situation demonstrates the degree to which we depend on cues other than words for communication.

Many people with this particular ability have attended my workshops over the years. I use these people to demonstrate how easy it is to read the particular bodies of any human being. People who have been "unreadable" turn into expressive beings — by a change in the point of view of the participants. The experience goes like this: I have the "unreadable" person agree to stand and face a group and think about his or her response to some statements without speaking. Then I describe various situations, one at a time, to the person. As I describe each one, the group will attempt to guess whether the person likes or dislikes the situation.

With this type of person, the group is never able to make consistently right guesses and they are never certain of the guess even when correct. After the person's "unreadability" is established, I have that person turn backwards to the group or make some similar adjustment in position. Then I repeat the process and the group soon guesses correctly every time and begins to know when they are right.

What causes the change? How can it be easier to know what is going on in another person when you can't see his or her face? The change represents the difference between body "language" and calibration. When the person turns around, the "normal" signals which the person has learned not to show are not available to the other participants. They are no longer confused by the lack of "meaningful" signals. Presented only with someone's back, you have to discover a set of signals which have no meaning except in the particular situation with that particular person. And these signals always exist.

Body language is a term which implies that specific gestures, postures, movements, have specific meaning — in the nature of a language. We do have specific signals which are *Body Language* culturally accepted to have a particular meaning and *Is a Starting* we use them that way. Most of what is referred to as *Place to Read* body language, however, is not in this category. The *Meaning in* major use of body language is in providing a starting *Communications* place for determining the meaning of particular physical communications or signals. The most likely meaning for any posture or expression is determined by the cultural setting. It is a meaning which must first be tested before it can be confidently used. Even the standard, accepted gestures such as crossing of arms may mean something opposed to its standard indication. I know someone who has a bad back and sits with crossed arms only when feeling comfortable and "open" to what is occurring.

Calibration is the ability to detect signals and compare them to that particular individual's reactions. Each person will have a fairly regular

48

Calibration Allows You To Detect Signals and Verify Them set of signals, of outward manifestation of internal states, which can be relied upon with much more success than any accepted body language. Posture, breathing, muscle tone, and other more minute — and larger — changes will accompany all significant changes of internal states. Each individual is unique in his or her reactions. The cheeks of one person will get darker when they are angry. The cheeks of another will get whiter. Each will be different for different degrees of similar emotion.

The source of the ability to detect these reactions and respond appropriately is to make distinctions between what is actually seen and heard and the meaning it might have. Looking for something called a smile which has a particular significance is very different from simply observing the movement and muscle tone of a mouth. Looking for a smile will cause the distinctions in the physical changes to be blurred or missed completely. Looking for the particular changes, one will also register that a smile occured if, in fact, it does. This latter approach will contain far more information.

Our minds work in such a way that they will automatically compare what we see and hear to what we have seen and heard in the past. The level of body language information will result in evaluations whether we want it to happen or not. The training which is most useful is to develop the ability to detect individual reactions and patterns and differentiate them from the general meanings we automatically attach to body "language." Each communication is a unique experience and we require the ability to receive the specific feedback we are being given.

Flexibility

Flexibility in communication requires a variety of behaviors, of use of words, body posture and movement, voice tonality which are available

Flexibility is Detecting Differences and Adjusting Accordingly for use as required. Flexibility implies having a wide range of possible responses to any situation. It also implies the ability to detect differences in the world and make distinctions which call forth the appropriate response. The definition of flexibility contains as its root "an adjustment to" another person or a situation. Variety for its own sake is not a part of flexibility. Being open to the communication, however subtle, of another person and being willing and able to respond appropriately to that communication is the essence of flexibility.

49

The preceding skills are all pieces of behavior which will contribute to your flexibility. Each is intended to be responsive to the situation and the other person's needs in a way which will also meet your own requirements. The requirements of rapport make obvious demands of flexibility. Adjusting your way of communicating to that of the other person demands skills and the flexibility to use them at the appropriate time.

The problem of learning these skills from a book is the lack of experience of their effectiveness. A workshop environment is far more powerful if the presenter is able to model — to demonstrate — the skills and provide experience of their impact. You can get the most benefit from the above material by continually referencing your own experiences as you consider the individual techniques. Later, you can practice them in settings where there is no pressure to be right and you can be comfortable with whatever results you obtain. Restaurants, parties, and friendly groups are some places where both observation and behavior can be tested. Calibration can be practiced at meetings and social gatherings. You need never be bored again as long as there are people around.

All of the techniques presented may be used equally effectively with groups. They require minor adjustment in some cases and even more flexibility, yet the basics are the same. Each group is made up of individuals who require matching in some way. The individual adjustments may be slight, but each one which is made will also communicate to the group your willingness and ability to deal with each one. More than the ability or range of skills available, flexibility is the willingness to adjust to another person.

Summary

Having considered a number of techniques and skills which will dramatically increase the power of your communication, it's time to turn to the level which integrates your behavior. A common reaction to these ideas is, "How can we keep track of all of those things and still accomplish what needs to be done?" It seems hard enough to concentrate on the content of a conversation without the added consideration of nonverbal behaviors and controlling all of our responses. The concern is legitimate. There is far too much for our conscious minds to handle.

With or without the above considerations, there is far too much for the conscious mind to handle. You are already receiving more information than you know how to use. You are already communicating far more than you can possibly control. We human beings are complex systems who give and receive more information than we can possibly keep track of. Yet that is the environment we are "designed" to operate in. We have built-in mechanisms to screen out information that is not important even though it strikes our senses. We are programmed to pick up important sensory signals even though, moments before, it was part of the "unseen" background. And we already communicate with a coordination of more verbal and non-verbal activity than we can keep track of.

The controlling element for all of this is intentional — our intention or purpose organizes what we receive and what we send. If our intentions are mixed or unclear, our communication will be the same and what we receive will be that way as well. Congruence in communication is the agreement or matching between words, actions, expressions. It includes appropriate receiving of messages sent and responses to them. Intentions are made clear only by their physical appearance through action. Congruence will produce the desired result without particular attention to skill. Skills which have been developed will be available at the appropriate moment without effort.

Congruence is the End-Result of Appropriately Sending and Receiving Messages

Skill development and development of intention proceed together. It is difficult to arrive at optimum, congruent intentions regarding other people if you lack the skill and experience of effective communication. Knowing your potential impact on others and theirs on you affects your intentions. Theory Y, Win-Win, and similar approaches have been around for a long time and are not the experienced norm. Few people are able to make them work consistently and therefore the intention behind attempts to do so often include contradictions which defeat them. The behavioral skills to make them work are often poorly developed or unavailable. On the other hand, being technically skilled and lacking a congruent intention will also produce mixed results. Smooth operators with mixed intentions are not trusted. The two areas must be developed together to produce significant results in the world. Your organizations will not change without complementary development of both of these aspects.

Congruent communication occurs when an intention is organizing all of your words and actions. Intention will select all of the behaviors to contribute to its realization. The task becomes simple at that level of skill. The greatest difficulty will be experienced in creating a unified intention from a complex being (yourself) and a complex situation (organization, family). An effective Performance Management System requires that the intentions be thought out and an appropriate structure provided for those intentions to be realized. Within that context, these communication skills will produce dramatic results.

PERFORMANCE MANAGEMENT

2.

Creating a Framework

Planning

Intention

The intention of the Planning session of a Performance Management System is to turn the organizational goals into action plans. This assumes that goals have already been set at the next higher level of the organization and that the manager or supervisor conducting the Planning session has agreed to division, department, or team goals. The purpose here, then, is to develop the plans and agreements necessary to achieve results and assign accountability.

The existing plans have been determined according to what is "normal" procedure for your company. This may include elaborate methods for involving all levels of the organization in determining the goals or may simply be directives from the top of the organization which work their way down. No matter what method has been used, turning these plans into actions is the overriding intention. What is appropriate during a Planning session will be guided by that intention.

Intention—Turning Plans Into Action

What is expected to happen during a Planning session? Think of your own best planning sessions with your people. Think of the worst planning sessions you have had with your bosses. What would you like to happen in the sessions which you conduct? Stop for a moment and consider your own experiences and goals before proceeding.

The Planning model which follows assumes that you and your organization value growth, creativity, and cooperation, and expect management to develop people. I have made this assumption because it is a challenging target, not because it is usually true. While the vast majority of companies would agree with these goals, most of them do not, in fact, support activity which is congruent with this concept. This model is designed for those ideals to be put into action and to *work*. If you or your organization do not actively uphold such values, I recommend that you adjust the models presented here accordingly. Congruent behavior is more effective than agreeable but insincere words.

The Planning session is expected to develop detailed plans to achieve existing goals, not to revise goals or create new ones for the organization. Within the framework, other goals *can* be realized. Employees can be given a chance to express their goals and interests and to create the plans for their own development within the organization's goals. And, in fact, the organization will grow if each employee continues to grow — planning for new ways of doing anything better, from whole jobs to single tasks, will provide the continued improvement of the organization.

The Planning session gives employees a chance to express their degree of ambition. Discussing the kind of rating an employee wishes to get at evaluation time will be the first step towards eliminating surprises at that session. There is a security in knowing that the rating will not depend simply on the whims of a manager at the end of the performance cycle. Knowing what it will take to get a particular rating beforehand gives the employee the opportunity to attempt it or not.

Throughout this book, "performance cycle" will be used to indicate the time period expected between Planning and Evaluation. In most instances, this should be less than one year. Often, it could best be only a month or two. Occasionally, it may be more than one year.

What of the danger of an employee selecting a low goal and coasting during the performance cycle? If, in order to achieve a satisfactory rating, an employee has to maintain standards and *Planning Allows* improve in at least one area, then there is likely to be *Employees To* little room for coasting. This is the time for the *Define Goals* manager to present the benefits and create the conditions where an employee *wants* to perform at a level appropriate to that manager's view. There may be times when low but acceptable goals are all right, but if standards are set to be *met*, not merely as challenges which only some will meet, then the organization should achieve its basic goals when all employees meet their standards.

To summarize, the Planning session is intended to achieve understanding and commitment to specific action plans. These plans will be as challenging as you, the manager, are willing to make them and will depend on how much you commit your own resources and support to their being actualized. The final outcome of the plans you make is your responsibility.

Framing

Most of us tend to function best when we know what is expected of us. This is particularly true when we are dealing with those we perceive as having power over us. We like to know whether we are expected to provide information, be creative, ask questions, sit quietly, or say how we feel. Most of us are willing to do any one of these things so long as we know what it is and don't expect it to be used against us.

The way to create a reasonable expectation for what will take place is by setting the context, or *framing*. It's one of the first things that needs to happen in any but the most informal contact. If we

Framing Sets Up Expectations for What's to Come

know what is expected and what is coming, we can adjust our behavior and many of our own needs accordingly. How many times have you been called into someone's office, failed to hear much of what was said, and failed to respond appropriately because you were waiting to find out what was going to happen to you? This can happen in any interaction but is frequent when one of the parties is perceived as having most of the power.

Setting the context will often be the first step in putting the other person at ease. It sets the stage for what may be the most important element in effective communication — establishing rapport. Framing will not only make establishing rapport an easier task, in most cases, it will be a major element in that rapport. Framing should occur at all interactions of any significance.

For the Planning session, rapport consists of the following statements by the manager:

1. A statement of intention from the manager's point of view as a representative of the organization.
2. A statement of intention for the employee, that is, what is expected and how the employee may look after his or her own interests.
3. A review of the process to be followed and what is appropriate in each separate function.

Knowing these things ahead lets the employees organize their own internal resources in the most appropriate manner. They will be better able to put irrelevant issues on hold, knowing that there is a place for them, or that this meeting is *not* the place.

The framing may be prepared before the meeting. It may be distributed to employees beforehand, and it, or some condensed version, can be read at the start of the meeting. The optimum results will be obtained by the maximum direct, personal contact and communication. Reading will provide the minimum direct contact. It will, however, be better than no framing at all.

The purpose of the framing is to meet the basic needs of the employee as much as to smooth later processes for the manager.

A fairly complete example of framing might go something like this:

> The purpose of this Planning session is to develop an action plan that meets the requirements of the company goals and satisfies your needs. I want a plan which includes some specific ways for you to improve your performance and I will help provide coaching, training, or information for you to do that. We want your creative help in establishing these goals so that both your needs and mine are met. After we have finished, we want the plans to be specific enough so that we can make adjustments as we move to achieve our goals and so that we both will know at the end of the planning cycle whether or not they have been achieved.
>
> The Planning session is being done so that you can influence your own goals and develop your own ways of achieving them. It gives you the opportunity to spell out what I or the organization need to provide you so that the goals can be achieved. It gives you a chance to choose what level of performance you want to aim for over the coming period. I want you to be sure that you understand what is expected of you before we complete these sessions.
>
> We have an opportunity now to arrive at an action plan which satisfies us both. We both need to know what standards will be used for evaluating performance so that neither of us will have any unpleasant surprises throughout the planning cycle. This way, you'll know where you stand and what is expected of you and I'll know whether I'm providing you with the resources you need.
>
> How does that sound to you? Do you have any questions or comments? *(Pause after each question in a way which indicates that you really do want participation.)*
>
> The procedure we'll follow has five steps. The purpose is to make sure that you can influence the plan and that we don't finish this session until you understand what is expected of you.

The first step is for me to give you the specific goals which I have agreed to for our part of the organization and to tell you your part of those goals. Then I'll give you the resources available and any restraints which we must work within.

Second, we'll explore ways for you to get the most satisfaction from your job and your part of the goals. This is the time to talk about your special interests and we'll be as creative as possible in exploring ways to satisfy them.

Third, we'll develop a specific plan of action for the planning cycle. We'll end up with a plan which is detailed enough so that we both will know that we are talking about the same thing and we'll know whether it is actually happening as the cycle goes on. This includes what you need and expect from me as well as what you are going to do. I'll also indicate to you which are the most important parts of your work in my opinion and we can discuss that.

Then we'll establish Early Warning Points for each of the major items. These are the points when you will know that part of the plan is in danger of not being met *while there is still time to do something about it*. If these points are reached, you will contact me so that I am aware of what is happening and we'll work out a plan to recover or correct the problem — or even change the plan, if necessary. These will allow you to work independently, give me confidence that everything is going as expected, and eliminate any serious unpleasant surprises for both of us.

Any questions about the procedure?

We won't have completed the process until both of us understand what is expected. Participate fully and I'm sure we can develop a plan which satisfies you. Settle for specific plans only when they are ones which you are willing to commit to.

The first goal we should agree to is, What rating would you like to work towards for the next evaluation?

The above example should be changed according to the beliefs and desires of the organization and the individual manager. After the system has been in place for some time and employees have gone through the process, an abbreviated form would be sufficient. If the planning cycle used occurs only once per year, I suggest that the framing be reinforced each time with a fairly full presentation. A full framing should be done for all new employees and for those with whom relations have been less than comfortable throughout the last period.

An external visual aid such a flip chart for writing the intention and the basic steps of the process will help the Planning session flow

Visual Aids
Help Framing

smoothly. It will be easier for both parties to stay on track and will serve as a reminder of where you started and where you are going. Using an external visual procedure such as a flip chart in developing plans will help ensure that you are both agreeing to the same thing and that nothing is left out. An alternative is to have the employee take notes and then review them together at the end of the session.

• *To recap —*

The *Intention* of the Planning session is to turn organizational goals into action plans. A Planning session is intended to achieve understanding and commitment to specific action plans and to create the opportunities for employees to express their goals and interests.

Framing is the first step to meeting the intention. It's a means of setting a context for the session that puts employees at ease, allows them to organize themselves, and encourages participation.

Establishing rapport, a requirement for effective communication, is an important component in framing and will be dealt with more fully below.

In summary, here are the main points you'll cover in successful framing of your Planning session:

State the purpose of the Planning session.
1. Develop an action plan that satisfies both company requirements and individual needs.
2. Be sure that at the end of the session employee clearly understands expectations.
3. Be sure finished plans are specific enough to allow adjustment throughout process and to allow measurement of success.
4. Encourage employee to establish own goals and spell out resources needed from organization.

Rapport

Now, we'll look at the importance of establishing rapport in your interactions with employees. Pacing and leading are two elements we'll examine within the overall process of establishing and maintaining rapport.

The first step of any communication, one that is so significant that it warrants special consideration, is establishing rapport. Although there are certainly specific non-verbal techniques for establishing, enhancing, or maintaining rapport (see Book 1, *Communicating for Results*), here we will consider the verbal requirements. What would take place at the start of a Planning session if it were with a person with whom we had a mutual liking? Stop for a minute and consider what would happen before we got down to business.

We can use this as a model for what needs to happen, no matter who it is — with one caution. Our model for content and style are created by an existing relationship which makes sense of the

Matching —
Of Primary
Importance

interaction. In a meeting with someone you have had a poor relationship with for the past year, the same words and style will not be appropriate. How might you adapt what would happen in the first, friendly situation to help you in this more awkward one? One of the key issues in establishing rapport is that we match what makes sense for the other person *regardless of the situation*. Many people believe that making small talk, finding points of agreement, being friendly are the means to establish rapport. However, if the other person in the situation expects to dispense with business quickly and directly, then small talk will work against rapport.

Some personal contact is usually expected in boss-subordinate relationships. If the relationship has been somewhat strained in the past, the expectation will likely be lower and the interaction less personal. In this case, after brief pleasantries, an adequate job of framing will be the most effective vehicle for establishing rapport. In this case, special effort should be made to engage the other person in the framing. This is effectively done by asking questions such as, "How does that sound to you?" and, "Is there anything you would like to add to that?" Pausing in the framing and giving space for response, verbal or non-verbal, will also indicate an adequate consideration for the other person.

Often, if previous relations have been strained, an explicit reference to them can be used effectively. Your first response to this suggestion may be, "What? Draw attention to the previous hassles? Drawing someone's attention to past states won't be useful now." Consider *when* it might be a good idea. Some explicit efforts at rapport have been made and the framing has been done. Yet as you look at your employee, you recognize that this person does not look cooperative. What you see and hear suggests that he or she is already thinking of or experiencing past problems. Now *is* the time. You will not be drawing attention to it but simply naming what is already in this person's attention.

This is the place to use a technique called *pacing* and *leading*. (See

Book 1.) The first step is to *name* what is apparently there and then *lead*
to the new desired state. Something like, "We're
Pacing   probably both remembering some of the times when
and   (I've yelled at you, we've been working at cross pur-
Leading   poses, I didn't respond to your needs very well, etc.)
and feeling, Why should this one go any better? I'm
thinking that I want to really make an effort at making the situation
better for both of us and that this Planning session is an opportunity to
start that. What do you say to giving it a try?"

The naming technique is a way to pace your words with the experience of the other person and it works most effectively if it focuses
on your own behavior or feelings. Speaking in a way which could be interpreted as putting employees at fault, anything which uses only their
behavior, will probably not match the way they are viewing the past.
Although blame operates as a major factor in many people's understanding of interactions, it is neither the issue here nor the way to get
the results you want.

At this point, you might choose to test for the existence of rapport.
The first test is to ask yourself, "Are things going the way I want them
to? Is the employee participating or seem ready to?"
Testing   If the answer is Yes, no further test is needed. If you
for   are uncertain, a non-verbal test may be in order. The
Rapport   simplest ones involve major body shifts. You can shift
your posture (say, lean forward or relax back) and
notice if the employee makes a shift in posture in response. It is not
necessary that the shift be identical to be "in response," merely that one
take place. A change in breathing (say, a sigh) or an increase in general
body movement may also be useful as tests. Pick one which is relatively
comfortable for you.

What if your calibration of the employee suggests he or she is not in
an appropriate state and your rapport test fails to get the desired
response? Do you press on or continue to try for rapport? On the
assumption that without the cooperation of the other person, without
being able to access that employee's resources, the goals of the session
cannot be met, there is only one good reason to push on. That is that
the next steps may provide what is needed to bring about the required
rapport, if done with that in mind. Let the option of pushing on be the
last. It is the one most commonly followed and which produces the least
success. Your pushing on will likely be in response to your own needs

and not to the needs of your employee — the very problem you are having with this person.

The first words to use if you are continuing to work on rapport can be something like, "Before we start into the actual Planning session..." These words can remove the formality of the situation and relieve the pressure that either one of you may be feeling. What follows could be a reference to a previous positive experience that you have shared, a positive work experience of the employee which you know about, or just a general reference to a positive experience which you are sure the employee must have had at some time. It might even be a story which will make your point, starting something like, "I'd like to share with you an experience I had..."

You might follow the "before we start" with a statement about clearing the air over past incidents which are getting in the way, by stating, "We don't seem to be heading in the right direction," or simply by asking, "What might I do for you before we start the session?" You might also start a summary of the Planning procedure or framing and notice which points seem to generate responses which might need some extra attention. Use the opportunity to stress the positive points as seen from the employee's point of view.

Before we move on, we need to consider one more aspect of rapport. The need for rapport continues throughout the process. Fortunately, it is much easier to maintain than to establish. Once the original work has been done, it is usually safe to remove your attention from the issue — but only as long as things are going well. Whenever the direction of the meeting seems lost or blocked, reestablish rapport before trying to make corrections based on the content. An explicit check with the other person, accompanied by a shift in voice and body posture, if indicated, will frequently take care of any problems. They will always make good leads. When things are working, you can assume that you have rapport.

As we've emphasized here, establishing rapport is a major element in effective communication. It's a pivotal point in the success of this system and one that we'll come back to frequently. And it's based on this premise: *to achieve the best possible results in communication requires that you are genuinely willing to respond to someone else's needs.*

Here is a quick review of some of the elements in establishing rapport:

1. Match what makes sense for the other person regardless of preconceived ideas about rapport. (Small talk may not be appro-

63

priate for everyone.)

2. Framing which involves the other person helps establish rapport and determines what will be included in the session.
3. Referring to past negative situations will help clear the air. Use pacing and leading to set the tone for current session.
4. Testing for rapport tells you if it's appropriate to continue.

A Model For Use

Now let's go on to look at the specific content of your Planning session. We'll go through the specifics of a model Planning session using these five steps as the framework:

1. Give Goals and Review Resources
2. Develop Common Goals
3. Develop an Action Plan
4. Early Warning Points
5. Understanding and Commitment

1. *Give Goals and Review Resources*

The purpose of this function is establish the parameters within which Planning is to take place. What are the fixed goals, outputs, responsibilities, and standards that must be met? What are the fixed resources available for their achievement and what other resources can be considered? This portion of the meeting might be considered as a more explicit extension of the previous framing. That is, it tells the employee what resources are expected and what the boundaries of consideration are. These boundaries should be expressed in terms which allow the maximum behavioral flexibility. We want the employee to apply his or her creativity in the widest possible area. Most of the boundaries are specific goals which you, the manager, have already committed to. To the extent possible, these goals should be expressed in terms of results or output rather than behaviors.

Make Explicit Statements — Expect Flexible Response

For a managerial subordinate, the goals might be stated something like this:

> Our division is required to show a return on invested capital of 20 percent with a sales increase of 12 percent over the next year. I have committed to this goal and, according to our previous team planning meetings, you will have to make slightly less than what your projected figures indicated was possible. These goals are the standard required for

an adequate performance rating.

So that our division can meet its goals, your department is expected to show a return on invested capital of 15 percent with a maximum of 10 percent in increased investment and no overall increase in staff. An increase in staff requires special approval. We are installing a complete Performance Management System and you will need to make time available for at least three formal contacts with your people over the next year. Our training department will be available for a minimum of 36 days of training for your department. You are authorized to spend $2,000 on your own development before special authorization is required.

In line with this division's policy for continual growth, we need to come up with a plan for a mutually agreed goal of performance improvement in one area of your department. Do you have any questions about goals, resources, or limits before we continue?

For a subordinate who is a supervisor, the goals might be stated something like this:

Our department's share of the organization plan requires that we increase production 7 percent in units while changing our product mix to increase the specialized product to 50 percent from 30 percent. We will be allowed as many as four full-time new employees under your supervision to accomplish this.

As we agreed in our supervisor's meeting last month, we are shooting for a reduction in absenteeism, turnover, and grievances. We will need a specific action plan for working on these items before we finish the Planning session. We will also need a specific plan for production scheduling to make sure the product mix change occurs as required.

These will take care of the improvement requirements of the organization for your department. We will also need a plan for your own personal growth within this company. Each employee is required to plan for personal improvement in the area which is of most interest.

Would you like any clarification before we move into planning?

For a production subordinate, the goals might be stated something like:

Our department is required to increase production by 4 percent per person. With no capital expenditures planned, this means we will have to find ways to improve our own productivity. Your areas of responsibility will be the same as last year with a shift in emphasis toward giving more assistance to the assembly department.

We have allocated one hour every two weeks on company time for our department to meet and discuss possible areas of improvement. In addition, we need to arrive at measures for your own major areas of responsibility. In line with the company's policy of continual growth, we need a specific plan of action for one area in which you will concentrate on personal improvement. As a minimum, any one of the training department's three-day courses will be available to you.

Do you have any questions before we start developing plans?

Overall, we want to give the employee the maximum amount of freedom without ignoring fixed (and certain) limits. If we ask for creativity and then veto ideas because they violate preexisting but unannounced boundaries, we are likely to leave the employee with the feeling of having been set up. For many, the areas of planning will revolve around projects and improvement areas rather than the day-to-day activities. Where this is the case, production goals or volume figures which need to be achieved will place constraints on the time and resources available for special projects or development.

All Situations Contain the Same Basic Steps

All of the above examples include a context or larger plan within which the individual goals are required. They state the required results in varying degrees of specificity depending on the nature of the goals — from exact production requirements to the need for a development plan. They all mention company policy regarding growth, demand a specific action plan, and refer to or imply the possibility of varying levels of employee performance ratings.

All finish with a request for more information or a confirmation of understanding. This is the minimum requirement in this area. It is expected that the manager's non-verbal behavior will have indicated the possibility of interruption and clarification throughout. One way of accomplishing this is to pause frequently and look at the employee. The request for a response is phrased in such a way as to indicate the organized nature of the procedure being followed and allow the employee to keep track of where we are in the process: "Would you like any clarification before we move into Planning?" "Do you have any questions before we start developing plans?"

2. Develop Common Goals

The function here is to develop a set of common goals which are mutually understood and agreed to with the maximum amount of employee creative input. At higher levels of management, most of the goals within a specific return-on-investment goal can be generated by the employee or will already have been done by them in organization planning sessions. At the lowest level, where no management functions are involved and production requirements are set, the employee may still contribute to both company and personal improvement goals.

This part of the process will set the tone for use of employee creative participation throughout the rest of Planning. If goals have been given in terms which allow no room for addition or adjust-

Allowing Maximum Employee Creativity

ment from the employee and you move directly into developing an action plan, the strong message will have been given that it is your plan and the employee has no choice but to follow it. If preceding goals have covered the behavior of *how* they are to be done, there will be little room for creative input here. What can we expect in active participation after that?

The first goal to elicit, if not already done, is what level of perfor-mance rating the employee is aiming for. This will affect the specific goals of quantity and quality that need to be planned for. This is a goal which can truly be the employee's own and will tend to provide a strong ownership of the resulting plans. It is important that any performance goal which is within the acceptable range for the organization be receiv-ed as legitimate. By that I mean that the manager's non-verbal signals as well as verbal ones should confirm the acceptance of the choice. This can be accomplished relatively easily if thought through and accepted before the Planning session starts.

Although the level of performance is the employee's choice, it may be appropriate to register your own opinion and attempt to influence the

Creative Development of Mutual Goals

employee otherwise. One test for yourself is that if you try to influence everyone upward, you are not really allowing them a freedom of choice. If, on the other hand, you are genuinely surprised at an employee's choice and believe a different choice makes sense for that person, it would be appropriate

to indicate that and even persuade that individual to make a change. Notice that the above does not suggest the *direction* of change. There are times when a downward shift might be beneficial. The first steps in this part will be to suggest the opportunity available in positive terms and to explicitly ask for creative input. To the extent that the previous step in-cluded boundaries and limits, it is important to present this phase as an opportunity for creative development of mutual goals. The intent is to remove any feeling of restriction while maintaining the explicitness of fixed boundaries.

You might start this phase by restating its objectives and inviting participation, something like:

> We've established the broad goals that the organization requires, now let's explore what your own personal goals for your department and yourself might be. I'd like us to be as creative as we can in developing goals which you can really be interested in. I'm sure that if we work together we can arrive at goals which will satisfy both of our needs.
>
> *(Insert a shared experience here in which some positive results were achieved or a "story" about the kind of experience you want which you or someone else was involved in.)*
>
> I'm excited about the possibilities of this Planning session. Do you have any ideas about what you would like to accomplish in the next period?

In the event of the most-feared response — none at all — you will want some back-up. If rapport has been established, adequate framing has been done, and you in fact do want some creative employee input, there will be few instances where you will fail to get appropriate responses. However, in those few instances, what can you do? First, don't rush in to fill the gap. It may be that this employee needs a little time to think — or to check your sincerity.

The following questions may be asked, making sure that each is followed by a pause adequate for the employee's full consideration:

> Think of the most interesting part of your job. Is there some way we might make it a larger part?
>
> Think of the least interesting part. Is there some way we might eliminate it or make it more satisfying?
>
> If you could set one personal goal for yourself this year, what would it be?
>
> What is the one area of improvement that would pay off the most for you?

If none of these elicits an answer to provide a springboard into useful planning, I would assume that there is not adequate rapport to continue — although there are exceptions. It may be that a new employee who is struggling to keep afloat will not be in a position to view his or her situation with creativity. That person will simply want to be told in detail what to do. In other words, the appropriate behavior is always determined by the situation.

There are other alternatives to the question approach. Anecdotes which mention previous situations where the employee contributed an
Alternatives for Eliciting Response
expanded goal or a new approach can be told. Another approach is to suggest one or two possibilities that come to mind, if necessary, prepared beforehand. Another approach is to go back to the original goals and explore the possibilities of changing the way they are expressed to allow more flexibility. Even though the goals themselves are fixed, they may be expressed differently or achieved in different ways not indicated by the first presentation. All of these have the purpose of involving the employee and accessing that person's creative resources.

The way in which the initial approach is made will strongly influence the outcome. For example, if one or two ideas are presented by you for lack of any response from the employee, they should be done with words and manner which clearly show that they are only ideas to consider and may be used to suggest yet other ideas. Words like *maybe, might, may*, etc., sprinkled throughout and a voice tone which is slightly hesitant or questioning will encourage participation. A quick "You could try A or B" followed by a request for an opinion will likely suggest that one or the other should be taken and reinforce the feeling that participation was not really wanted.

Maintaining rapport non-verbally as suggested in Book 1 will contribute to your success. The major impact on creative participation will
Respect the Other's Processes for Rapport
come from creating an atmosphere which is not threatening and which conveys the message that any ideas will be accepted for serious consideration. One of the major messages required will be that you respect the mental processes of your employee. This includes giving time for employees to think, assistance with that thinking, and the feeling that they might have something worthwhile to consider.

After some input has been received from the employee and discussed, you will want to add some goals of your own or clarify the relative importance of specific goals. The areas requiring clarification will be apparent from the previous Evaluation session if one has been held. If there has not been an evaluation, extra care will be required to ensure a common understanding of the relative significance of each goal.

This phase will end with a summary of the goals being as explicit as deemed necessary by the situation (employee, relative importance, and past evaluation) and will include at least a commentary on which are the most important.

Finally, of course, there will be a question such as:

> Is there anything we should clear up before moving on to developing specific action plans?

A test for understanding at this point may be made by requesting that the employee give a summary of his or her perception of the goals which

Test for
Understanding
By Getting
Feedback

have been agreed to and their relative importance. It is often useful to provide an opportunity for explicit demonstration of understanding rather than relying on non-verbal confirmation. When you ask, "Do you understand?", the most reliable part of the answer will be non-verbal. Often it takes more courage than

we have at the time to say No. If a person is confused, he or she seldom knows how to talk about what they are confused about.

3. *Develop An Action Plan*

This step is to arrive at a sufficiently detailed plan of action to ensure that responsibilities are known, that adequate resources are available,

The Contract —
Specifying
Plans and
Standards

and that clear standards of performance for later evaluation are set. The results will be a kind of contract between employee and manager for performance. Like any contract, it will contain provision for responsibilities on both sides. There are a large number of responsibility areas in most jobs which

are taken for granted. Those that have been done satisfactorily in the past are expected to continue in the future. Little is said about them. These areas, however, often hide the potential for significant improvement. One way of tapping the potential is to develop measures of their performance and then ways can be found, on a selective basis over time, to improve the standards. The very act of developing such measures will tend to increase awareness and attention and produce positive results.

The requirement for detail depends on the ability, experience, and responsibility of the employee. Although it may take a little longer to go

Determining
the Degree
of Detail
in a Plan

into sufficient detail, the effort will pay off in the reduced time it will take for improved performance. Let's take the case where too little detail is included in the plan and there is only one planning cycle per year. In many areas, substandard performance will

70

not be obvious enough to attract adequate attention for correction and will *not* result in major goals being missed. ("Substandard" is often built into the system.) The less-than-adequate performance is not likely to be addressed until evaluation time. The employee then is likely to profess a lack of knowledge about adequate performance with, "Sure I agreed to do that job and I did it just the way we said — or I understood it. I didn't know you meant *that*."

What are you going to do? It is the employee's responsibility to understand goals. However, our basic premise is that it is the manager's responsibility to ensure understanding and agreement to goals. Employees shouldn't be evaluated on goals they don't understand. Goals which are not clearly understood indicates a need for future clarity and possibly training for the next period. On an annual schedule, inadequate performance in minor but cumulatively significant areas may take years to improve.

Performance standards which are clearly described will reveal training, coaching, or other means of improvement at the time of Planning and that's the place for corrective steps to be built into the plan. This approach is an active one for growth, rather than simply reactive to surfaced operational problems. It has another major advantage. If the employees are not clear on plans and performance standards, the manager must constantly monitor all areas of performance to detect areas needing correction. Besides being an onerous task, this approach ensures that only major areas ever get any significant attention. If the employee, the person doing the work, is fully aware of plans and standards, that person can exercise his or her own vigilance and attend to problems which can be corrected as a normal part of the working procedure.

The manager's responsibility in this contract is generally to ensure that adequate resources are available for the agreed performance. These will primarily be material and manpower, information from other departments, training and coaching as well as time allowed for experimentation, meetings, or information-gathering directed at areas of improvement. Specifically, the manager should contract for the amount of coaching or supervision that will satisfy the needs of both the employee and the manager. The employee's evaluation will be influenced as much by the manager's performance on the contract as by the employee's efforts: Responsibility operates from the top down in organizations.

Start each specific planning item with a bit of creative problem-solving, particularly if it is one of the areas chosen for improvement.

*Creative
Thinking
Starts the
Process*

There may be many ways to approach a problem and some early exploration will help to tap the hidden resources of employees. Although they have the detailed knowledge available from direct experience, they may never have attempted to access it in ways which may be useful to the desired result — improvement in performance. A bit of "brainstorming" may surprise all participants.

This might be done simply by saying something like:

> Before we develop any detailed plans for this goal, let's see if we can come up with a variety of ways to solve the problem...kind of brainstorming. Anything which might solve it, no matter how far out it seems now, is OK.

The major task for this session will be to maintain rapport while insisting that growth and alternatives which meet your own requirements are

*Setting
Growth
Requirements*

arrived at. The requirement of growth may range from demanding significant new effort to insisting on more specific language before a plan is finally agreed to. The non-verbal communication will of course be significant. Verbally, the task is to acknowledge the feelings or needs of the employee and then return to your own needs. Once you have acknowledged the needs of your employees in a way which gets that message across, they will be more receptive to responding to your needs.

This might go something like the following:

> I know this seems like more detail than is necessary. You're probably beginning to feel impatient with the way I'm going about this. *(Pause to let that sink in and give an opening for a comment. If there is one, acknowledge that in a similar manner and pause to let the fact that you heard it sink in.)*
>
> I want to let you work in your own way over the next planning cycle and I want to feel confident that our agreed goals will be met as well. If I'm not sure that we understand the same thing now, I'll feel uncomfortable and want to keep checking up on you. That won't be good for either of us. When we take these extra minutes now, I've found we can work together better throughout the cycle.
>
> The kind of information I need now is ...

Setting goals in an uncertain world means that the results will frequently be different than planned. Some goals will be exceeded and some not achieved. However, a specific action plan will generally be accomplished or not depending on the activities which are within the control of specified individuals. For this reason, I put equal emphasis on action plans and on achievement of goals specified in terms of results.

A goal to reduce scrap 10 percent, reduce staff turnover by 30 percent, cut costs 5 percent or increase sales 20 percent may be achievable but will frequently be influenced by factors outside of the control of the planner. A specific plan of action for achieving these results can be measured for performance and achievement. That is, what particular studies will be made, what actions taken, which areas concentrated on, what new controls started — these are the totally controllable elements and each can be measured in terms of performance as well as results.

The resulting action plan should be specified in enough detail to ensure a common understanding and the ability to measure progress and final results. The detail necessary will be determined by past experience, the importance of the job, and the ability of the employee. The manager must test whether or not an adequate level of specificity has been reached. Over-caution will generally be appropriate. A failure due to lack of shared understanding will take longer to correct and be costlier than the personal dissatisfaction resulting from too much detail.

How do you, as a manager, select the required amount of detail? The theory sounds fine, but how do you know what is appropriate in the real world? The answer, of course, lies in the total of

Testing for
Understanding

experience and information which you have. Your experience with the job and with the particular employee will provide you with an information base. Next you can devise tests based on the current situation. One of these will be to use active feedback, that is, have the employee explain the agreed steps rather than simply asking if he or she understands. Asking such questions as, "How will you know whether the plan is going as agreed?" will elicit information about understanding.

The other major area of information is what the employee conveys in addition to his or her words. The gestures, expressions, and voice tones all indicate degrees of certainty. Notice also whether the words make sense only because you fill in the blanks from your own understanding. This, combined with evidence of uncertainty, give a strong indication that more detail is needed. Finally, when erring on the side of safety, notice any non-verbal signs of boredom or irritation which indicate you are going into too much detail. These should be taken as indicators and, at the least, used to maintain rapport. They are not necessarily valid signals for too much detail.

After noticing a response of irritation when giving or asking for detail, a comment such as the following made soon after will address the requirement for rapport:

> This detailed planning can get tedious at times. There's just a little more that I need for my feeling of security. Maybe then we should check and see if there is anything more we need from your point of view.

You might want to add a short story about another time when you, or someone you know, got into a pinch when they stopped a Planning session before they were both satisfied with the amount of detail.

This part of the session should conclude with some specific measurements, specific times and dates, and the relative importance of the items related to each other and to the routine actions not specifically covered in Planning. Clarity at this stage will make all succeeding management actions easier for both parties.

4. *Early Warning Points*

This phase of Planning is to ensure that there are no unpleasant surprises as the planning cycle or project progresses. It provides for explicit signals that plans are going off target and ensures *Avoiding* adequate feedback for in-time corrective measures. *Unpleasant* It serves as a link between intentions and the actual *Surprises* operations required to realize them. The first step is to select the crucial functions. What are the critical events or actions which need to happen and upon which the appropriate sequence is dependent? These are the things which, if they don't happen in time, will prevent the goal from being reached. These critical events become the focus for establishing Early Warning Points. Major events of important plans should require active feedback.

It is not enough to report that one of these critical events has not happened on time. The nature of these events is such that if one is late, the whole project or goal is in jeopardy. What is needed is the earliest point at which the event is in doubt *and* there is time to take some form of special action to have it occur as planned.

Let's consider some of these events:

- In a construction project, obtaining permits is a critical function. The Early Warning Point would occur at some specified length of time before the permit is needed if it has not yet been reviewed by the authorities. The time will be one which might allow someone with special influence to expedite its movement through channels so that things are in place at the required time.

- A quality-improvement project to cut the percentage of defects in machined parts has a major function, the statistical analysis of specified flaws. The actual group problem-analysis meetings must be held before the busy season commences. Therefore, the statistical analysis must be completed by a specified date. The Early Warning Point would be the time when compiled data could be analyzed by the quality control/computer people only by special request from a department head.

- A sales department has an annual quota of $1,000,000 to be met by five sales representatives. A major function might be to have twice as many qualified prospects as would meet the sales quota six months before the fiscal year end. Experience has shown that it takes one month of concentrated work to convert a prospect into a qualified prospect and that about 80 percent actually qualify. The Early Warning Point would occur about eight months before year-end to allow enough time for adequate prospects to be developed.

- A training department has a goal of developing and delivering three new courses within the coming year. A critical event will be the completed design of the course and a critical function of that might be an outline ready for approval three months before the first planned workshop date. The Early Warning Point might be a time for completion of a partial outline which would require rescheduling of the time and resources of some of the department to meet that goal.

Each of the critical events has a specific time and specific measure. The Early Warning Points may not be as explicitly specified. They will, however, always be clear enough to provide an adequate signal some time before the actual critical event is to take place. The worst offense of an employee is to miss a critical event without providing active warning. The next worse is to miss an Early Warning Point and wait until the critical event is reached.

What about the problem of being continually pestered by employees fearful of missing the critical events and Early Warning Points? These employees are indicating their need for more assistance or direction. You ignore it at your own peril. What about the problem of employees not providing you with early warning of unpleasant surprises? The common experience is that the effort of the first is much preferred to the frustration and lack of control of the second.

The nature of the feedback required at the Early Warning Point needs to be clearly specified. All critical events should require explicit action by the employee in the event of failure. Timed Early Warning Points may call for explicit feedback initiated by manager or employee. All others which are dependent on quality of result, previous events, or personal judgment may require anything from formal meetings whether or not they are met to notification only when the Early Warning Point has not been met.

Setting Early Warning Points is the transition from the Planning stage to real operations. They serve to complete the requirements for

The Transition from Planning to Real Events
Planning and establish the points of feedback which will ensure optimum performance. These will be the triggers to make things happen as intended. Without them, we will have a system which can allocate blame for goals not met but which will be unable to meet operational requirements. Most evaluation systems fail to improve performance because, although they attempt to place blame and suggest improvement, they do not provide feedback in adequately small time frames.

This step also serves a major function in checking for shared understanding. Most of the Early Warning Points should be created by the employee. This will demonstrate an understanding of the major requirements. Establishing critical events may be done jointly. Many of these will be based on the manager's experience and other reporting requirements. Knowledge of major functions should be shared by both. With this information as a base, the employee should be able to determine appropriate Early Warning Points. This final step of Planning will indicate whether adequate understanding has been achieved.

5. *Understanding and Commitment*

This is not a formal step so much as the necessary result of the preceding phases of Planning. If, at the end, it is apparent that there is not adequate, shared understanding, then the manager has missed signals which should have been seen or heard — if the goal is to involve the employee in any meaningful way. Even though there appears to be understanding and commitment, it will seldom hurt to spend a minute to check that conclusion. All that the alert manager will need will be a simple question or two which elicits congruent responses from the employee.

We have considered the issue of understanding at length but not that of commitment. Understanding is a necessary first step. Commitment has been dealt with in a more indirect way, since each effort at maintaining and establishing rapport, the intention of framing, and the efforts at involving the creative resources of the employee have all been contributing to commitment. Goals, action plans, and Early Warning Points have all been developed in a manner which shares experience and creativity. The spirit of cooperation which has been fostered will include a tendency for commitment on the part of the employee.

The test for commitment will be the words and the non-verbal signs of commitment such as voice tone, body posture, and expression which provide the confirming evidence. Commitment, *Recognize the* along with understanding, will have been achieved, *Signs of* increased, and maintained throughout the process, *Commitment* or not at all. If there are signs that one or both are missing, a major restart will likely be required. Adding patches of involvement to a program which is solely yours will not likely produce the desired results. If there is a need for restart, recognize the importance for more employee input, and pay more attention to the non-verbal signals throughout the process. And slow down — if you don't have time to do planning right, you won't have time to correct all the misunderstandings that happen later.

Before we leave this section, what kind of tests might be employed to ensure there is adequate understanding and commitment? One will be to summarize the major points. A better one will be to have the employee do the summarizing. Both require at least as much attention to the non-verbal signals as to the content.

Some of the following series of questions may be useful:

Is there anything more you'd like to discuss before we finish this session?

Which parts of the plan are likely to give you the most trouble? Which the least? *(and notice the difference in quality of non-verbal response)*

Which parts will turn you on the most? Which parts turn you off? *(check up on the last casually but more frequently by creating your own checkpoints)*

Does this plan satisfy you? Do you think you can do it?

The content has already been covered to this point. The most valuable information will be provided by the accompanying voice and body signals. Use the information you get respectfully, by going back to issues without needing to comment on the reason.

That is, noticing that my voice and posture indicated doubt about a particular item, you might re-open that subject like this:

> I'm not sure we have the same understanding about item number three in our plan. Maybe we should review it in a little more detail. (?)

This comment would likely be made at the end of a summary rather than as an instant response to the perceived uncertainty. The suggestion to review is made in a questioning manner and careful observation of the response is made. Both the explicit answer and the non-verbal signs will indicate how much needs to be done.

Summary

As stated at the beginning, I have assumed the ideal situation (and the biggest challenge) of attempting to get full involvement of the employee. Anything less requires the same vigilance regarding the responses of the employee. Lack of understanding and covert resistance will ensure that a Planning session is wasted even in the context of the most authoritarian environment. If the above model is followed, great gains in results can be translated into the realities of production. The major key is to remember that it is an interaction between two human beings — they just happen to be named manager and employee — both of whom have needs and goals.

In summary, these are the five steps in the Planning procedure:

1. *Give Goals and Review Resources.* Manager informs employee of specific goals he or she agreed to in meeting organization's goals, and to inform employee of his or her part in meeting that goal.
2. *Develop Common Goals.* Explore ways for employee to state special job interests, ways to get the most satisfaction from the job and explore ways to arrive there.
3. *Develop Action Plan.* Develop specific plan of action for the coming period — through a detailed plan that allows specific agreement on elements and verification of success. Includes stating specific needs of manager and specifics of what employee will be doing — manager will spotlight his or her view of most important parts of employee's work.
4. *Early Warning Points.* Establish Early Warning Points — signals that current action may not allow goals to be met — gives

employee chance to work independently, gives manager the confidence that all is progressing, eliminates unpleasant surprises.

5. *Understanding and Commitment.* Natural conclusion to previous steps. Manager should be aware of non-verbal signals that conflict with verbal response. Employee involvement throughout the process is key. Check for understanding by having employee give summary in own words. Voice and posture give valuable information about understanding.

Coaching

Intention

The intention of the Coaching contacts in the Performance Management System is to develop employees while achieving goals, or adjusting those goals in a timely manner. The requirements will change only slightly in terms of procedures even if employee development is not, in fact, a major goal. The time spent at different steps may vary considerably depending on the specific needs of the employee. *Coaching* refers to the regular, continuous activity of a manager in the operation of a business. Employee development and achieving specific goals are both the essence of management. Planning and Evaluation will make it much more effective, but the major gains can be expected from improvement in the area of Coaching.

Intention —
Developing
Employees While
Achieving Goals

One of the things that's required to ensure the timely adjustment of goals is a high-quality information flow. Most executives will admit, unofficially at least, that the uncertainties of competition, the economy and human systems make strict adherence to numerical plans an unrealistic operational assumption. Many organizations, however, communicate their plans and budgets downward through the hierarchy by numbers alone. The result is the kind of horror story reported regularly in the Wall Street Journal where illegal or merely unwise business practices are discovered only when they have severe if not terminal effect on the organizations involved.

Using High-
Quality
Information to
Adjust Goals

80

The information needed to adjust plans is the same as that needed to take corrective action and channel employee development. And the first step in creating an environment where information flows on time may be the willingness to change plans in a timely manner. High-quality information is your guarantee that changes are made only when necessary.

Coaching contacts are much more frequent than the formal sessions held for Planning and Evaluation. They include every personal contact with employees; particularly relevant are the con-

Every Employee Contact Involves Coaching

tacts which needed to happen and didn't. For our purposes here, I will consider each contact as a major session, or "worst case," to illustrate the principles involved. You will probably recognize that many of your contacts require must less energy and time. Many of the elements should remain the same but take little time and be more informal.

Let's start to consider the issue of Coaching. What do you want to happen as a result of the regular contacts between your managers and their employees? Rather than considering this question session by session, think of the overall effect you want to achieve. Although each encounter will be different, the cumulative effect will leave an impression of the particular manager and of the organization. What do you want that to be? If all of your contacts — whether emergencies, support, training, or social — went the way you wanted, what would you have achieved?

Much of management systems work has a negative emphasis. It concentrates on how performance can be monitored, problems identified, warnings generated, and (implicitly) employees coerced into doing what needs to be done in an adequate manner. The control aspects are important. This is particularly true for a system where decisions are being made many times removed from direct, sensory experience.

By contrast, the positive emphasis of this Performance Management relies on the knowledge that rapport and face-to-face contact will

Face-to-Face Contact Brings Positive Process and Results

produce higher-quality information faster than any formal system and achieve the maximum in creative cooperative results. You should not be surprised to learn, then, that Coaching provides for, above all else, frequent face-to-face contact. It underscores the important recognition that we are human beings dealing with other human beings. From here, we can develop employees, by providing expert advice, training, or personal observation of performance. Finally, we can move into personal assistance with agreed behavioral changes which an unaided employee is unable to make alone.

These contacts give the employee the opportunity to respond as a fully functioning human being. They increase the likelihood of confrontation and emotion as well as the information flow which is more directly related to operations. While at first we may want to avoid these situations, they are a necessary part of human interactions if we are to access the full resources of everyone involved. We can come to see these contacts as exciting, even fun, when we accept them as simply part of that information source we are dealing with. In time, the added life and energy they bring to any endeavor will be seen as positive even while some of the encounters are uncomfortable.

The Coaching model which follows assumes that you and your organization value and believe in continuous improvement for every employee. It suggests that it is possible to positively influence other people and that they are likely to have important knowledge and abilities to contribute. It encourages the active development of people on the basis of personal contact.

Framing

Coaching contacts cover a wide range of contexts, while explicit examples of framing can cover only a few instances. A major factor in the framing will depend on who initiated the contact. The initiator will normally set the context or frame with the other person questioning or amending it. If the employee initiates the contact, however, the framing will often be left up to the manager. In this case, the manager can state what he or she is doing and then elicit a statement from the employee.

The purpose of framing is to be sure that both parties have a common understanding and each can organize internal resources in an appropriate manner. How many times have you been involved in lengthy discussions with employees before you found out the purpose of the contact? Sometimes you didn't ever get really clear on it. This type of contact tends to produce irritation and the resulting communication generates negative feelings — usually on both sides.

How do you know when it's time to use framing if the employee initiated the contact? If an initial casual contact doesn't require any particular framing, then there will be times when you will sense the need for it at a later point. When will that be? Many times the signal will be your own internal state. As soon as you notice a feeling of frustration or confusion, that is the time to make an explicit frame. Also, when an employee has left you with a puzzled feeling a number of times, it would be appropriate to use a short-timed trigger. If within the first minute of conversation you are not clear about its purpose, begin to develop an explicit frame.

The procedure might go something like this:

> Jim, I'm not sure how to contribute to this conversation. I feel a lot better when I know where we're heading and what is expected from me. Can you tell me how you'd like me to respond to what you're saying?

If the employee is not able to respond adequately to this invitation, or seems not to understand the request, the manager might follow with some assistance along the lines of:

> I listen differently if I'm to offer expert advice than if I'm sitting down to do some problem-solving. And differently again if what you want is a sympathetic ear or to simply report the status of a job. Each of these also takes a different amount of time and it's easier for me to focus my attention if I know about how long that will be.

> Sometimes I find that just taking the time to be explicit about what I want from another person helps me to organize my own thoughts better. I find that conversations usually go better if we both have the same understanding of what it's about. Lots of times I find myself jumping in with advice when the other person didn't even want it. *(pause)* What would you like to happen in the next few minutes?

If no satisfactory information comes from this attempt, you might try something like:

> I really need this kind of framework to operate effectively, Jim. Sometimes I may seem a bit slow, but this seems to get us where we want to go. Let me see if I can express what we're trying to do here and if you don't agree, you just say so. Then we can change it as we go if we need to. It's sort of like having an agenda for a meeting; and you know I always like that. Right now it seems you want me to hear about a problem you're having with meeting some deadlines and then to offer some advice for speeding up your work. Is that right?

If the above has seemed cumbersome and time-consuming, it has been in response to a worst case. Remember, the contact was initiated by someone who has repeatedly left you with a feeling of frustration or wasted time. It also went long enough for you to recognize it wasn't merely a social call — or was a social call you didn't have time for. The other major consideration is that these types of conversations will not happen frequently with the same person. After a few encounters such as this, the employee will learn to organize his or her thoughts before coming to you. As in most of the models, *the practical applications provide the necessary training.*

Having established a frame by the above process, or more directly with clearly organized employees, the procedure you intend to follow should be outlined next. As the manager, you are in a

Establishing the Procedure for Continuing

position to decide procedure from your position as an expert in this area and by your own time requirements. In your role as manager, you are like a consultant who is an expert on process, recognizing that the employee is the expert on content, that is, has the direct experience which is being used.

The procedure part of the framing might go something like:

> I have fifteen minutes available right now. How would it be if you spent just a couple of minutes giving me an overview of the situation? Then I'll ask some questions about what is happening and what you'd like to happen and you can add any details you think are important. After that, I should be able to give you some useful assistance. If not, we'll meet again on Thursday and spend more time doing some serious problem-solving? Do you think that will do it?

In most cases, setting a limited time will be productive for both parties. Time limits often force us to organize our thoughts more efficiently. A second meeting, if required, will allow both participants to process the basic information in their own time and manner. They can do any information-gathering outside of the meeting and come to the next meeting fully prepared to complete the task.

• *To recap —*

Before we go on to establishing rapport, let's recap the intention and framing stages of this Coaching section.

The *Intention* of the Coaching contacts is to develop employees while achieving goals — and making necessary adjustment to those goals in a timely way. Obtaining high-quality information provides the basis for the rest of the session.

Coaching, in fact, is a regular and continuous activity of a manager and takes place in every personal contact with employees. This step is intricately linked to the more formal Planning and Evaluation sessions and is greatly aided by their being accomplished effectively.

Framing in a Coaching contact depends on who initiated the contact. Even if initiated by the employee, the framing will often be deferred to the manager. Eliciting a statement from the employee is a significant part of the manager's role here. The manager is the expert on process, the employee is an expert on content. Ultimately, the purpose of framing is to see that both parties have a common understanding and can then adjust their own internal states accordingly.

Here's an outline of the pertinent elements in framing:

1. Be aware of timing — if conversation continues for a minute and you are still unsure of purpose, start to elicit a frame:

   a. "I'm not sure how to respond/contribute. I feel a lot better when I know where we're headed and what's expected of me. How would you like for me to respond?"

   b. More explicit request: "I listen differently if I'm asked to problem-solve, respond sympathetically, or just listen to a status report."

   c. More explicit (in extreme cases where there is no clear response): "I really need a framework to operate efficiently, I'll express what I think we're trying to do here and if you don't agree, just say so."

2. The procedure you intend to follow should be outlined next:

   a. "I have 15 minutes right now. Why don't you review the situation with me right now, etc."

   b. Include setting up second meeting if necessary.

Rapport

The next stage, *Rapport*, will examine some of the elements in an interaction with another person: where different responses come from, how we influence those responses positively and negatively, and how we can come closer to obtaining the responses we want. This, with the intention and framing you've done, will all come together in an actual Coaching contact.

What do we want most of all from another human being? On first contact, it is quite basic. We would like to leave an interaction with feelings of acceptance, respect, or positive regard. At the initial point of contact, however, what we want most is a response. The kind of response we want is one which is appropriate to our internal state, but more than anything, we just want a response.

How can we give this kind of response to another person? Think of someone who gives you the feeling of really paying attention to you. You

Respond to the Emotions First

tend to feel good about your contacts with this person, don't you? What is it this person does that gives you this feeling? You'll probably find that something happens immediately on contact that

starts this feeling of attention. Whatever the situation, whatever the problem being presented, however strong the emotion, the first response required is *to the emotional state of the other person.* People are not machines presenting you with facts or problems, but human beings with personal needs and wants. The most important thing about me at this moment is that this is *me.* I am more important than my facts, my problems, or your present preoccupation.

Your body and voice tone are more important than your words at this moment. A shift in posture will indicate that you are shifting your internal state from wherever it was. The direction of your eyes and the tone of your voice will indicate attention to the other person. Voice tone, body posture, and words which reflect what you see and hear at first contact will provide an immediate feeling of responsiveness. All of these will work even if your next words are, "Wait a minute until I finish this report."

Employees want a response which seems appropriate to them. How will they make that judgment? How can they know what is appropriate?

Give Response That Is Appropriate to the Individual

Their own present and past experience, generalizations they have made, their previous observation of you, and their current internal states will combine to establish a context in their minds against which your response will be compared. Rapport will be achieved by acting in a way which makes sense *in*

their context. Employees who have worked with you for any length of time have a set of experiences which includes how you treat people in general and them in particular. All of their experience of your behavior is observed from the outside and filtered through their own understanding. You have been a major contributor to the experience of the other person in an active way. Your response at this time will be interpreted in relation to your previous responses. For this reason, when we suddenly decide to treat people differently, they "don't respond" immediately and we often revert to our old patterns without getting the desired result.

Because of this interplay of personal histories, there is not one ideal response to another person which is right for everyone. We can say, though, that a shift from your usual or existing state toward your employee's state will always be appropriate. The nature and amount of the shift will depend on your ability and your past behavior. A manager who is loud and cheery with everyone might temper that a bit if an employee is disappointed or usually quiet. An excitable manager who talks in a fast, high-pitched manner might slow down a bit and lower voice tone somewhat when talking to an employee who is normally slow and deliberate in speech. Another manager who normally makes significant adjustments to those above might make the same adjustments to employees.

An employee whose manager is loud and cheery with everyone else but suddenly quiet and subdued with him might begin to wonder what was wrong. A complete change of pattern will seldom be appropriate if a basic style or pattern has been established. Another consideration is based on the internal states of the employee. It may be that even though an employee's behavior seems quiet and withdrawn, that person still expects or would like others to respond in a cheery and friendly manner. A shift towards such an employee would still be appropriate as long as it wasn't a complete match.

The basis for this seemingly complicated decision is fairly simple. Other people have expectations and desires which are significantly influenced by their experiences with you. Some part *Matching Others'* of your behavior will have to match their expecta- *Expectations Is* tions and understandings of the world which were *Part of Rapport* created independently of you. Some part will have to meet their desires as human beings. The simplicity of this concept rests with the basic needs and desires which we share, however different our behavior makes us appear.

There are times when you will be too preoccupied to respond appropriately to your employee. You may be upset about other dealings, annoyed with this particular employee, or simply too busy to concern yourself with other issues. Whenever this is the case, longer term rapport will be best served by respecting your own needs. A simple statement like, "Not now, Ralph, I'm too busy" will generally have a better result than the incongruent communication which is more common. "Sure, Ralph, what's on your mind?" said in a distracted manner with frequent glances at your watch does not accomplish the goals and shows a lack of respect for both parties. In most cases, a response which suggests another time and place is even better.

87

Two additional techniques will help maintain a positive relationship while respecting your own needs. The first is to make a note to yourself to follow up on your own initiative with the employee who requested time. The second is to keep a simple record of the number of times you are too busy and whom you are too busy for. A manager who is regularly too busy has a problem with people-handling abilities or with a few employees who need to be developed. A little time spent with "problem" employees can save a lot of time and aggravation later.

A good manager need not be superhuman. He or she will be able to recognize and deal with the needs of various employees most of the time. There will always be times, however, when *Communicate* personal needs will be too strong for that to happen. *Your Needs* In the main, these will be related to the priorities of *Realistically* the organization. At times, they will be related only *and Congruently* to the manager's needs as a human being. The ability which separates the better managers is that they recognize when their own needs must take precedence and communicate that in congruent ways. Paying attention to your own internal states without being driven by them provides you with the maximum information. Many times, these internal states will be the cue to recognize that a conversation has gotten off track or out of frame or that the frame needs to be changed. Using these cues to generate explicit statements about what needs to be done or what you, personally, can or can't do will tend to produce efficient use of time while maintaining rapport.

The overriding task for maintaining rapport is to recognize that *every action of another person makes sense to that person* and to discover what conditions make it that way for him or her. You can contribute significantly to the process by using words which make it easier for your employees to make sense of *your* actions. This is not a call for psychological analysis. It is not even a call for more openness, although I think in many cases that might go a long way. It is simply a call for sensible explicit statements about what is needed, what process is being followed, and brief explanations where they seem appropriate.

Rapport, once established, is maintained by continuous responses to the internal states of others. Our responses are to the external signals of those states: the words, voice tones, gestures, posture shifts, etc. The major areas in a continuing interaction are maintaining a frame which makes sense of what is happening, responding to particular changes in emotion, and communicating congruently when feelings or values are involved.

88

The frequency and timing of your contacts with employees will also have an impact on rapport. If the only time you approach an employee is when there is a problem or some kind of trouble, the employee will soon connect the two experiences. If the only time you contact employees is to satisfy some formal requirements such as Planning and Evaluation sessions, they will likely create a meaning which is contrary to rapport. Informal, seemingly random contacts mixed in with formal, scheduled ones will be most likely to create the conditions for positive human contact. We usually have this type of contact with employees with whom we naturally feel comfortable and avoid those who don't fit our personal models well. To discover your own patterns, keep a simple checklist of contacts with employees to determine their frequency, distributions, and cause. A solution to any significant imbalance is to mark your calendar for each quarter to schedule contacts with employees who might otherwise be neglected. These should be randomly scattered throughout the period and merely be for the purpose of establishing and maintaining rapport and gathering high-quality information through direct contact.

Avoid Expectations of Only Negative Contact

- *To recap —*

This outline reviews the main points in establishing and maintaining rapport:

1. Initially, what we want most basically from another person is a response.

    a. Whatever the facts/problems of an individual situation, the first response required is to the *emotional* state of the other person.

    b. Most immediate ways to do this are through body movement, posture and voice tone, even if the verbal response is not ideal.

2. Employees want responses which seem appropriate *to them.*

    a. "Appropriate" is based on what makes sense in others' context: their past and present experience, generalizations they have made, their previous observations of you, and their current internal state.

    b. Whatever the personal histories, a shift to the employee's state (as observed) will always be appropriate.

   c. It is rarely appropriate for you to make a complete change from a basic style or pattern (you are also matching others' expectation of you).

3. Overall, it is better for your communication to be congruent with your time/attention span.

   a. Suggesting another time and place is ideal.

   b. Part of a manager's job is to recognize when personal needs take precedence over others' needs and to communicate that congruently.

4. A key to successful communication is the ability to pay attention to your own internal state as a cue to a conversation off the track, or "out of frame."

5. Another key element in maintaining rapport is recognizing that *every* action of another person makes sense to that person *and* to discover what conditions make it that way: explicit statements about what is needed, what process is being followed, with brief explanations is helpful.

6. Throughout, matching words, voice tones, gestures, posture shifts are all ways to maintain rapport. Another basic is frequency of contact — informal, random ones with formal, scheduled ones is a good mix.

A Model for Use

Having established that a particular contact is more than a social interaction and with a frame set for that meeting, the following model of a Coaching session demonstrates how the basic requirements are met. The model is based on these steps:

   1. Gathering Information
   2. Select the Appropriate Intervention
   3. Modify Plans and Make Revisions
   4. Reset Checkpoints
   5. Give Feedback and Document

1. *Gathering Information*

A major function of any manager is the gathering and processing of information. Any manager who relied solely on reports would be likely to encounter many unpleasant surprises. The quality of information and timeliness will never match that of direct experience. The value of the total visual and auditory experience of direct, personal communication has been too frequently overlooked. If the value is recognized, then the conditions need to be created for the information flow to occur such as outlined in the preceding Rapport section.

We have been considering the value of regular contact from the point of view of its effect on the employee and rapport. The manager can gain immense value from these contacts by the information which becomes available. Where a manager's communication is congruent with his or her desire to gather information, that manager will receive early warning of problems, signals of potential areas of improvement, and relevant information regarding related areas of operations. Unpleasant surprises will be a thing of the past. Before any communication takes place, you can gain a great deal of information by observing employees at work. By going to them rather than calling them in to your office, you observe them regularly as they typically function. The direct, sensory experience you obtain will be the highest-quality information you receive.

Use Your Direct Experience As Information

Congruent communication at this stage will be a request for information and the behavior which indicates that any information is wanted and acceptable. What is this behavior? What does it look like and sound like? One of the requirements is to show some respect for the internal processes of the employee. Another is to take responsibility for adequate understanding. Another is to demonstrate that unpleasant information is valued equally with pleasant information — simply as information.

Open questions such as, "Are there any problems?" or "What can I do to make your job easier?" or an invitation such as, "Tell me more about the problem you mentioned yesterday" indicates a willingness to listen to an employee tell it in the way most appropriate to that person. These may be used as openers, before a frame has been established. If used after a frame has been established, they will tend to elicit fairly focused statements even though they are extremely general questions or statements.

Where an employee has a method of approaching things which you can't understand or which seems to waste too much time, you can begin to direct the flow of information by asking specific questions based on the words used by the employee. (See Book 1, *Precision Model Questions* and *Precision: A New Approach to Communication*.) These same types of questions are required to elicit the more detailed information contained in the employee's experience but not explicitly stated in the communication. As a manager, you often want to obtain information from the employee's direct, sensory *experience* in preference to the employee's conclusions based on that information and many other personal factors.

The questioning format recommended will demonstrate that you want information based on the employee's experience. Using the employee's own words in your questions will indicate that you are listening and trying to understand. This is particularly important with an employee who is trying to make you understand in a manner which is not getting the message across. The common outcome of this is for the manager to become impatient and dismiss the employee with both of them knowing that understanding was not achieved. The employee is left with the message that the manager doesn't want the information he or she has to offer.

This process usually ends with a summary which demonstrates that understanding has occurred. Jumping to conclusions, offering expert advice, starting to problem-solve, or cutting off a *Find Ways To* conversation without using a summary to discover if *Demonstrate* there is shared understanding demonstrate a lack of *Your* concern for that understanding. Even though you *Understanding* do, in fact, understand, it is necessary that the employee also knows that you do. The other person's subjective experience will be satisfied by your appropriate response to the situation or by a summary which makes your understanding explicit.

There are many stories of executives, business and military as well as government, who never hear negative information until it is totally obvious and too late to do anything about it. Most of *Use Words and* us have similar personal experiences. The executive *Action That* in this position has created the conditions for these *Invite the* results. Few of them have explicitly said to anyone, *Negative and* "Don't tell me those kinds of things." They have, by *Positive* more subtle behavior, given that message quite strongly. The emperor who killed the messengers carrying bad tidings never said, "Don't tell me those kinds of things," but the message got across!

What are the more common forms of sending this message that you are familiar with? There are probably some major ones in your experience, but it is the minor ones which are cumulatively the most harmful. Failing to ask the obvious question, responding in an annoyed tone of voice, failing to ask about overt displays of discomfort or negative emotions, and using leading statements such as, "No one disagrees, do they?" are some common examples. While we can learn to monitor and control these behaviors and choices of words, if we are congruent in our desire for information whether good or bad, our behavior will tend to be appropriate. Think about any objections you had to the preceding material. They will indicate the likely problem areas for you.

Finally, when you are asking for information, what do you look and sound like, apart from your words? Voice patterns for asking questions rise at the end of the sentence to indicate a question. A demanding or aggressive voice indicate something other than simple information-gathering. Facial expressions such as raised eyebrows and gestures such as open palms also suggest questions. Eye contact and other behavior indicate whether attention is being paid to the answer or not.

Besides gathering information for the manager for later use and processing, effective information-gathering at this point will be a major time-saver. Getting involved in problems or issues before gathering adequate information will result in a great deal of time spent in affairs which should be solved by different people, often at a different level.

A major area for employee development is the ability to gather and use information effectively. Often, a manager will have the experience to solve a problem or offer advice after only a small amount of information gathering. Unfortunately this answer comes from the hidden internal processes of the manager and has little developmental value for the employee. Not knowing how the manager arrived at the answer, the employee must repeatedly return for the answer. Any explanation by the manager might improve the situation but will tend to be time-consuming and inefficient. Not knowing the parts of the process which the employee already has, there will be little effective teaching that matches individual requirements.

Further questioning will be the quickest way to effective teaching. Using short, explicit information-gathering questions takes only a little time and produces a lot of information. This information

Effective Information Gathering Techniques

will reveal the gaps in knowledge of the employee or mistakes in his or her way of approaching a problem. These are the areas where the employee needs guidance for personal development. Now, the manager can use direction, give information, or ask more questions to lead the employee to an understanding which will provide the required solution at the same time as improving

93

the employee's ability to handle similar situations in the future. A little time spent at the beginning can save a lot of time later.

This dialogue between a manager and employee provides an example of using questions to obtain the required information:

E: We'll have to replace everything.

M: Or what will happen?

E: The machines will continue to break down.

M: Does *everything* have to be replaced for the machines not to break down?

E: Well, no. But all of the moving parts do.

M: Are there any exceptions?

E: A few are new and some may not be wearing too badly. I guess a few may not need it.

M: What parts, specifically, don't need replacement yet? *(The introduction of "yet" separates the current breakdown from future ones.)*

E: I don't know. Each time it breaks down it seems to be a different one.

M: *(offering expert advice)* First find out which parts are wearing or worn and which are not. Then you can develop a schedule for replacement which will continue to keep this problem under control.

A few repetitions of this kind of questioning will direct the employee towards more efficient, practical information-gathering and less-exaggerated urgency towards problems. A manager may choose to make an explicit learning point at this time by commenting on the process used. In the situations where there is frequent contact with employees, the repetition of this behavior will usually remove the need for explicit comments and teaching. Consistent behavior of the manager will soon shape the behavior of employees along more desirable lines.

A different example illustrates gathering adequate information related to the process used by the employee:

E: Sales are 15 percent below our target and unless we hire another person, I don't see how we can meet our goals.

M: Tell me what the situation is now. *(An open question likely to be used with an already competent person.)*

E: With the competition greater than expected, we're closing a lower percentage of our prospects than we have in the past. It works out like this. Each salesperson can make eight calls per week, and we can expect 50 percent to request bids. That's four bids, which average $45,000, and we can expect to get a favorable decision on

30 percent of them. We've tried to change all of those variables but nothing seems to improve them. The only answer I can see is more salespeople.

M: How have you tried to change them?

E: I sat down with all of the salespeople and we tried to come up with new ideas for each area. But we found we'd already tried to improve our calls, our closing ability, and even to make more calls per week. We seem to have tried everything for all of those. We considered trying to increase the average dollar per bid but we're already concentrating on the best areas and we have to take what business we can get. You can't make more calls per person because you need the face-to-face contact and that just takes a certain amount of time.

M: It sounds like you've got the situation pretty well analyzed. Problem-solving often gets stuck by evaluating suggestions as they are being made. Another way to get creative new ideas is to think of things differently — try to create new problems to brainstorm. I'll ask you some questions to suggest how it works. Okay?

E: Sure.

M: What's the purpose of making eight, or more, calls per week? What will it accomplish?

E: Well, you have to get your pitch in front of as many people as you can.

M: Okay. Then one of the things to brainstorm will be, "How can we get our pitch in front of more people." Do any calls which generate bids get more than one bid from the same person or company? *(Question based on expert knowledge)*

E: Yeah. Some do.

M: Then you might also consider how to generate more than one bid per interested prospect. If you sit down again with your salespeople and try these two items, without any analysis of suggestions until the end of the session, you may discover some new approaches. Also, you might take some of those areas in which you think you "have to" do things and apply the process of finding what they accomplish — *why* you have to do them — and try to find other ways.

In this case, had the manager started in with helpful suggestions, the response probably would have been overtly or merely silently, "We've already thought about that and it won't work."

Creating New Alternatives and Patterns of Thinking Gathering some information allowed the manager to build on the work that had already been done. It also indicated the kind of approach to the problem that had been lacking. The employee's words — "we

95

can expect," "we've tried to change all," "the only answer, "already tried," "have to," and "can't" — suggest boundaries in that person's thinking that are probably reflected in criticizing ideas too early and an inability to think of things in new ways. The manager's suggestions deal with *the process of creating new alternatives, of thinking differently,* rather than the content of a solution.

The kind of response needed in any situation varies with the external requirements of the business and the internal needs of the employee. Development will be achieved most effectively by matching the response to the gap in knowledge of the employee whether it be content or the process of arriving at answers. It is usually much easier to supply the content than discover the incorrect process, but the latter produces far greater rewards.

2. *Select the Appropriate Intervention*

The most common intervention is to offer expert advice. This is normally in the form of content — solutions or information — and provides the minimum in employee development. It also allows little opportunity for employee creativity and frequently is given based on less-than-adequate information. With all this against it, why is it the most common intervention? Surely most managers realize its limitations.

Let's review its attractions. First is probably time. Even with adequate information-gathering to ensure dealing with the right problem, it is usually quickest to offer advice. Stepping through a process or leading employees to discover answers for themselves may *Offering Expert* be quite time-consuming — and often frustrating due *Advice Limits* to our general lack of skill in assisting the internal *Employee Growth* processes of others. Another factor is that we are confident of our own ideas and processes; after all, we are experts. We feel good about being able to solve problems; we'll tend to like the resulting answer.

The major factor which should affect the choice to give expert advice is time pressure. In a crisis, there is seldom time for anything but expert advice and this is the situation where the manager as an expert is highly valuable. If you find that you are constantly giving such advice and justifying it by referring to the need for speed — crisis — then you or your company need to look at the way things are being done. The definition of crisis is that it is occasional, not constant.

Even expert advice can be used for employee development. Simply offering a solution or giving directions transmits the minimum possible information to employees. Exposed to enough of these interventions, some will detect the underlying patterns and learn more general rules. Most will fail to detect these patterns. To increase the employees' chances of learning from the intervention, spending a little time on the reasons or general background will increase their ability to make sense of the intervention and to generalize from it in the future.

A technique which can multiply the developmental value of expert advice is to use the technique of thinking out loud. Offering reasons for

Thinking Out Loud Helps Develop Employees

an answer will often provide the logic or proof for that answer. What can be of much higher value is the process by which that answer was arrived at. Reviewing how you got that answer, or thinking out loud if the employee is present during the process, will give employees a great deal of information about

how to arrive at similar answers on their own. Knowing how to organize information or solve a problem is far more valuable than having ready-made answers from past experience.

You need not have neat models for what you do internally. Some of us are much better than others at explaining how we think. Most of us are not good at all. Thinking out loud doesn't require such organization. Nor does it require explanation of what is happening. Do not allow yourself to be interrupted or caught up in justification. If interrupted say, "I'm just thinking out loud for your benefit. Learn what you can, but please don't interrupt." You are merely reporting anything which might seem significant during the process of arriving at answers. It will reveal the use of expert information as well as the organization and sequencing of mental steps.

A simple example might go something like this:

We have to make a decision on whether or not to accept this batch of parts which have been manufactured outside of specifications. The major alternatives seem to be:

1. reject and wait for a batch within specifications

2. accept and ship a substandard product

3. accept and allocate to noncritical uses

I don't see any other alternatives. That feels complete to me.

If we reject, I see a string of major delays down the line. The customer will have to be told the reason for the delay and I imagine we will have to offer assurance that this won't be repeated. Because we don't have a track record with this customer, if I put myself in his shoes, I'd feel very insecure in future dealings. The really important part is the impact on the customer. I don't like the feeling that gives me.

If we accept and ship substandard, I'd have to tell the customer. I imagine that we'd lose a lot of credibility and the customer would want assurance that it wouldn't happen again. I can see them starting to look for other suppliers right away...and maybe our substandard product being returned. We'd really have to get shipping approval first. Our image with other customers and prospects might suffer if we don't. That's not acceptable either.

Accepting and allocating to a noncritical use looks pretty good from the point of view of customer experience and our own scheduling. We'd have to shuffle jobs a bit but there wouldn't be any major lost time over all. The major problem will be ensuring that our standards are met in the future. I can hear the comments being made in the shop if we accept this substandard batch and don't explain what happened. This approach still leaves a bad feeling over our own quality control but the customers shouldn't experience any significant negative effects.

As I compare the alternatives, the one I feel the best about is to accept for noncritical use. If we can do this one without more than a four-day delay to any customer, let's do it. If not, we'll go to the reject choice. The idea of shipping substandard seems like it would have the worst consequences. Our image would receive the most harm and we could end up in the same production bind. We have to tell the customer anyway, so the reject choice can be given to the customer. We will let the customer know that we don't just ship products outside of specifications and that we still give the customer maximum alternatives.

Going through this kind of procedure will not take very much extra time and will assist employees in learning how to make decisions in a way which matches your process. Besides a lesson in learning how to think, it provides the kind of information which makes sense of a decision without necessarily proving its rightness. Many of the decisions in business which cause apathy, lack of involvement, and worse are the result of resolving conflicts which are apparent to employees but where the basis for resolving is invisible. This is a particular problem in the area of quality-control conflicts such as the example above. Seeing faulty products shipped without knowing the circumstances produces an understandable skepticism.

The intervention of offering expert advice is the most frequent one. I recommend that it be the alternative of last choice: sometimes necessary but seldom best for long-term operation. If that is last on the list, what would be first? What sort of intervention can be made that will produce operating results in reasonable time as well as provide development of employees?

The greatest need in the area of employee development is education in the area of thinking: How to approach a problem. How to sort out useful information. How to establish priorities. How to make decisions. How to use their creative resources. How to communicate their internal thoughts and states. How to turn ideas into reality. These internal processes each have a basic structure which can be taught and learned. As children we have learned many of them unconsciously from those around us. Many of us still learn that way quite well if given the opportunity. Thinking out loud is a useful aid in this process. Even with this aid, though, we each have our own individual ways of doing these things. Most of us follow our own steps which are related to our own way of processing and may be of no use or even a hindrance to others. A tool is required which can accomplish the desired results without depending on the individual processes of the manager.

Educating Employees on Thinking Process

This tool is the use of models. Whenever problem-solving or any other identifiable process is required, giving an explicit model of the steps required and how to accomplish each step will provide learning for the employee. You can present these models by memorizing them, reading from notes, or displaying them on a flip chart for shared use. It is important that they be explicit and that the individual steps be clearly separated as the process is being followed. A model for each of the common major interventions that affect more than one person such as problem-solving and negotiations could be available to employees and shared with them by all managers.

Using Models Is a Good Way To Teach Employees

Each of these interventions starts with an introduction of the model, that is, a specific statement of the steps to be taken. The employee learns the explicit steps by being exposed to them in this way. It also allows employees to organize their own internal resources for what is to come. Next, the manager returns to the first step and begins to go through the process with as much employee participation as feasible in the circumstances. Even when there is little opportunity for participation due to time constraints or lack of employee ability or knowledge, this can still be useful if it is structured as a "thinking out loud" process.

99

If the manager accepts the role of a "developer of employees" apart from what is imparted in specific task-oriented situations, similar models can be developed for any activity whether a physical task or a mental one. These are a base for organizing and presenting the required process regardless of the content. After first presentation and use, they can be modified according to the individual requirements of the organization and the sophistication of the employees. These provide a means for managers to get actively involved in the improvement of performance of employees as well as their more general development.

The final intervention which we need consider separately is the one managers feel most uncomfortable with and handle poorly. It is an area which managers tend to avoid. When an employee is supposed to do something and doesn't, what is the best way to get that thing done and ensure that it will be done without intervention in the future? The most common approaches, when used at all, are penalties of some kind or incentives. These usually come into play only after a situation has gotten out of hand.

This area tends to be most uncomfortable for managers because they lack the ability to help employees with the required changes. Repetitions of non-performance tend to lead us to view the employees as resistant, lazy, or trying to sabotage our efforts. We generally don't want to deal with those kinds of situations. The best result would be if the employee would change behavior and then continue to act in the desired way without further intervention. This supposes that we do have goals in common with the employee and that at least one of us knows how to effect that behavior change.

The starting point for this kind of change is an assumption that the employee is a worthy human being. It is simply a part of his or her behavior that is not appropriate to the situation as you see it. *Each person can be assumed to be acting in a way that seems best to him or her under the circumstances as experienced by that individual.* The starting point of behavior change then becomes a discovery of how the situation is considered differently by the manager and the employee. It is critical at this point to realize that this is simply a time for information-gathering; judgment or solutions are not relevant here.

The first step of a Coaching contact for behavior change will be to gather information to ensure that you and the employee share the same understanding of what was agreed on. If you discover it was not shared, you will correct the information and assume that appropriate results will be obtained. Before leaving such a step, you can spend a worthwhile few

Intervention To
Change Behavior
Starts With
Information

minutes determining what caused the missed communication so that it will happen less frequently in
the future. Going through specific steps to change
behavior is required only when behaviors are
understood and agreed on by both parties. Let's consider an example where a particular behavior has been demonstrated to
produce more sales, has been agreed to by the salesperson, and is not
being done. The manager has noticed the lack of performance, first in
sales goals and second in this particular behavior, and is initiating a
Coaching session.

Here's how the exchange might go between manager and employee:

M: Harry, I've noticed that your sales are below their target level for
the first quarter. I'd like to take a few minutes and review your performance to see if there's anything we can do about this situation.

E: O.K. My sales are down a bit, but the market just isn't going too well
right now. People don't seem to want to buy as much.

M: You've noticed the drop in sales, too. *(pause)* I've noticed when I
walk by your desk and you're talking to customers that you aren't
asking for a specific amount of money when you close. I've also
checked the sales tickets and notice a lot of 100 share orders in your
sales. It appears that you aren't following the sales model we agreed
on as far as asking for a specific dollar investment. Is that correct?

E: Yeah, I guess so. I just don't feel comfortable doing that. It seems too
pushy and I used to get pretty good sales without doing it.

M: It's not a very comfortable way of doing business for you.

E: No.

Agreement has been reached that the manager and employee share the
same information and that the behavior had been previously agreed on.
So far, no judgment or solution has been sought. The manager has given
a little additional information to the employee and listened to some input
from the employee. The employee has also been given the feeling of
respect by hearing the manager acknowledge his position.

The next step is to review the intention of the expected behavior or
result. This is an extension of the information-sharing process. In a high

Reviewing the
Intention of
Behavior

percentage of situations the employee is not aware of
the reasons for a requirement or its priority with
the manager or organization. In these situations, the
employees' behavior makes sense to them and they
are not convinced of the need for change. While
some managers may think that "because I said so" is good enough, it

seldom is. Besides treating employees with more respect as functioning human beings, there are few of us who have not issued conflicting or unclear statements over time which are not possible to be carried out in full. We also tend to assume that many of our intentions are obvious and have been agreed to when we have not made them explicit. Many of these intentions are obvious *in the context of our own knowledge.* Unfortunately, those that work for us often do not share that information and thus make different assumptions about priorities and intentions. *The next step, reviewing the intention, might go like this:*

M: I'd like to brief you on the importance of asking for a specific dollar amount. We've done a lot of study to determine what makes a good salesperson and what produces the highest production per person for the least amount of time. An important part is how closes are made. It is our policy that if individual production is above target, sales can be made with an individual style within broad limits. However, if sales fall below target, we insist that our model be followed because it produces more income for the company and, in our experience, benefits the salesperson as well. Does that make sense to you?

E: Yeah. It's been a while since I took the course and no one's really said much about how I sell until our Planning session. I know about closing, it just doesn't feel right.

M: Yeah. *(In tone of voice to match "doesn't feel right")* Maybe we can find a way to make it easier. I want to make sure you understand its importance first. *(Wait with an expectant attitude.)*

E: I can see it is important and it makes sense. It just isn't comfortable.

The manager has achieved a mutual agreement that certain results are not being met, that certain behaviors are not being done, and that the intentions behind them makes sense. The employee

*Get Agreement
That Results Are
Not Being Met*

has also been responded to in a satisfactory manner around his discomfort with the expected behavior. It has been fully acknowledged without being resolved at this point. The next step will be to agree on a new behavior which the employee will be able and willing to carry out. In most cases, it will do no good to simply restate the already agreed on behavior and expect it to be carried out. If the previous information-sharing revealed a major discrepancy, then we might expect behavior change without any further assistance. In those cases where there already existed a basic understanding yet the behavior didn't take place, more work will be needed. The employee's behavior revealed an inability or unwillingness to act as required. Some other change will have to occur before we can assume that the behavior will change.

The process of agreeing on a new behavior will involve getting more specific information about what is actually happening and then discover-

Agreeing on New Behavior

ing a change which will fit the employee better. This may involve training the employee or discovering a way which fits his or her present understanding. We must discover whether it is a question of skill (unable) or attitude (unwilling) and provide the remedy. The remedy for *unable* is training — simple "how to." The remedy for *unwilling* is often also "how to," with explanations or adjustments to fit the individual's existing beliefs or system. If intentions have been previously agreed to, in fact, then *unwilling* is simply *unable* in a particular context. Lack of agreement and positive results in this step indicate a difference in intention which needs to be dealt with.

Let's continue with our example:

M: Let's see if we can make it comfortable for you. There is probably another way to accomplish the same result which will fit your style better. Maybe we should start with what you are doing right now?

E: Well, it depends on the customer. Sometimes I just ask if they would like to buy some and the other times I usually ask for "a hundred shares."

M: How do you decide which to do?

E: If it's somebody who's been buying in larger lots, I leave it up to them. If it's somebody new or who buys in small lots, I suggest one hundred.

M: So, based on your experience with them and what you think their resources are, you vary your close.

E: Yeah.

M: It sounds like you never ask for a dollar amount. Is that right?

E: That's right. I feel more comfortable asking for a specific number of shares if I'm going to ask at all.

M: Part of our model is to gather information from the client and decide what an appropriate amount might be before attempting to close. Do you do that?

E: Yeah. That's how I know whether to ask for a hundred shares or not. I review their previous record before I talk to them.

M: Okay. Before we look for solutions I'd like to tell you how I view this situation. The first thing that strikes me is that the new customer you get, unless they are the type who just jumps in and buys larger amounts on their own at the start, will soon be "trained" to buy in

103

lots of 100 shares by your approach. I also think that part of the service we provide is to help a customer allocate resources between different kinds of investments. Many people do not know what to do in this area and really appreciate the assistance we can provide. *(pause)*

E: That makes some sense. I hadn't thought of it that way before.

M: You've said that you are more comfortable suggesting shares than dollars. Perhaps you could figure out how much investment would be appropriate, convert that into a number of shares and suggest that to the prospect. Remember, in the sales course they also suggested that you give the customer an alternative as well. Do you think you could do that?

E: Yeah. I think I can.

M: Okay. Do you agree to give it a try for the next month and we'll see what results it produces?

E: Yes, I'll try it.

M: Good. If it doesn't work — if you can't do it or it's still too uncomfortable — you can come and see me and we'll try to find a different way.

E: I think it will work.

Most managers who get this far would stop here. We have, after all, got agreement from the employee for a behavior which meets our needs. What more could we want? After experience with many encounters where behaviors or actions have been agreed to but have not happened, many a manager is skeptical of the above process. What we want is performance in reality, not simply agreement in our office.

The next steps then are designed to increase the likelihood of the transfer of the learning and agreement to the actual work situation. This involves a test for the ability to perform the agreed *Employee Has* behavior and some assistance in ensuring that it will *To Transfer* be carried out at the appropriate times. Things can *Agreement to* sound easy and more agreeable in a manager's office *the Work Place* than back in the real world. An enthusiastic manager and a persuasive presentation will make the task seem easier than it is for that employee. The manager won't be there and the environment won't be the same when it comes time to act. The next step is a test for ability to determine if the employee is, in fact, able to carry out the expected behavior. In the type of situation just described, a role-play can be used on the spot to determine if the behavior is possible and to develop it a little. Another effective method is to set up a real-life trial. A role-play, a simulation, or a test under special conditions can help develop the skill by removing pressures and the added variable of a real-life trial. A final test would be on the job with a report on its success after the first attempt.

Finally, the event which should trigger the desired behavior is reviewed. We want to ensure that the employee knows when the behavior is supposed to occur and that they recognize the time when it arrives. We can help the employee greatly by providing a strong automatic connection between the desired behavior and the triggering event. This event might be a signal within the employee, a signal from the environment, or simply some preceding step in a process. In our example, we want to ensure the salesperson's ability to ask for a specific number of shares based on a preceding calaculation.

Here's how it might go:

> M: The last thing to review to help you start using this close is *when* to use it in your presentation. When will you know it's time to ask for a specific number of shares?
>
> E: I do a trial close and when I get a positive response, I know it's time to go for it. I get a feeling of excitement and tension.
>
> M: Good! And when you get that feeling, you...*(pause)*
>
> E: I plunge right in with, "Shall I put in an order for 500 shares or is there some other amount that seems right to you now?"
>
> M: You'll need to have that number ready before you get to this point then.
>
> E: I already do that before I attempt a trial close.
>
> M: So each time you get that feeling from the trial close — can you feel it now? — good! You plunge right in with...
>
> E: "Shall I put in an order for 500 shares or is there some other amount that seems right to you now?"
>
> M: Good! That should do it. Will you get back to me in the week if it doesn't seem to be working for you?
>
> E: Right.

This intervention can influence major behavioral changes in a cooperative spirit which can be comfortable for all. It is respectful of the needs of the full personalities of each participant while getting the results required by the operating realities. The appropriate non-verbal behavior such as posture and voice tone as well as the respecting words will likely come spontaneously to the manager if the basic assumptions are kept in mind: *The positive worth of the employee is held constant even though the value of his or her behavior may be questioned.*

After the intervention has been made, the Coaching contact needs to be completed in recognition of its part in the overall system of managing. That is, it relates to previous Planning sessions and will be a part of future evaluations. The next steps close the session and are intended to meet the system needs as well as those of the employee.

3. *Modify Plans and Make Revisions*

Many Coaching contacts will originate from checkpoints not being achieved or other problems which may delay reaching goals or affect how they are to be achieved. If the plan needs to be revised, it should be done explicitly and any other affected people or departments advised. Many times, the only plan which needs to be modified is that for the individual employee. The original plan is the contract against which later evaluation will be made.

It is common, however, for plans to be changed. In some situations, it is the rule that plans will change frequently. Most often these changes are not recorded and there are many disputes and

Making Changes
Is Predictable —
Record Them

misunderstandings at evaluation time. Formal recording will help to avoid this problem and also provide some organizational information regarding changes affecting others and the frequency and causes of changes. If plans change too frequently to make such recording feasible, that is a signal that Planning and Evaluation sessions should be held on a different basis. This might be shorter review periods, on a project basis or some other variation.

4. *Reset Checkpoints*

Whenever plans are changed, the nature and timing of checkpoints is likely to be changed as well. Revising plans without changing checkpoints will lead to the same difficulties as planning without checkpoints in the original situation. The worst result is unpleasant surprises which cannot be corrected in time.

A case in point: The software development department of a computer company set quarterly plans, with checkpoints, two quarters ahead of

Expect to Revise
Checkpoints and
Keep Them

expected performance. With that time lag between planning and performance there were very few projects started when planned and therefore also very few completed on scheduled time. The company required that all projects be formally reviewed based on the planned checkpoints and employees were penalized if checkpoints were not met. The review process had become a mockery

106

which failed to serve any of the control functions it was designed for, because the original checkpoints were never revised. Planning and Evaluation was based on scheduled start time, an event outside of the control of the employee, rather than actual start time. The large computer manufacturer using this approach was generating employee ill will and dangerously assuming that it had an adequate product-review function. Checkpoints needed to be changed with actual job-starting times.

It should be noted that checkpoints may often need to be reset even if the original plans are not. If problems are solved which will bring operation back on line, there need to be some new checkpoints to ensure that the solution is being put into effect in a timely manner. Our behavior-change example above included a one-week checkpoint to make sure that the new behavior was being carried out even though there was no explicit change in the plan.

The worst event is for a checkpoint to be missed without any follow-up. We recognize that conditions change, that plans often cannot be met as originally expected. The best possible response to that situation is early warning so that appropriate corrective action can be taken. A checkpoint missed is worse than a plan not achieved. The latter may simply reflect reality and provide information about our planning process. The former suggests that we have no control over what happens or our ability to respond to it.

5. *Give Feedback and Document*

The final step meets the needs of the employee and contributes to the coming Evaluation session. Giving feedback to employees provides them with the information about the relative importance of the item under discussion and lets them know if there is any significant change in the manager's attitude toward them. It may include the kind of behavior needed in the future to achieve a particular rating or reward. It is an answer to the frequent employee demand "We want to know where we stand." Once a year is not enough. We as managers don't like unpleasant surprises and want the opportunity to adjust what is happening to counter unwanted results; just so, an employee doesn't want an unpleasant surprise at evaluation time when it is too late to adjust behavior for better results.

It has been shown many times over that simply providing immediate feedback in a useful form will improve performance dramatically. A variation of this takes place at each Coaching contact. By giving immediate feedback on the meaning of the meeting and the employee's behavior, the manager provides the maximum in incentive and useful information to generate positive change. Many employees report walking away from a manager not knowing quite where they stand, or worse, thinking they stood in a completely different light than their manager saw them in.

When was the last time you gave positive feedback to one of your employees? Has every employee received some in the last month or so?

Giving Positive and Negative Feedback Will Improve Performance
While most managers say that they think positive feedback is good to receive and good to give, very few do it consistently. Those that give it usually miss a few problem individuals. A common question is, "What if they don't deserve it?" Before I answer, I'd like to point out that unless your answers to the first two questions indicate a high level of positive feedback, the question of deserving is not the appropriate focus. My response to the question of being deserving is, "Why is someone still working for you if you cannot find a positive behavior?" If you say you can't, things have already progressed to the point where some outside intervention is required or that person should be fired.

The feedback to be given, of course, need not be positive. There are times when negative feedback is appropriate and it need not be tempered by positive. To be effective, the feedback does need to be given in a particular form and with recognition of the other person's needs. Any situation which has got to the point of having no possibilities for positive feedback, expressed or not, indicates that an inadequate job has been done *by the manager*. Proper feedback, negative and positive, and coaching should have produced behavior change long before this point is reached.

Proper negative feedback requires that the behavior be identified in sensory-grounded terms. That is, the focus is on what is actually seen or heard that is objectionable or counter-productive. It should also contain an expression of at least one of the following:

its effect on the manager and its importance, *or*

its effect on the organization, or its outside contacts

This form of feedback gives the employee a description of the behavior which can be understood and accepted or disputed on grounds which are demonstrable. If a judgment or opinion is given without the behavior base, there can be much argument and disagreement which has no satisfactory resolution.

The statement of negative feedback can be given in a format called the Problem Description Statement.* The structured format of this statement can assist managers in providing useful feedback in a manner which respects the individual personality of the employee. *It goes like this:*

When you *(do something),*
that means *(specific negative result),*
and I *(feeling or corrective action).*

This format ensures that all necessary parts of feedback are included and encourages the use of sensory-grounded language.

Let's consider some of the phrases which might be used. For the first part, starting with an event that did happen rather than a negative or non-event will help to reduce resistance.

"When you agree to have a report to me on a particular day (event), and I don't get it by then..." This states first what did happen which makes the non-performance serious.

"When you don't get reports in on time..." This doesn't clearly specify which events — is it all reports? — and the generalization will likely increase defensive feelings.

"When you goof off on the report..." This is a statement about a portion of your behavior which I do not have information to support. Worse, in this case, it is expressed in terms that imply your character or motives are bad.

When you agree to have a report to me on a particular date and I don't get it contains only factual information about which I am certain and which can be even more explicitly stated if required. The particular agreement, report, and date received are all readily identifiable. The factual basis is clear and can be verified if necessary. If the facts are agreed to, the following parts must be dealt with.

The second part might go something like, "...that means I have to work overtime to prepare my report to the executive or use estimated figures...". This part states the meaning *to me* which may include the impact on customers, other personnel, or the organization. The key in this part is that we are not presenting cause-and-effect justification — proof — but merely the meaning that the event or lack of performance has for us. We want the terms to be meaningful to the other person without necessarily giving the idea that it is a total and necessary cause

*See Book 1, *The Required Communications*

of a problem. To help meet this condition, this part of the sentence can start, "...that means I..." A statement such as, "...that means the company can't organize its affairs properly..." is far too general to be supported or accepted as reasonable.

The final part is often avoided — at least until the feelings are escalated beyond the point of useful expression. In many organizations it is culturally inappropriate to talk about feelings. What tends to happen in these organizations is either that there are periodic explosions, that feelings are expressed in more subtle ways, such as with voice tone and sarcasm, or that the organization suppresses all emotion and becomes a sterile and boring place to be.

Recognizing the existence of this cultural bias, I invite you to attempt to introduce the final part of this sentence into your negative feedback.

This Statement Provides An Appropriate Place for Feelings The feeling expressed need not be vehement. It can be toned down and still serve as a useful part of the feedback to your employees. We all know that feelings are there. The hard part is when we have to guess what they are. They are much easier to deal with on an explicit level. It also serves notice that your feelings count. The earlier demonstration showed a willingness to take account of employee feelings. The other side of that coin is that you are prepared to insist on your own being important when necessary. The feeling which completes our example might be any one of the following:

> "...and I feel let down by you."
> "...and I get annoyed at the extra time it takes me."
> "...and I'm uncomfortable using estimates which may turn out
>   to be inaccurate."
> "...and I'm unsure about our other agreements."

To be effective, this part of the statement must be expressed congruently. That is, your face and voice should match the feeling. A common action is to smile as you are saying it. The smile takes away the significance of the words. Notice that this part didn't introduce any new factors about the employee's behavior. Each phrase was short and contained an explicit internal state.

The words that follow "I feel" must be emotions or internal states rather than thoughts about something. If the word following feel is "that," we have a good indication that the next phrase will be simply more judgment or opinion rather than a description of an actual internal state. The particular trap which is generally used is to express thoughts as feelings and therefore stop any challenge (e.g., "I feel that you were just avoiding work.").

To review this step, the Problem Description Statement contains each of the basic elements in a situation expressed in an explicit manner. There is no room for challenges or defensiveness in the language used. If the facts, the sensory-grounded information, are incorrect, they need to be corrected for the satisfaction of both parties. Once they are accepted, the meaning to the manager and the feelings involved are expressed in ways which are statements of fact that cannot be disputed. The employee will have heard a message that is clear and requires a response leading to a change in behavior.

The follow-up to the Problem Description Statement will depend on the situation. It may be another statement by the manager indicating what needs to be done about the situation now and in the future. It may be an invitation to jointly consider what needs to be done. It may be simply an expectant pause awaiting a solution or appropriate response from the employee.

The Problem Description Statement may also be used as a structure for giving positive feedback for managers who have difficulty doing that. It provides a somewhat formal structure for getting started in what is for them an uncomfortable situation. All of the elements of useful positive feedback are there. It is, after all, easier to reproduce a situation which generates positive responses if you know something about the events and feelings which produced those responses before.

The final part of the feedback and document step is to record the contact in some simple way. Besides meeting organization and legal re-

Keeping Records Helps in Evaluation

quirements, it will be a useful reference when evaluation time comes around. All too often, evaluations are based on a few outstanding events or the events closest to the evaluation date. If the Evaluation session is covering the period of a year, a fair evaluation requires a balance of the year's events. This is extremely hard to do without a record of the past Coaching contacts to refer to.

Remember our earlier discussion of observing and checking employee attitudes and non-verbal behavior. The approaches mentioned in Planning should carry over into Coaching. In Coaching, the nature of the interactions is varied; the exchanges are generally reduced in formality, and so the specifics will be modified according to the situation. The general approach, however, is the same. The need for using appropriate non-verbal behavior and for checking participation with employees has been assumed. Words, voice, and gesture need to be selected to convey respect for the needs of the employee as an individual. In Coaching contacts, the manager will need to organize these elements in a way to meet his or her own needs as well. The Problem Description Statement was introduced as a tool for achieving that end.

Although the Coaching contacts are less formal in structure and are generally not planned events, they are the most important part of the process. Planning and Evaluation are required to

Coaching Keeps the System Responsive have a system of Performance Management. The regular contact provided by Coaching makes the system human and responsive to the needs of employees, managers, and the organization. The direct, operating contact provides regular, high-quality information and the human contact which we all require. It will usually be better to provide this contact even though it contains negative elements than to provide none at all.

Evaluations are generally avoided by managers where possible and frequently looked upon with dread when they must happen. The factor which can make the biggest single change to this is a history of effective Coaching contact. The exchange of information and the support provided by the manager provide the best insurance against either person having to deal with unpleasant surprises in an Evaluation session. The Evaluation session becomes pretty much a review and summary of what has already been dealt with as a basis for future growth.

Here's a review of the steps of the Coaching session as presented in the model:

1. *Gathering Information.* Also reveals gap of information. Of major importance is the visual and auditory experience of direct, personal communication. Actually observing employees at work provides another kind of useful direct, sensory experience. A request for information should elicit responses from the employee's direct, sensory experience, rather than conclusions.

   In asking for information, summarize to demonstrate understanding. Do not jump to conclusions, giving advice, etc. Use employee's own words. Listen to key words: *can't, won't, have to, only answer* suggest boundaries in employee's mind. Be aware of sending "don't tell me" messages:

   By failing to ask obvious question.

By responding in annoyed tone of voice.

By failing to ask about overt displays of discomfort or negative emotions.

By asking leading questions, "No one disagrees, do they?"

Avoid above pitfalls by *asking* — through facial/body expression, eye contact, etc.

2. *Selecting appropriate intervention.* Giving expert advice provides *minimum* of employee development. A positive approach is thinking out loud:

Reveals thought process and alternative solutions, and gives employee model for similar problem-solving.

Beyond "thinking out loud," using explicit step-by-step models will provide learning for employees — you can memorize, read from notes, use flip charts.

When things don't go as expected:

As a starting place: the employee is a worthwhile person whose behavior makes sense as he or she understands circumstances.

Be sure to gather information to see if you and employee share information about what was to happen.

Agree that behavior/results are not being met.

Review intention of expected behavior/results.

Reach mutual agreement that certain results are not being met and that intentions behind them make sense.

Agree to new behavior which employee is willing and able to carry out — which fits his or her understanding.

Test for ability to perform agreed behavior (in safe surrounding).

Check trigger (anchor) for desired behavior.

3. *Modify Plans — Make Revisions.* Do explicitly. Record changes. Inform other affected people/departments.

4. *Reset Checkpoints.* Can reset even if original plans are not changed.

5. *Give Feedback and Document.* A reponse to employees' need to know where they stand.

Give immediate feedback. Model for negative feedback — Problem Description Statement:

When you *(do something)*,
that means *(specific negative result)*,
and I *(feeling or corrective action)*.
Follow-up includes recording the contract, for smooth operation and as reference for future evaluations.

Evaluation

Intention

The intention of the Evaluation session of a Performance Management System is to create a shared understanding for reward and growth.

A Summary of the Past and a New Place to Start
There is a likelihood of this occurring *only* if an adequate job of planning and coaching has been done already. This session will consistently be considered useful and fair by the employees only if they have known what is expected of them and how they were doing along the way. Ideally, employees have participated in creating their own plan, committed themselves to the achievement, and received some feedback along the way. This is one area where you must allow employee involvement if you are to produce a positive result. Any successful system requires goals, feedback, and adjustment on a continuous basis. These elements have already taken place. Evaluation, then, is a summary of the important points from the previous Planning sessions and Coaching contacts. The Evaluation closes the cycle for any particular planning cycle, provides formal feedback for the organization, and creates a starting place for the next cycle, which again will depend on Planning, Coaching, and Evaluation.

A major concern of most organizations is that employees experience the system as fair. The minimum requirement for creating this experience is an evaluation which is understood by employees and which is based on agreed conditions. It is desirable that the evaluation itself be agreed to but at the least the facts upon which it is based should be agreed to.

If we've said that the system must be fair, how do we decide what is fair? How can we create the experience of fairness when individual values and expectations are so varied? Before we consider the elements which contribute to an experience of fairness, let's consider the area of subjective experience for a moment. An experience of fairness is, after all, subjective, dependent on the beliefs and understanding of the individual. I cannot decide what you will consider fair, I can only create a set of conditions which will match your idea of fairness or not.

The subjective experience of others is profoundly affected by communication. The first opportunity you'll have to influence the experience of fairness is at the first contact with the employee or prospective employee. Providing information about how the system works and what it is intended to accomplish can go a long way towards setting a framework within which fairness will be judged.

Fairness Is Perceived When Expectations Are Matched

Related to this is the requirement that the organizational system matches the expectations we have established. From this point on, our behavior will be compared to the expectations we have created and we will be considered fair to the extent that they match. Communication, as perceived in your behavior and the organization's intentions, will be the largest single factor in the subjective experience of the employee.

Most of us recognize that motivation and incentive also arise from subjective experience and that if an organization is perceived as unfair, motivation and incentive are unlikely to occur. An Evaluation session will not, by itself, be enough to create an experience of fairness. However, assuming that the organization is actually attempting to be fair, to operate within its own policies, most experiences of *unfairness* will be a result of lack of communication.

The Evaluation session is intended to provide formal feedback to the organization for future management needs, for future promotion and firing decisions, and to ensure that the system is being followed as intended. It also sets minimum requirements for formal review and closure between manager and employee regarding performance. It is intended to provide a fresh start from a current base of information. Specific training needs often develop out of these sessions. Inadequate performance in a particular area will become obvious. Agreed goals which have not been reached, even with the best coaching that a manager can

Evaluation Reviews Performance and Reveals Training Needs

116

provide, indicate training needs for that individual. The summary provided by this session may indicate future development needs even when all goals have been met.

This is generally a good time to discuss career paths. The execution of previous plans and the review of resources needed will provide a realistic background for consideration of future plans. Discussing the specific strengths and weaknesses provides the content for what will have to be done to attain the career goals of the employee. The manager will also be in the best position to personally determine the appropriate goals for the employee within the organization.

The employee's experience of fairness will be significantly affected by what happens in the "real world" related to the evaluation of performance. The "real world" will consist largely of two factors: pay and promotion. We might stop for a minute and consider the relationship of pay and promotion. Do they necessarily go together? That is, does performance which merits a pay raise necessarily also contribute to promotion? In my experience, the answer is that they are frequently unrelated. Although it will normally take an above-average performance in all departments to merit consideration for promotion, there may be many cases of exemplary performance where promotion is not considered. The famed "Peter Principle" is the result of confusing these two factors.

The value of continuous growth for all employees as the route to continuous growth for the organization has been an important part of this series. The Evaluation session is an integral part of *Evaluations Are* a system for growth. It ensures that periodic reviews *Difficult to* provide a basis for development originating in the *Conduct and* individual circumstances, that training is based on *Essential for* individual needs, and that frequent new bases are *Growth* established for measurement of that growth. Evaluations are the most frequently stressed part of Performance Management Systems in most organizations. Often there is a regular evaluation without any complete system. Outside of the context of Planning and Coaching, evaluations tend to be extremely difficult to conduct and accomplish little of their intended results.

In many large organizations, evaluations are avoided or poorly done even though required. This is frequently due to the discomfort we expect to experience when evaluating another human being. The techniques we're presenting here will go a long way to removing that discomfort. The biggest factor, however, will be what has preceded the evaluation. Adequate Planning and Coaching will solve most of the problems.

Framing

Setting the context is particularly important in any encounter which may be expected to generate strong feeling. An evaluation which contains any negative components can be expected to *Framing —* generate some defensiveness. A generally negative *a Way* evaluation will likely produce strong negative feel- *to Deal with* ings such as antagonism, anger, depression, and *Negative* extreme defensiveness. These will have to be dealt *Responses* with as they occur. The framing which is done at the start lets employees know that they will have a place to air their feelings and contribute their facts. This in itself will allow them to better control those negative feelings and reduce the obstructive behavior which might otherwise be shown.

The framing may also assist in removing some of the personal discomfort which we as managers feel at evaluating another person. With a known and shared procedure to follow, the flow of the meeting will not depend on the feelings of the manager or the employee in the same way as they otherwise might. The progression will be agreed to by both parties before the emotions are hot.

The framing will contain all of the elements of every effective frame, namely:

1. A statement of intention from the manager's point of view
2. A statement of intention for the employee
3. A review of the process to be followed

The basic format and method of presentation have been covered earlier in *Planning*. A prepared outline which is read from or even simply handed to the employee will be better than no framing at all. It is also extremely helpful to managers, at least at the start of the system, to have a written outline which they can refer to before the Evaluation session takes place even if they intend to make the framing in their own words on the spot.

The framing example which follows could be used as the basis for a written outline to all managers. It is the kind of framing which assumes a full commitment to employee development and involvement. If the organization or individual managers do not intend to follow through in this manner with appropriate action, the example should be adjusted.

Here's a fairly complete framing model:

118

The purpose of this Evaluation session is to make sure that we have a shared understanding of your performance as the basis for pay increases and for your future growth. I want to make sure that I have based my evaluation on a fair representation of the facts — of your actual performance and the context we provided — and make sure that you understand the situation in the same way I do. Then I want to provide any information you need to make sense of what has happened and my evaluation of it and make sure that you have a clear understanding of your rating. After that, I want to review your goals and begin to plan what I can do to help you reach your career goals with this organization.

This session is intended to make sure you have a chance to have your say and to make sure you understand what's behind your evaluation and rating. I'll try to be as clear as I can and I invite you to ask any questions or add facts as you see the need. My goal is to get the performance we need here and to help you develop in ways that interest you the most. You'll also have a chance to criticize my performance and the rest of the organization's if you think we got in your way or if you have ideas about how we might help in the future.

I've made the session sound a little heavy, and I'm sure it will go better than that. My goal is to use this session to help us both get increasingly better at what we do.

How does that sound to you?

Do you have any comments or questions?

The procedure we'll follow has five separate steps. Although we might have to double back on occasion, I'll try to complete each one before we move on to the next. If we do it this way, we should each get to say all we want and still get it done in a reasonable amount of time.

The first step will be for me to give you the basis for my evaluation. I'll give you what seems to be the important facts and then explain any which you are unclear about. If you're not sure about any of them or think I've missed an important part of what happened, make sure you ask me about it.

Second, we'll agree on the facts which should go into the evaluation. If there are any which I've missed that you think should be included, this will be the time to mention them. This is the time to clear up any disputes, to discuss relevant circumstances, and add any items which may have been overlooked. It is important to me and the organization that we agree here. If we don't, we'll proceed with the evaluation but it will be "under protest," that is, we will have to get agreement at a later date and possibly change the evaluation, or a higher level of management will decide what needs to be done.

119

Third, I'll give you the evaluation and what it means in terms of pay and promotion. I'll attempt to explain to you the reasoning behind it if there are any surprises. The most common cause of misunderstanding is a different view of priorities and if we discuss them now we can work better together in the future.

Fourth, you get to evaluate me. You get to tell me what I did to hinder you, what I might have done to help you, how the organization has supported you or could have done better, and what you'd like to happen in the future. This part is your forum and I encourage you to say anything you want. The company wants me to hear what you have to say and I want to hear it. I'll try to "bite the bullet" and just listen carefully to you.

Finally, we'll review your goals, your likes and dislikes, and begin to think about how I can help you achieve them. We'll use this time to discover what we need to plan towards in the way of training or new experience to reach the goals you have for yourself. I can tell you what I think is indicated based on the evaluation and we can lay the groundwork for our next Planning session.

Any questions about the procedure?

We won't have completed the process until we agree on the facts or a method to get agreement, until you understand clearly the evaluation, until you've had your say, and we've started moving toward the coming period. This session will complete the planning cycle and give us a new start for the future.

This procedure should be adhered to fairly strictly until you are comfortable with the process. You will find as you use it that many anticipated problems don't appear; the problems that do can be handled much more easily. This type of experience is what is necessary to remove the dread of evaluation sessions that most managers have. Even negative evaluations can turn into positive experiences — even though they may not be totally comfortable.

Separating factual basis from evaluation and allowing the employee a special time to air thoughts and feelings will keep control of the process. The employee will more easily participate knowing he or she will have a chance later.

• *To recap —*

The *Intention* of the Evaluation session is to establish a shared understanding for reward and growth. The total system depends on goals, regular feedback, and adjustment. Evaluation is the place to summarize the previous stages. It closes the cycle, provides feedback to the organization, and provides a starting place for the next cycle.

An important element is that the system be perceived by employees as being fair — a subjective judgment by the employee that is heavily affected by communication and congruency in the manager's and the organization's actions.

Framing sets the stage — the context — so that an employee knows what to expect and how to participate.

Rapport

Of all the interactions we have considered in this book, evaluations have the greatest need for rapport. Evaluating another person is likely to be uncomfortable for both parties, at least at the start, and the emotional charge is likely to be at its highest. Rapport may also be hardest to achieve at this point, particuarly if there has not been adequate rapport in the past.

Imagine you are preparing to go in and talk with your boss about your past performance and you know it has been below the expected and agreed levels. You have some anger at your boss, *Rapport Is* a feeling that you didn't put as much as you might *Crucial In* have into your job, some defensiveness, and a lot of *Evaluations* apprehension about what is about to take place. What could your boss possibly do to get rapport with you in that state? Remember that your boss wants the rapport to last throughout the meeting and that this is only one of a series of interactions, including evaluations, which you will have together. Since the evaluation is going to be negative, your boss cannot simply set your mind at rest by assuring you that everything will be pleasant and positive.

In these situations, we are usually so concerned with our own internal states that we leave little of our attention for awareness of the external world. Both the manager and the employee are likely to be in this kind of state at this time. If both are responding to negative internal states of their own, the amount of effective communication occurring is likely to be minimal. The objective of Evaluation sessions is to accomplish something positive, not merely to go through a formality of saying words to an employee.

The *greatest single source of rapport* is the ability to take in all of the communication offered by another person and to respond in an ap-

*Respond to
Other's
Understanding of
the World*

propriate manner — appropriate by *the other person's* understanding of the world. Failure to respond in this way seriously reduces the ability of the recipient to receive our communication. Assuming that our manager wants us not only to hear what is said but to participate in the Evaluation session, what might that person do or say to establish enough rapport to proceed? What would it take to get you to a frame of mind where you had most of your normal resources available to you, where you could listen without an overbearing need to defend or attack? What feeling would you need inside you to get to that state and where might it come from?

Let's take your manager's role now. As the manager, you are feeling uncomfortable too. You are about to give a negative evaluation which you wouldn't like giving under any circumstances. To make things worse, you imagine that the employee coming in is going to be angry and defensive. You are working towards a point where you simply want to get it over with and don't expect anything good to come of it.

But wait. Our need at this point is to set aside these feelings and remember that our goal is to have an Evaluation session involving our employee which will meet the intentions we established earlier, particularly a session which will lead to a better future performance and better relations. How can we set aside our feelings and do a good job with the evaluation?

By focusing on our intentions and the positive outcome desired, we can put our feelings in a less dominant position and gain access to our power and resources. Then we can consider what actions we can take, what things we can say to get the result we want in spite of the negative feelings we have. As the manager, we need to remember that the employee is probably feeling so negative that he or she will not gain anything from the session. And, as the manager, it is up to us to create the conditions to change that situation. We can hardly expect the employee to ease our own discomfort.

The first requirement is that we establish contact with the employee when we first meet. This means that we see and hear the employee and

*Pay Attention
to What Is,
Not What
You Anticipate*

respond to the other person's present state as we experience it. Not to where we expect that person to be. Not to our own internal states. Simply to what is obvious in front of us. Responding to what we expect will probably ensure that we get it. Responding to our own needs based on our internal states will probably get worse. How can we detect another's state and respond accordingly? What is an appropriate response? Each individual contact will have a different requirement. By listening to the words, by paying particular attention to the voice tone, by observing posture, by noticing gestures and expressions, we can get a quick impression of what needs to be done and what the employee is feeling.

Our first response should be to that state. It can be made without mind-reading accuracy by mirroring the physical and voice qualities. This activity will help accomplish two things. The act of mirroring will help you to recognize the internal state of the employee. It will also give an immediate non-verbal message that you are aware of the employee as a human being and are responding to him or her. At this point, you have made a start without any concern for what words are chosen. It has occurred while normal social amenities are taking place.

Assuming that the employee is apparently uncomfortable, it will be most effective to mention it in a way which makes sense to him or her. That might be a comment on the person's condition. The least elegant choice: "You seem really uncomfortable with this meeting" and a follow-up, such as, "Let's see if we can make it a better meeting than you're expecting right now."

A better choice than commenting on what you see and hear in the other person but which is yet unacknowledged might be to comment on the circumstances which cause such feelings, such as, "These kinds of meetings make most people uncomfortable. Never knowing quite what's going to happen often causes people to expect the worst." And then follow up with, "I expect we can make it a positive meeting and the worst won't happen. Let's see what we can do."

Another choice which is often most effective is to comment on your own internal state (or what it might be if you were the employee) indicating complete understanding of the situation.

Start By Commenting On Your Own State That might go something like: "I usually start these sessions feeling a little awkward. I remember when I was being evaluated, I always had the feeling 'I wonder what's coming next'...and my boss always seemed pretty uncomfortable. Some of that's still there when I get evaluated by my current boss."

These kinds of words, accompanied by a manner and tone which match the words and state of your employee, will go a long way to establishing rapport. You can maintain that rapport by noticing the changes in body and voice — in expression — in your employee, by listening to his or her words and by responding in appropriate ways. The first step is simply to notice all of the communication which is being sent to you. The ability to do this will be enhanced by looking and listening for changes without guessing what they mean. Being willing to see and hear and to respond to that will go farther than any techniques which can be learned — although techniques can make it easier.

Before the formal start of the Evaluation session, one other useful thing can be done which might be considered an extension of rapport. A positive internal state can be elicited from the employee before the session begins. This might be related to a work experience which is shared, a part of your relationship, or another experience which can be expected to be part of the employee's reality. The purpose of this positive state is to provide an internal state which can be returned to when useful.

When an employee becomes angry, depressed, or when some other negative state intrudes in the session, that employee loses a significant part of the resources which might otherwise be useful in the session. Many of us cannot even see or hear very well when in one of these states. The session won't be completed successfully unless the employee participates with something like his or her full resources. As managers, we need to be able to restore resources to our employees, by helping them recall, usually through subtle means, that positive state.

Heavy Emotion Blocks Full Resources

The extra effort may be made at any time. We consider it here because of the amount of fear and apprehension which the manager usually feels over the possibility of negative emotions arising during Evaluation sessions. Experience with this model indicates that such is not usually the case, but until you have experienced it, a technique for assisting you in that event seems worthwhile.

The kinds of things which might be said to elicit this positive internal state might include:

> You really did a fine job on that accounts conversion, Jim. Everything got done on schedule with fewer hassles than I expected. You must have gotten a lot of satisfaction from that.

> *or*

> We've had a couple of productive meetings on planning for your staff for next year. We've got a lot done in a short period of time and I've really enjoyed them. I feel like we're working well together.

or

I was just thinking about our last Planning session. Whenever I have a session like that I get really enthused about the coming year. It's like the excitement I felt when I first started to work. I didn't know what was going to happen but I felt a lot of anticipation over the exciting new challenges that were ahead. I knew things were going to be different and that they would be better.

Each of these approaches is designed to elicit a positive state in the employee as he or she accesses his or her part of that experience or a similar one. Said in a congruent tone of voice — best done by actually re-experiencing the situation yourself — the employee will likely remember the situation with a similar internal state. By using a technique called *anchoring*, you can elicit that same internal state at a later time. The internal state you elicit will be connected with the voice tone, expression, and posture you use as well as any gestures which might accompany your words — the anchor. Whenever you want the employee to access that private state, you can repeat the voice, expression, posture and gestures — without explicit reference to the same words — and the employee will tend to feel the same way as in the first situation.

Although this can be used anywhere during the session, it will generally have the most beneficial effect when it is assisting the employee in accessing resources when the employee most wants that to happen. Just before you consider what needs to happen in the coming year would be a likely time to use the anchor. Just before you ask for feedback on your own performance would be less appropriate. Used every time the employee is about to express a negative reaction to you will be looking after your own needs at the expense of those of your employee. The long-run impact on rapport is likely to be negative if you use techniques such as this to meet your own needs instead of those which your employee has in the conditions which you create.

A Model for Use

The model which is being used for Evaluation can be used to assist in gaining and maintaining rapport. By making the model explicit and letting the employee know what's coming, you can take away a lot of the uncertainty which causes apparent resistance. It is hard to pay attention to the business at hand if we feel we had better look for the first opening to defend ourselves. Knowing that we will have a place for that makes it easier to pay attention to the present.

The model is based on these five steps:
1. Give the Basis for Evaluation
2. Get Agreement on the Basis
3. Give the Evaluation
4. Elicit Feedback From the Employee
5. Review for the Future

1. *Give the Basis for Evaluation*

An evaluation is a measure of performance. Within the context of a Performance Management System, it is a summary of how well an employee's performance matched the original plans set at the beginning of the planning cycle. The Evaluation will measure all of the explicit performance plans made, all of the items which were not made explicit but assumed as commonly understood, and all of the revisions made in Coaching contacts throughout the time period.

The basis for the evaluation is that set of facts, of actual events, of particular behaviors, which make up the performance of the employee. These are all items which could be witnessed and verified under appropriate conditions.

An expression of your opinion about some particular performance at this point will not be within the boundary of giving the basis for evaluation. If you find that employees are justifying and defending behaviors, review your language for evaluation comments. If I say to you, "I'm disappointed that you held only a few planning sessions with your employees in the last six months," you will likely experience a desire to defend yourself. I have indicated the behavior and my evaluation of it. If, however, I say to you, "Our plan called for at least one planning session with each of your people and four of them have still not had planning sessions," you will likely accept that as fact (if it is) and possibly add some relevant facts of your own in the same manner. I have, after all, simply stated some facts.

Many times our performance is judged against a standard which we have never known or understood. In most situations, the best format will be to name the planned item or the specific unstated expectation against which the performance is being compared and then specify the actual performance. This will give the employee the basis for your evaluation and allow him or her to provide information about either item if it seems relevant.

The language to use here is explicit, sensory-grounded words. These describe a situation so that it cannot be mistaken. It is usually better to

126

err on the side of too much detail than to assume the employee knows what you are saying.

Compare these contrasting examples:

> You were late far too many times last year.

> You were late a minimum of four times a month last year and a total of 70 times. *A statement about acceptable limits set by agreement or company policy would normally follow.*

> Your attitude towards customers with complaints was too abrupt and unfriendly.

> You frequently interrupted customers before they had finished telling you their complaint, you often pointed your finger at them, and sometimes never smiled throughout the whole exchange. I saw a number leave who looked more angry than when they came in and we've had 14 complaints about your attitude.

The Evaluation should contain no major surprises. Unless it originates from a very recent event, any fact which is a surprise to the employee indicates that an inadequate job of coaching has been done. The details of the behavior should already have been covered in earlier Coaching contacts. If the behavior is continuing in an unacceptable manner, then the specifics should be repeated with the assumption that the employee is still unclear about what is expected.

Noteworthy behavior should also be mentioned in some detail. We often neglect to tell employees in enough detail about the good things that they do. There is merit in saying "good job" but there is a great deal more benefit in specifying what exactly made it a good job. This has particular impact when it is stated in terms of the positive behaviors and abilities demonstrated. Surprises shouldn't occur here either. Good Coaching contact will have provided the employee with some positive feedback. It will be beneficial to remember it at evaluation time.

Managers sometimes feel that an evaluation should be all bad or all good. There seems to be a feeling that one will take away from the other.

Evaluations Will Contain Some Good and Some Bad The reality of any situation in which I have been involved is that there are some good and some bad in all performance. All goals are seldom fully met or fully missed. The basis for evaluation should be a summary of all performance. Any significant point, positive or negative, should be included in the explicit basis for the employee. The significance of each can be explained later in the session. At some point in an evaluation containing any negative information, we are likely to encounter excuses, justifications, and other defensive arguments. How are we to deal with them? If the purpose of this step is to give the basis for evaluation, there is no place here for such behavior. However, as I'm sure you have already thought, your employee may not feel that way and be quite insistent on continuing to press for such defense.

Here is a strong test of your personal ability. How can you maintain rapport, maintain control of the process, and get to your stated outcome? There seems to be a conflict here in which one of the desired results must be lost: either maintain rapport or complete the evaluation. People or results. Frequently, it is at this point that the situation degenerates into an argument which the manager wins in the end by using his or her position of power. But who really wins? Usually nobody.

Remember what it takes to maintain rapport. You must respond to the needs of the human being you are communicating with. This must be done in an appropriate manner for that person, but it need not violate your own needs in relation to the previously specified outcome. The first step is to give a response which acknowledges what is important to the employee. The important point will revolve around the employee's feelings rather than the content of what is said.

Let's consider an example and then develop the components that make it work:

M: You frequently interrupted customers before they had finished telling you their complaint. I saw a number leave who looked more angry than when they came in and we've had 14 complaints about your attitude.

E: Well, sure, I got some complaints. The kind of people who come in to complain about their purchases are often unpleasant types who'll complain about everything. I can't keep everyone happy and still maintain the store policy for returns.

M: It's not an easy task dealing with those people at times.[A] *(pause, then voice shift)* What we're trying to do now is just establish what actually happened during the year.[B]

E: Well, I had the same sales responsibilities as everyone else and I had to handle the complaints too. I really think if I'd got a little more help from some of the others, it would have gone better. Some of them sell things to people when they know we're going to get them back.

M: There are some things which might help you do a better job next year. Maybe you'd make a note of that and we can discuss it when we start preparing for next year. *(Maintain rapport by acknowledg-*

128

ing — pause) I'd like to make sure you understand what facts I took into account and to add any others you think might be relevant. *(Re-direct, lead back to process — pause)* I think 14 complaints about your attitude is too many, and reports and observation of the effect of your behavior on customers doesn't match up with the store policy of having satisfied customers. We say that satisfaction is guaranteed or your money back. [C]

E: Yeah. We did talk about that a few months ago and I think it's gotten better. I was having a tough time at home for quite a while. There haven't been any complaints about me in the last two months have there?

M: No, there haven't been any in the last two months. I'm glad to see that.

[A] Rapport is maintained after each employee defense with pacing and by acknowledging what was said. The acknowledgement should match the tone of what was said in voice and meaning. Notice that in doing so, it never adds an opinion which relates to the evaluation. The employee needs to feel that he or she has been heard and responded to. The importance of the comments relating to the evaluation can then be put on hold until that time comes.

[B] The manager then leads or directs the discussion back to the outcome of this particular step. The defensive statements are acknowledged and then directed back to the appropriate step of the process — "Giving the facts." When the first attempt is met with more defensiveness, the choice might have been to proceed without added comment. It is generally unsafe to do that if a series of statements have been followed by defensive responses. It indicates that the employee has not fully registered the situation being presented.

[C] When the first pace and lead doesn't produce the desired response, the manager repeats it with different words and follows with a more detailed explanation of expected performance standards. In what appears to be an obvious area, such as customer reaction, the expected performance may have been only implicit before. The employee, of course, has heard it all in the context of a Coaching contact. Again, this representation should simply be a summary of what has gone before.

The pacing and leading have created the conditions for the employee to acknowledge the previous Coaching contact and respond with some information and feelings about current performance.

Guide Employee's The employee also indicates a desire to have im-
Behavior By provement acknowledged and the manager does that
Providing a Time quite simply. The manager takes control of the
for Response situation quickly by providing a place and manner
for the employee to add facts for consideration. The employee has started off in a defensive manner and the session will lead to argument and dissatisfaction if that path is followed. By indicating the appropriate timing and nature of employee input without attempting to

stifle such input, the manager begins to direct the employee's behavior into productive channels. This manner allows the employee to control his or her own behavior in a manner most useful to the desired result for the session for both participants.

All input from the employee should be accepted by the manager. The "redirect" which follows irrelevant information or defensiveness — and little distinction need be made between them — does not imply that the preceding comment has been ignored. It is allowed to stand by itself and then a return is made to the business at hand. To explain how it is irrelevant would simply lead further from the desired track. All information can be accepted from the employee without making explicit reference to the weight of the new input. The evaluation has been kept out of your own presentation so it need not be applied to the facts contributed by the employee.

Throughout the summary, the manager should be doing some checking to ensure that the employee understands and agrees with the facts presented. Any changes of emotional state or obvious disagreements may well be pursued at the time they are noticed. Otherwise, they should be noted for further development in the session. Completion of this step will involve obtaining some input from the employee.

2. Get Agreement on the Basis

In most cases, substantial agreement will be reached as you give the basis for your evaluation and accept input from your employee. In that case, this step will be a sort of summary closure for the preceding one. You will need to go to greater lengths here if you have elicited little participation from your employee earlier. The completion of this step requires that the employee contribute all that is needed in the way of facts and that he or she understands and agrees with the manager's facts. The evaluation should not be given until this part has been completed.

In the preceding step, each item was dealt with individually. Agreement and understanding were reached and the employee contributed relevant additional material. If agreement was not reached, a method for determining the facts was established or the item was held "without prejudice." Any major item in this category might require that the session be terminated until the appropriate information can be gathered. Before asking for explicit agreement to the facts from the preceding step, the manager should present a summary of what has occurred. The employee may feel that he

All Information Is Now Summarized and Agreed On

or she agreed to and understood each item as it was covered but have a very different feeling when they are gathered together as a summary. Considered together, things often seem different than when considered separately. The impact and significance of certain items may appear to change or we may have left out large areas of pertinent material.

The need to deal with emotion will frequently occur here. The employee who could deal with each item individually may find that a summary of mainly negative items will trigger a defensive response. The need to explain and justify may not appear until this point. This summary also indicates that the basis is complete. When an employee was expecting the better things that they remember to come last, they may react to what they perceive as an unfair representation.

Since you recognize the need for rapport, your first response will be to acknowledge the feeling of the employee. He or she can then be led toward providing additional information which might be relevant to the evaluation. Elicit the necessary information and acknowledge hearing it without indicating its weight in the evaluation. It may be important to establish whether or not the new material is fact or how that will be decided. If there is a significant amount of information or if a part of it will change the overall picture, it will usually be effective to summarize again with the new material included.

Completion of this step requires that the employee explicitly agree to the facts upon which the evaluation will be based. If previous contacts have been effective and the employee has been *A Basis Has To* responded to appropriately, this should not be a dif-*Be Agreed To* ficult step. Disagreement indicates that the outcome *Before Evaluation* of the Evaluation session cannot be achieved and that *Is Given* some other course of action needs to be taken. The overriding objective was to achieve a mutually understood basis for reward and growth. If the basis cannot be agreed upon, the outcome cannot be achieved.

How could such an impasse arise? How might it be overcome? These are questions which management must take into account when they set the objectives of the system. The manager involved should step back and review the process followed with the employee and attempt to reach the desired outcome. If it cannot be reached, there needs to be some procedure within the system to handle it — if the system is to maintain its integrity. This might involve a disinterested arbitrator or a higher level of management. No evaluation should stand without this level of agreement being achieved.

3. *Give the Evaluation*

The evaluation is the statement of the net effect of all of the behaviors, actions, and results that go into performance. It is the subjective report of the manager which is the result of all of the factors throughout the year. The evaluation is a reflection of the relative importance of each of the elements of performance to the manager. Although there are objective elements, such as sales quotas, budgets, and productivity figures, the rating will include the subjective experience created in the manager by the employeee.

An extra bit of framing will often be useful at this point. If the rating is less than the employee might expect, there will often be some significant emotion and a desire to interrupt or protest. *Use Framing* Setting a context for what is about to happen and the *To Assist the* employee's part in it allows the employee to better *Employee Here* control his or her own behavior. This is not a procedure for softening what is to come but for assisting the employee in organizing personal resources. Including a phrase such as, "I'm giving you a rating here just because the company insists that it be done" doesn't change the rating or its effects. This kind of phrase merely removes the personal responsibility of the manager for the rating. The employee is left with no one to object to or to express anger or frustration to. The manager should make it clear that he or she is responsible and is the one to receive any such response — to ensure that this important event is personal.

The framing might go something like this:

> Now that we've agreed on the important facts for the year's performance, it's time for me to give you your overall rating. I'll summarize the major points and talk about the relative importance of each and then give you the rating. The purpose is to make sure you have a clear understanding of what the rating is and that it makes sense to you. It will probably work best if you just listen until I've gone through each item and give the rating. Then I'd like you to give your opinion of it and ask any questions you have which might help you to understand it. When we've finished this part, you should know what to do next year if you would like a different rating. Once that's done, we can leave the past year and concentrate on where we go from here. Is that all right with you?

The frame should be given with as much observation of the comfort level of the employee as possible. You will want to know whether that

132

person does, in fact, feel comfortable with the process and understand it. You will also want to observe whether he or she is ready to proceed and decide if you want to go back to expanding the basis for evaluation. You then can respond to the signals you get in a way suitable to your judgment of the situation.

The perception of fairness which we want the employee to have is a result of making the elements of the manager's subjective experience

Full Information Helps Contribute to Fairness

sensible. The facts which have been given and agreed to should result in a similar evaluation by another manager. The major element in the employee's perception of fairness is a knowledge of the components going into the manager's decision. The

next most important element is an understanding of the relative weight attached to each one. The procedure to get that result will include a summary of the facts and a comment about the importance of each. This summary will indicate the weight which has been attached to each of the additional items which the employee has contributed in the preceding steps. Major items should include a statement of these additional items and a statement of the effects of actions in understandable terms. The primary factors in an evaluation should relate to observable results which can be seen to affect the organization's performance.

The summary should include both positive and negative and lead up to an overall rating appropriate to the system. The final rating needs to be clear and to be in simple terms. A surprise relating to pay or promotion based on a mistaken understanding of an evaluation is unpleasant and unproductive.

One way to give a rating is with a standard set of words or numbers which have meaning in the organization. (Part of that meaning will come from the monetary consequences of the rating.) If the organization has no formal rating system, the manager can create a short — a sentence at most — simple, overall rating that cannot be misunderstood by the employee.

Too often, an employee is left with a confused feeling after an Evaluation session. The complexity of people and their performance requires

A Rating Needs To Be Clear And Complete

that we provide them with an answer to the question "Where do I stand?" At some level they realize the subjective summarization which is involved and they are also aware that will be the basis for their future progress whether it is made explicit or not.

Managers who don't provide a simple statement or rating leave it to the employee to add the plusses and subtract the minuses and figure out where they stand. "Where they stand" is another way of referring to subjective experience, since it relies on the manager's reality and cannot be supplied adequately from outside.

Some managers resist the idea of giving a simple numerical or standard word rating to an employee. They feel that it is unfair and demeaning to an individual to receive such a simple and seemingly arbitrary rating. Because people are complex, there are bound to be both good and bad elements in their performances. That is the very condition which requires such a simple rating. Assuming that bonuses or pay increases are based on performance evaluations, there is no way around the "single arbitrary" rating. There is certainly *one* raise of a *certain* amount and that is the singular meaning of a rating to many employees. Complex statements of good and bad points are all summarized for the employee in a paycheck. That summary will likely be less clear than a complete evaluation which included a clear and specific rating.

One top executive of a successful, well-run company told me about a situation he was involved in on his rise which illustrates the problem. In one particular year, he was enjoying his non-working life to the detriment of attention to his work. At the end of that year, without receiving a clear evaluation, he received a large bonus for his "outstanding" performance. He had done some good work but put little effort into his job. The following year, he was determined to do even better and earn himself an even larger bonus. Again, without first receiving a clear evaluation, he received a bonus — the smallest bonus he had received in his career. To this day, he doesn't know why he received the large bonus or the small one.

A clear rating might be closed with a statement like:

> The two most significant factors of those I have just summarized are the reliable work you have done in meeting all of your technical duties and the failure to perform the management-related duties of planning and developing with Mary and Jim. This organization considers employee development of prime importance. Based on the importance of each of the points we have covered, your rating is satisfactory. That means you will get the basic pay increase for next year with the basic bonus added. To get a higher rating next year, you will have to significantly improve your performance in the area of people management. If your performance remains the same in that area, your rating next year would likely be only "acceptable."

The essence of an effective evaluation does not lie in merely giving a rating. The value comes from a clear understanding of the facts behind it and of the relative importance of each of these to the manager. The employee wants to know two things. The first is the rating or overall impact of the previous period's performance. The second is enough information to organize behavior in the coming period. Employees want to know how to alter their behavior to get greater rewards and then they can make decisions about what they want to do. The manager is providing the context within which employees will organize their own behavior.

Evaluation Gives Information for Making Choices

So far, you will have had the floor throughout most of this step. Now it's time to turn it over to the employee. Employees will likely have questions and feelings which want expression and, in many cases, will lack the ability to communicate what is needed. The manager's role is to elicit that communication in a respecting manner. What is a "respecting manner"? Where does it come from? We can all agree with what kind of behavior but it frequently fails to happen. Where it comes from is an internal attitude of respect for the employee. That is a result of recognizing the whole personality whether or not the particular needs have been made explicit. The situation of being evaluated by a senior person can be expected to generate feelings and a need for more information as well as some hesitation over expressing either. A "respecting manner" will result from that attitude and making some adjustment to the employee. The commonest adjustments will be in posture, choice of words, and voice tone — all towards matching the employee.

Some ways of eliciting this communication might include direct questons such as, "Are you clear on the rating?" and "Do you understand the basis for it?" These types of questions only invite a Yes or No and unless an employee is quite expressive or self-confident that is all they will elicit. Many of these types of questions have been used to lead employees to the desired answer. A better type of question is one that invites a fuller answer. These might include, "What questions do you have about the evaluation?" and "I'm wondering what you think about it..." (followed by an expectant pause).

Where direct questions do not elicit the desired results, some different approaches might include:

How does that compare to the evaluation and rating you thought you

135

were going to get before we started today?

or

Every time I've been evaluated in the past there's been a surprise in it for me. Sometimes it's the rating itself...sometimes it's one of the facts which was ignored or included...sometimes an event that didn't seem significant to me was really important to my boss. I'm wondering what part of my evaluation gave you the biggest surprise...

or

Many times after an evaluation it takes a while to digest what it was all about. We don't think of what we wanted to say or ask until we've left the manager's office. Take a few minutes to let what we've done sink in and when you think of something which isn't fully clear or anything at all you might want to add just go ahead.

The completion of this step will be achieved when you are sure that the employee has a clear understanding of the rating and of the relative im-

A Clear Context Helps Employees Understand the Rating

portance of the facts which went into it. Employees should also understand what would have to be different for a different rating. It is not necessary that the employee agree with the evaluation. It *is* important that the employee understand it. What is the difference between these two states? How can you get understanding without agreement? The understanding will come from making the context clear. It will involve a reference to the values and relative importance of different behaviors and results to the organization and to the individual manager. If I can make my values clear, then you can understand my assessment of your behavior. You may still disagree with my evaluation because you disagree with my values. You may disagree with my judgment about the impact of your behavior on those values. The involvement of the employee at this point will lead to the next step.

4. *Elicit Feedback from the Employee*

The success of this step will be related to the participation which has been elicited in preceding steps. If there has been little participation, you should not expect much feedback.

If the communication has been flowing both ways, then it will likely continue through this phase. *The response you get is the one you elicit.* That is, when a manager tells me that employees won't speak up or give honest feedback, I direct my attention to what in the manager's behavior is getting in the way of that feedback. There are some people who are easy to get feedback from and there are some who are difficult, but there are very few human beings who do not want to speak their minds given the right conditions.

What kind of feedback do you want to hear? What information might your employees have that would be useful for you to receive? There is an opportunity here to receive valuable information which is not available through the normal organization communication channels. Most reports are production-related and most personal contacts are task-related. Here is a chance to create the opening for that information which never seemed quite appropriate to say.

An opening which invites personal feedback after giving an evaluation is likely to be effective. A general question such as, "What did I do to get in your way over the last period?" or "What might I have done better to assist you?" invites any direct feedback which the employees might be holding. The question needs to be asked in a manner which implies that an answer is truly wanted.

Ask for Feedback In A Way That Will Elicit It

Besides the standard questioning actions such as raising the pitch of your voice at the end and raising your eyebrows, your posture should remain relaxed and gestures should be physically open. A reasonable pause to allow time for considering the response may also be needed.

The major requirement is an intention to listen to the feedback and consider it. Most of our non-verbal behavior will be reasonably congruent if our intention is clear. The major requirement at this point is usually to "bite the bullet," that is, to refrain from making comments or asking questions which in any way imply defensiveness or criticism. Questions for clarification are acceptable, although it is often wise to hold them for later. Comments which acknowledge that the information was received and understood are effective. The only other comments should indicate an acceptance of the feeling behind the statement. These might be things like, "Yeah, I can see how that would be frustrating," or "You'd feel more at ease if I checked in with you more frequently."

After the information has started to flow, you might want to direct it to specific areas such as company policies, staff interactions, organization support, or general working conditions. If these are used as openers, however, most managers end up controlling the type of information they receive and fail to give the employee the chance to say what he or she wants to say. This is an effective technique if you don't want certain kinds of feedback and gives the opportunity to receive some.

On occasion, these sessions will turn into attacks. If an employee has been a problem all along and receives a poor evaluation, the feedback session will frequently be used to vent anger and frustration. Before we consider how to deal with this issue, let's stop for a moment and think about the source of the problem. It would appear that the employee is unhappy with the situation and has been for some time. The problem has escalated to a state which is probably highly uncomfortable for all concerned. What is the cause? The employee is unable to deal with the situation in the normal course of events either through lack of skills or limiting beliefs (such as fear that speaking will result in being fired). The manager has also been unable to deal effectively with the situation. Where does that leave us? It seems that both the employee and the manager have been unable to handle the problem. The employee is now experiencing a need to vent pent-up feelings. The best solution might be to allow or even encourage that to happen. This isn't as bad as it sounds. Considering the source and the controlled environment, the results are likely to be only mildly and temporarily unpleasant. The key to this alternative is that the environment be controlled. Where is that control to come from?

This Is the Time To Allow Venting of Feelings

The situation itself provides some control. You are still the boss and you are probably in your own office. Knowing that you invited the feedback, you don't have to hold it against the employee later. The real source is your own ability to use communication effectively. The first technique to use is one of Responsive Listening. By feeding back the emotional content of what is being said in a way which demonstrates without a doubt that you have received and understood the employee's communication will soon take care of the employee's need to express that feeling. The facts behind it then can begin to flow and useful information can be shared. This does not imply that the information regarding feelings was useless — only that a limited amount is needed.

Control Comes from Your Ability to Communicate Well

Remember also the positive experience we anchored before the formal session started. You will be able to interrupt any irrelevancy and then reaccess that positive internal state to help bring the employee under control — his or her own control. If the situation gets to a point where you can no longer handle it or it seems to be past the point of usefulness for the employee, it will be time to use these and any other techniques to change what is happening.

If this situation is anticipated, the use of anchoring can be extended. You might, for instance, establish a gesture such as picking up a pencil or cup each time you interrupt the employee or start a new step in the process. This will give the employee's unconscious a signal of what is expected. By repeating that gesture, now, when you want the employee to wind down, you allow them to complete what they need to do quickly and stop themselves.

This is getting into an area considered manipulative by many. The considerations suggest to me, however, that it is highly respectful of the whole personality of both parties. The employee has lost control of his or her own useful functioning and/or the manager is no longer able to deal with the situation as it exists. If neither person does anything about it, the results will be a waste of time at best and could get significantly worse. An end needs to be called, somehow. The approach suggested above respects the needs of both parties without forcing an instant compliance, without using the positional power of the manager and without creating an overt action for further argument or bad feeling.

5. *Review for the Future*

Now it is time to move on. The past has been reviewed, its significance recorded, and each party has had their say. Whatever has gone before, it is time to gather our full resources to apply to the future. To prepare for that consideration, we might well recall the positive state which we created and anchored at the start. We want a creative cooperative spirit as we begin the new period. Particularly if the evaluation has been negative, we want to give the employee time and assistance in regaining full access to his or her internal resources. What better way than to recall a positive experience?

This is a brief session designed to signal a fresh start and to begin both the employee and manager thinking along lines for future performance. Each will be more fully prepared for the *Start to Plan for* next Planning session after this step. Elicit from the *the Future with* employee both personal goals and likes and dislikes. *A Positive State* The most productive effort is likely to come from what people are interested in and enjoy. The management task is to discover what these are and how jobs can be matched or to make the job fit the category through skillfully creating the environment. It is generally easier to discover what people like and figure out how to let them do it. Consider the longer term goals of the employee in the light of your own opinions as well as the desires of the employee.

If there is a mismatch, say the employee wants to be a manager and you don't think he or she is the right material, discuss what the employee will have to do to get from this situation now to where he or she wants to be in the future. Many employees' goals change when confronted with the requirements and they frequently begin to develop if they know what is required.

Complete the review with the next steps or preparation that each of you will do before the next Planning session so that you can maximize the benefits of that session. The employee may want to clarify goals or assess their own growth requirement. The manager may need to investigate the resources available for development, opportunities with the organization, and changes in job responsibilities.

Here's a review of the steps of the Evaluation, based on our model:

1. *Give Basis for Evaluation.* Evaluation is a summary of performance — a check on how performance matched original goals. It is not based on opinions, but on verifiable events. Evaluation requires knowing the standard against which one is measured.

   Throughout, there's a need to maintain rapport, acknowledge negative reactions, while directing process to the stated goal. It is important to check for agreement on the facts stated.

2. *Get Agreement on the Basis.* This summary closure for the preceding step must be completed before the evaluation is given. Here, the employee must contribute all that is possible in the way of facts and agree with the manager's facts, as they are presented as a unit. Acknowledge any negative responses. A mutually understood basis for reward and growth cannot be achieved without agreement about the basis.

3. *Give the Evaluation.* The evaluation is a statement of the net effect of all the behaviors, actions, and results of an employee's performance. It includes the subjective experience created in the manager by the employee.

   Setting the context, framing, plays a critical part in helping the employee organize personal resources. Take all evidence of comfort (or discomfort) into account.

Employees' perception of fairness is based on knowledge of the components going into the decision. This is accomplished through summary of facts, including positive and negative, with an appropriate, clear rating. Getting a clear response from the employee is important.

4. *Elicit Feedback from the Employee.* The response you get is the one you elicit — it requires an intention to listen to and consider the feedback. Handle negative feedback by responsive listening, or help change out-of-control behavior by using techniques like anchoring.

5. *Review for the Future.* Gather full resources to direct toward the future. Use positive experience to access resources. Review next steps to take place before next Planning session.

The emphasis of this session and in fact the whole Performance Management System is the continual growth and development of each and every employee. To be done well, it requires the same personal commitment from each and every manager. The system is not easy. It requires a lot of contact with people and the ability to relate to their individual personalities. The ability to deal with emotion effectively and to keep communications on target is one which needs to be continually developed. If continuous improvement is expected of employees, it needs to be demanded of managers.

PERFORMANCE MANAGEMENT

_____ **3.**

Creating A Working System

Planning

Planning within the Performance Management System is the process of aligning the outcomes of the organization and the individual goals of the parts of the system. Each manager, each department, and each employee are parts of a larger system. Each is a complex system in its own existence. Each has unique goals which are related but not necessarily complementary to those of the organization. And so the essential need for alignment is accomplished through adequate information about the organizational goals and adequate flexibility in how these goals are to be achieved.

Planning, in this light, involves setting goals and converting them into action steps within the context of the larger goals of complex systems. To achieve growth, the process must be creative. The process should be essentially a flow of information from the top down, with a mechanism for feedback up and appropriate provision for adjustment. Creativity will flourish only with this mechanism for flexibility, the feedback and adjustment, built into the system. Specifying outcomes should entail setting the minimum restrictions necessary to provide direction without confusion over the expected results. Each limit on *how* tasks are completed puts a limit on the creative input of those in the system.

How does creativity work best within a system? Each part of the system is made up of individuals who have creative potential. To fully utilize the resources available to it, an organization *The Purpose of* must be able to tap that creativity. We should *expect* *Goals Is To Set* each level to plan creatively and to set goals in such *Direction* a way as to encourage it—we're creating the conditions which produce creativity. Goals should

145

regularly be surpassed. We cannot adequately predict the results of creative efforts except to expect them to be on the positive side. The results we predict should relate to what has been done in the past. They are a control measure for maintaining past performance. Creative planning is a distinct process. The results, if positive, will be the basis for the next period's control figures.

The function of goals, then, is to indicate direction, provide control points or measures, and to determine appropriate behavior. Within a system, the goals provide the direction and the context for decision and action. Planning carried out within the Performance Management System is an activity directed by the overall goals of the organization. Again, the alignment of individual goals with the organization's larger goals is in effect.

How Plans Work: Concepts Into Action

How plans work becomes an interesting concept at this point. The assumptions which are made in the development of goals are often more useful than the goals themselves. They provide a context for shared understanding of the plans. The details developed in individual Planning sessions provide the standards for measurement of performance and control. The specific plans developed throughout the organization determine the appropriate actions and extent to which we can realize creative potential. Each level, in coming up with specific action plans, provides a balance between the conceptual world of strategic planning at the top and the requirements for actions and specific results at the bottom. The move from the conceptual to the specific is critical. It provides the transition to reality. To be effective as elements of control in the system, the plans need translation into results which can be verified and reported on in sensory-grounded terms—what can be seen and heard, what is verified by observation.

The organization is involved in an ongoing process of reaching broadly stated outcomes in the best possible way. This involves maximum use of all of the organization's resources. Maximum use of all resources. This means that a system must be developed which will provide immediate feedback for adjustment of inadequate processes or results. The processes and results must themselves be broken into their component parts. Each goal that isn't met should be so small as to not jeopardize reaching the end-result and large enough to indicate a trend or out-of-control condition.

*Maximum Use
of All Resources
and a System
for Immediate
Feedback*

146

The information provided as feedback should point to the area of cause or be significant enough to indicate the direction of correction. The emphasis is on *what*, not *whom*. The purpose of business is to achieve results, not to place blame. Placing blame fails to indicate what corrective action may be appropriate. Finding cause indicates potential corrective action. To satisfy this requirement, each task needs to be broken down into small-enough segments so that, based on time, quantity, or quality, the results are measurable and adequate control is attained.

Let's assume a unique type of organization. Imagine a business with an owner, a manager, and three employees. (If, as someone said, a successful complex system was once a successful simple system, let's start our system development with a simple one.) What will the requirements of this system be? What will it need to do in relation to our present concern of Planning? The requirements we develop will be the same for a business organization of any size. The implementation will differ depending on size and original desired outcomes.

Imagine that the owner is living in Greece in retirement and comes to the United States once a year to review results and plan for the coming year. He has already determined the basic goal of the organization and the subsidiary goals relating to employee compensation, investment, and technological innovation. In short, he has followed the procedure discussed in the *Outcomes* section of Book 4.
Here are the results:

> *Purpose*: To produce wooden toys which are priced in the lower third of the market at the quality of the middle third with a return on investment exceeding the prime rate.
> *Employees*: Compensation will be at competitive rates in the local area with a profit-sharing plan for return on investment over the prime.
> *Investment*: The company is to remain out of debt and finance its own growth from profits.
> *Technology*: No product innovation is expected. Improved processes will originate from employees with no capital required. New products will be imitations of competitors.

The data which supply the quantitative measures for these goals were established by the owner and a system for updating the information was established. The manager now gathers the data and sends it to the owner two months before their annual meeting. From this information and the annual financial reports, the owner develops specific goals for the coming year.

147

The Performance Management System begins at this point. The manager and owner meet at a resort on the coast of Maine each summer and establish agreed objectives for the coming year. The manager receives the specific quantitative goals for the coming year and any changes which relate to such areas as quality, new products, technology, and employee policies. He then verifies to his own satisfaction that the manager understands the goals and is able to achieve them. He also establishes with the manager what signals at which times will be used to assure them both that the goals are being reached. In this process, the goals are sometimes modified by the direct input of the manager. The manager frequently suggests new ways of achieving the desired results.

It is understood that if these points or signals are ever reached, the manager will contact the owner to discuss required changes in goals or to discover new ways to achieve those goals. These goals include events or quantitative measures with certain time limits. The owner returns to Greece where he can spend the year in comfort knowing that his business is operating effectively without him and will provide him with the return he needs to continue to enjoy his retirement. Before his return, however, he does one last thing. He goes to the factory, looks around, and talks to the three employees there.

The manager now must complete the Planning process by meeting with the two direct labor employees and the salesperson. He must convert the overall goals agreed with the owner into terms that are meaningful to the employees. The goals of a specific sales increase, maintenance of net profit, and an average increase in investment with no total change at year-end do not indicate to the employees what they are supposed to do or when they are to do things. The new directive "to meet the competition by developing new toys with working wheels" has to tie into the above goals in ways which they cannot be expected to readily understand as presented.

Examples of what needs to be worked out with the salesperson are:

- Maintenance of existing accounts
- Sales of new toys in second six months to result in a specific new sales mix which will provide return
- Specific new business activities
- Information-gathering requirements for future market development

Input from the salesperson will include what he can do, an agreement to results, and a statement about what he needs to do and will do to improve performance.

A similar process must take place with the two production employees about quantities, quality, timing, and new product development. The allocation of time between two people and the three main tasks of new toy design, manufacturing parts, and assembly must be divided between them or a system for division established. The employees will be expected to contribute ways of doing things better and how, specifically, they are going to do something different for improvement. A problem with quality—breakage of a particular part—must also be solved in the early stages of the year to maintain quality standards. A plan for change in design or production must be developed. Each of these new ideas and proposed actions must be developed with time frames for each stage and with specific responsibilities.

In the process outlined, the owner has little contact with the operations of the business yet he expects his goals to be achieved. The manager has contact with the owner to understand the goals, provide feedback for adjustment, and bring direct experience to the Planning process. He also has direct contact with the employees and their day-to-day operations. He requires the ability to translate the desired outcomes of the owner into reality, while meeting the needs of the employees and the changing situation of the business. The employees are concerned with the operating details of how to do their jobs and accomplish specific results which they have been allocated.

The Manager Is the Link to the Most Direct Experience

If the owner were to omit the manager, he would have to communicate in a totally different way to achieve his goals through the employees. He would require language that was more specific and would need more direct contact, more sensory-grounded experience, with the operations. He would also require a feedback mechanism that was outside of the system or he would need to become that part. In short, he would not be retired, he would be the owner/manager. In large organizations the owners are absent. Even in smaller ones, however, the requirements are essentially the same due to the complexity of dealing with numbers of people and complex systems. The sheer quantity of experience and information required is too much for one person to handle. This requires systems and more people, each further removed from direct, sensory experience.

Planning—First Step in a Performance Management System

Planning is the first of the three major functions to be performed to achieve a system of Performance Management. What is the outcome we want to achieve from this function? What are the needs of the system which require a planning function? The low-quality answer, the overall objective, is something like, "To translate organizational goals into specific action plans with appropriate controls." This is the step which specifies the plans in adequate detail for specific action and for establishing feedback points—the basic requirements of any system. The feedback mechanisms and the adjustment mechanism will be determined by the content of the plans. The processes have been established (see Book 4, *Managing for Performance* and *Outcomes*) but the triggering or critical events have not.

The outcome for Planning needs further specification of expected benefits related to the philosophy of the organization. What are some of these? In your own ideal system, what other goals would you expect this step to achieve or contribute to? These other outcomes give life and richness to the system. They convert it from a dry and technical system of controls which demand no input to a living system of achieving the outcomes for all who are involved in the system and of providing for creativity and growth. A system designed for humans should take into account the nature of the beings which are its parts.

First, let's look at the subsidiary outcomes which further describe the required functions. One of these is an Early Warning System for deviations from the expected and desired path. We want

Details for
Specific Action
and Feedback,
and a
Basis for
Later
Evaluation

to know as soon as possible when corrective action needs to be taken so that the original goal can be achieved or the goals can be changed and appropriate adjustments made in all parts of the operating system. The existence of specific controls is required if we want confidence in the system. Another requirement is that a basis for later evaluation of performance be established. Knowledge, understanding, and agreement are prerequisites for effective evaluation, if our goal is a participative process. Any contradictions or impossibilities will be discovered by this process and can be given further investigation or be more tightly controlled.

This stage will also determine the organizational resources required to complete the objective, such as equipment, training, and interdepartmental services. It will also be apparent, as more specific actions are described, whether or not they fit the overall objectives of the company and prevent sub-optimization. As I've suggested in the other books, sub-optimization refers to the undesirable results which occur when immediate goals, if achieved, do not contribute to organization goals.

Another category of these subsidiary outcomes is more challenging. What impact do you want the system to have on your employees? What results do you expect or want? Having taken care of the basic information requirements of the system, there is more we can get from a human system. One of these is the involvement and creativity of each employee. If our system is built to achieve only those organizational goals which are known and quantifiable, we stifle the possibility of creative input and growth from those in the system, a costly result when you consider that the people actually doing the work have information which we cannot possibly have. An ideal system will take advantage of this creative potential in the planning process.

Involvement and Tapping Creative Potential — The Real Payoff

Another major outcome is the commitment of the individual employee. We are not dealing with machines or robots. The whole human being is present at the workplace; using less is wasteful and destructive of the individual. Commitment provides the energy which will continue the system in positive and unimagined ways and produce better results than can be planned. Since we are not dealing with robots, a lack of commitment will result in a withholding of resources which could otherwise be available.

To summarize, some basic outcomes might be:

- To provide an Early Warning System for adjustment
- To create a basis for Evaluation
- To ensure the possibility and "fit" of all plans
- To provide the specific operational controls required
- To obtain employee creativity
- To get employee commitment

This list is not exhaustive but indicates the level of outcome which needs to be stated to determine the needs of the system from the Planning process. Add your own or subtract any which don't suit your experience. Then check the congruence of your resulting list.

Looking At Employee Outcomes

Most systems, if they get this far at all, fail to take another step in establishing desired outcomes which is crucial to maximum success. The outcomes have all been stated from the point of view of the organization and its managers. What of the outcomes of the employees within the system? Your job is to create the conditions for improved performance. How can you create those conditions without considering the outcomes of the employees who are to be part of it? The previous paragraph referred to commitment. The considerations here take care of that category. Let's look at the issues for employees from their own perspective rather than that of "motivating for company ends." The reason is that we don't really have the power to provide motivation—we can only *create the conditions* for its appearance. Whether elicited by survey or simply developed from existing experience, this is a worthwhile perspective in a system's development.

The most frequent complaint I hear from non-management, whether or not there already exists an official system of Performance Management, is, "I don't know where I stand around here." We all prefer to feel that we can control our environment, within the established boundaries at least. We want to be able to know how to act in particular circumstances to get the best result in that environment. The feeling of control, which we all value, is a feeling of control of our own selves, which comes from knowing the conditions, knowing what's expected, and being able to make choices about our responses to both.

Another frequent and related complaint is, "We have evaluations or appraisals but I don't know the basis of judgment." Of what use is an appraisal under these conditions? Only that it tells employees what they should have done and adds to their information or experience so that they have a better chance of guessing right next time! Far better to know what the basis was going to be before an action is taken or not. You can remember the same feelings even while you have been in a management position, I'm sure. "Nobody listens to me or wants my ideas" is a common response to employees being asked about possible voluntary contributions to the work they do. The attitude "It's not my problem, I just do what I'm told" is far more prevalent than suggested by those who will say it aloud. Feelings of inclusion, of being valued as a potentially creative human being, of being treated as an adult individual is generally lacking. The systems are not organized to accommodate the necessary behavior, and many managers feel comfortable only if they are in a position to insist on their way in an impersonal manner, or as though in a parent-child relationship.

Employee Outcomes Are Directly Related to Feelings of Control and Getting Information

Expanding our outcomes to include those of employees would involve these categories:

Meta — To ensure that employees know what's expected
Subsidiary — Employees have the ability to self-monitor
Know what resources are available
Have the ability to predict impact
Experience acknowledgement of creativity

Add or subtract starting from this basic list as you desire until you come up with a set of operating principles which can guide the development of the system and the manager's use of it. The list can become the basis for assessing the kind of job a manager is doing. It is the first step in being explicit about *what* good managers do and *how* they do those things.

What processes will have to take place to achieve these outcomes? The type of outcomes you choose will determine the nature of the interactions required. As we proceed, we will develop a model for a Planning session which would meet the above outcomes. A model provides the steps required to reach an outcome. It isn't a theory. It is a behavioral series which says if you follow these specific steps you will reach the desired outcome. It isn't the "truth"—it simply works. The most significant thing we can aim for is an elegant model, one which contains the minimum number of steps required to reach the outcome—and also the *necessary* number. Too many steps means it will be difficult to remember and probably will not be used. We will discuss the essential elements and then create a simple model for practical use.

Developing the Model

The starting point of the function we have labelled Planning is the organizational goals which have been developed or approved by the top management of the organization. These are the most

Managers Must Translate Low-Quality Language to Higher Quality

general level of information. Each succeeding level in the organization will receive plans which need to be made more specific for its own action or passing down to the next lower level. If the CEO says, "We need to run a tight ship this year," the management level which receives that communication needs to translate it into some specifics and verify with the CEO that these would meet his intended outcome. If they feel that they can't do that, due to the communication environment, passing the same statement to lower levels of the organization must be expected to produce little in desired results. If the level closest to the CEO can't make the translation and check it, who can?

153

Let's look more closely at an example of a low-quality outcome: "We want to add another 20 retail outlets during the year." Notice that while this has a specific number, it lacks information about size and timing as well as what operational changes are going to have to be made for this to happen successfully. The translation process is required *no matter what* the quality of the statement at the top of the organization. If it's not required, it shouldn't be coming from the top. Each level is paid to operate at an appropriately *different* level of detail. The Planning process will be a set of plans which have already been developed at higher levels and are ready for translation into achievable goals at the next lower level.

We are all familiar with the quantifiable goals which are part of all organizations which use any form of official planning. Qualitative goals are much less frequently used. *How* a job is to be done is seldom part of the goals. Yet it is often more important and is used covertly in evaluation. Let's take an airline hostess. She has certain goals in relation to hours in the air, numbers of passengers to service, meals to serve, and a quality goal of "courtesy." Although she has been trained to be "courteous," she hasn't been given a behavioral model of how we would both know that courtesy is in action. It is based on subjective opinion and complaints. There are, however, ways for her to act which will meet the standards, generate no complaints to the airline, and still lose customers and good will.

The average manager is in a worse position. He or she is expected to conduct effective interviews and coaching and evaluations, with various subjective results, without the training that the airline hostess received. A component of any planning for these types of jobs should be a description of the behavioral model against which they are to be judged or which will indicate how to achieve the desired quality of result. It is not good enough that a manager have a quantified record of the employee evaluations that were held during the year. *The method and actual results are what count.*

• *First Step — Give Goals and Review Resources*

The first step of Planning will be to review with your subordinate the plan which has been developed for your level and the outcomes for his or her level. This will provide a context for subsequent steps. A review of the available resources will expand this context even further. Budget, interdepartmental cooperation, expected training, time available, etc., are all parameters which will focus the potential creative resources of

Clear
Outcomes
and Context
Open the
Door to
Creativity

your subordinate. At this stage, the more information about outcomes and context that is made available, the more flexibility is left to the potential creativity of all involved. Refinements and "how to" can then be developed jointly to satisfy the needs and outcomes of all concerned. Passing down explicitly defined steps developed in the privacy of my own mind excludes creative potential and communicates to the employee that only *my* outcomes count—his or her desires are not important in this environment. That person's response is likely to be covert but measurable in minimal results.

Rapport must be established before this first step can be considered completed. It may be done even before formally starting the model. It is not included as a "step" due to its overriding importance in all communication. *No successful communication can take place without rapport.* Even attempts to directly pass information require some level of rapport to be successful. Any attempts at persuasion, at obtaining creativity, or any other accessing of particular internal states is bound to fail without a significant amount of rapport.

Establishing rapport can be considered as a preliminary step superior to the model. Or it can be accomplished as part of the process of establishing the context and presenting the existing plan and resources available. Throughout the model, each step will be presented separately, but there is a continual overlapping and recycling in any actual meeting or continuing communication.

• *Second Step — Access Creative Resources & Develop Plans*

You are being paid to influence the internal states of others. You are paid, explicitly, to achieve actions and results in the external world. However, the source of those actions are results of the internal states of others. You cannot do your job, you cannot be held responsible for results, unless you have significant influence over the causes—and the causes of human action are the internal states which motivate, or provide meaning to, an action. At this stage of the process, you need to be able to obtain the creative participation of your subordinates. Commitment will also depend on this step of the process.

Having established the context in Step One, your next step is to access the creative resources of your subordinates. The idea of creating the conditions for results as the responsibility of the manager now becomes obvious. You can demand that certain goals be met. You can demand

155

some external behaviors. You cannot demand *internal* states or their results, such as creativity. You can ask. You can create the conditions which make those states attractive to another. You can obtain those states *without* asking by making them simply the best choice in the circumstances. But you cannot demand and expect to receive.

The second book of this series details the behavioral processes to establish rapport and access creative resources. In the context of Planning, Book 1 gives detailed instruction in the art of rapport.

What are some of the ways we might use to help us access creative resources in others? We have just considered two—creating the context and establishing rapport. Another is simply the use

Ask the Right of questions which allow as much freedom as
Questions possible. "How might this be accomplished?" "How
and Recall might this be done better?" "How would you suggest
Past Success doing it?" These are some simple examples of using questions to encourage response. Another way is to recall, out loud, some previous time when the employee has done a creative job, come up with a new solution, or used resources appropriate to the current desire for creative participation—something like, "I remember when we were faced with that bottleneck in the materials flow and just couldn't seem to get around it. After some discussion, you saw a possible solution that no one else had thought of and developed it into a practical plan. That was an exciting time." Said in an appropriate tone of voice, this kind of comment will recreate similar mental states in the listener.

An activity which will continue throughout the Planning session is continual review of the resources available to meet the objectives. The plans passed down will constantly be under view for possibility of achievement and for alignment with the other goals and plans which are known. The achievements of the employee are always in the context of the organization. Other departments' input, the cooperation of fellow employees, and new training and investment are all factors outside of the employee's control which will affect performance. It will be the responsibility of the manager, in many cases, to arrange for the appropriate resources to be provided by the organization. The most effective managers are able to obtain the maximum in required resources from the organization. The issue of possibility and fit at this stage are in relation to the resources which are needed compared to those which are available.

The *Outcomes* section of Book 4 refers to the different requirements for control for maintenance, compared to managing for continuous growth. Both types of activity are required in the Planning stage. The first will require little in the way of creativity. The latter, managing for continuous growth, is mainly a creative process and will occupy most of our attention here. The goals for maintenance of previously satisfactory operations are already known and need only updating of quantitative information and review of warning for out-of-control conditions. These operations will be expected to continue unless certain signals appear. Once these signals are known in relation to the quantified results, little attention or energy should be required beyond that of the actual operators as they perform their tasks.

The major management challenge is to set goals for growth which engage the creative resources of employees, stretch their capabilities, while maintaining appropriate control of activities. Setting goals for growth and "stretch" means that there is no previous shared experience to count on, no readily available control data, and no absolute knowledge of possibility. The creativity for developing such plans requires that the problem of certainty and control be left until ideas are developed. Brainstorming techniques or the more controlled process called Pathfinding in *Precision—A New Approach to Communication* demonstrate the need for separation of control restraints from the creative process. The later, full development of *what, how,* and *who,* in specific sensory-grounded terms, will provide the means to control within the system proposed here. The emphasis on creativity for our purposes here is on your ability to *create the conditions* for its emergence. *Precision* and other books deal with some of the external or structural requirements for it to flourish. The factor which I stress is your own personal contribution to creating those conditions. Your attitude and how it is reflected in your words, body, and actions are the most powerful factor in accessing the internal resource of others, thereby tapping into creative potential.

How might you set the stage for some specific contribution to continuous growth right now? One way is to differentiate two processes for the employee—one is maintaining operations and the other is growth—and then ask for some growth suggestions.

The following indicates to the employee what you want and also that a certain kind of response is expected:

> We are having this Planning meeting so that you can contribute towards the goals of the organization in ways that interest and challenge you from your own point of view. We expect to maintain our

regular operations at the present standard *and* we expect every branch, department, and person to do at least one thing each year which is a significant improvement over last year. Our department goal is to find a way to eliminate the defect which caused fifty percent of returned products last year.

My personal goal is to conduct a full Planning and a full Evaluation session with each person in our department and to hold three group Planning sessions with all of you. My question to you is, "What can you do differently in the coming year to make a significant difference to this department in a way which will benefit us all? What will make your job easier, what will add to your productivity, what will make things more interesting for you and benefit the organization?"

Be warned: Statements such as these also indicate to the employee your intention to support and follow through on the results. This is intended as a serious request for contribution from the individual's own resources and needs to be taken seriously and supported. Every suggestion will not be feasible but each must be given and new ones need to be elicited. This is a considered demand for continuous growth of all involved. If ideas are not followed through, this process will turn into another corporate joke. Ideas which *are* followed through will produce spectacular benefits to the company.

• *Third Step — Creating the Action Plan*

The world is full of good ideas that never quite happen. The plans for growth which are developed in Planning sessions need to be translated into the language of action. The question to follow any suggestion is, "How are you going to accomplish it?" Approval should not even be considered until the means and method are indicated. The goals for any growth option are less important than *how* they are going to be achieved. What steps are going to be taken? What resources will be needed? Where is the time and effort going to come from? How is it going to be directed? The answers to these types of questions provide the assurance that the goal can be achieved. These same answers provide the means for a system to establish checkpoints, feedback requirements, and adjustment mechanisms.

Decide on the Methods for Accomplishing Goals

• *Fourth Step — Establishing Checkpoints*

The checkpoints are what qualify our approach as a system. Business regularly has intentions, actions, and results. The most significant lack is in the area of feedback, or checkpoints. Most of business is more like a game than a system; that is, the only measure is the final score. Budgets, yearly goals, production quotas are generally too general and remote to serve as guides for adjustments within the process. They are merely scorecards which show whether the goals were achieved or not.

The distinguishing feature of feedback is that it is received in time for an adjustment to be made which will satisfy the original intent or goal.

Setting Checkpoints and Making Adjustments Is Essential
The information content will be an indication of existing control or point to the direction of corrective action if an out-of-control condition exists. Out-of-control is the first signal that the variations from expected standards are significant in amount and/or direction. This is a specific condition which can be calculated for manufacturing processes. The processes of management are subject to the same approaches, with a different set of tools. Although the development of the specific tools may take some time, each step along the way will produce worthwhile returns in itself.

The manager and the subordinate must ask themselves which functions or actions are critical to success. Each of these functions need to be assessed for its timing in relation to the success of the total goal. Next, determine when you would need to have indication of inadequate completion so that these functions could be expected to be completed in time for the overall goals to be met.

The detail at this level will depend on past experience with each employee. It is the employee's responsibility to complete agreed-on objectives. It is also the employee's responsibility to report as soon as there is a likelihood of inability to complete. The manager, however, is still responsible for results to higher levels.

Let's look at an example before we go further. Suppose that you are Vice-President of Operations and one of your project managers has a plan to complete a particular building by year-end. One of the functions critical for success in this particular project is to obtain the appropriate zoning and building approvals from the city. The required date to complete the approvals and still finish the project on time is three months away. However, if approval isn't obtained by that time, the whole project will not meet its deadline completion. The checkpoint is therefore established in two months' time; that's the critical deadline for determining that the overall goal will not be met without additional resources. If the approvals are not obtained at that time, there is still time to establish another strategy to ensure success for this particular function.

159

A natural tie-in to this process is to contract for consulting. That is, the manager is a primary resource for subordinates and will generally have involvement in growth projects. The contract *The Manager* may specify that the manager act as an advisor, for *Still Needs* direct technical contribution or for ensuring that *To Be Available* required organizational resources are obtained.

Each situation is unique; each person is a different stage of independence for different tasks; each growth objective will have different requirements. The manager's needs for control have been satisfied by the previous step of establishing checkpoints.

This step will satisfy the employee's need for the ability to exercise self-control. Self-control may mean that the employee has all of the information and ability within his or her control to complete a function with assurance of quality. It may also mean that the employee has understood checkpoints at which time he or she knows where to get the required assistance if goals are not being met. It may mean only that the employee knows when and how to call for help. This contract should provide enough contact to provide control and only enough to satisfy the needs for development and achievement of the employee. A manager hanging over your shoulder while you are performing independently and adequately is just as bad as not having any assistance when it is required, particularly if the need was anticipated.

• *Fifth Step—Understanding and Commitment*

The planning process cannot be considered complete until the manager is sure of the subordinate's understanding and commitment. If the preceding steps have been undertaken with the congruent attempt to involve the creative resources of the employee, this step is little more than a formality. If there has in fact been participation of the employee, if the manager has adequate listening and observing skills, if both have asked questions and supplied information, there is every reason to assume agreement and commitment. How many meetings have you left with the feeling that an agreement had been reached only to find that it wasn't carried out? Do you attribute that result to a failing in the other person? If it happens frequently, there may be something in the situation itself which would have told you the result. There may have been something you could have done.

Many of us find that understanding and commitment weren't reached until it is too late — when the consequences have been realized. The

Look for Understanding and Commitment in a Variety of Signals information is available to assure you that an understanding has been reached. The words, posture, and voice tone, to name three, are all adequate signals to indicate the appropriate agreement. People tell us in many ways when they don't understand — even when their words say they do. You have been using these signals all along if you have been communicating effectively. However, you have been involved in the content of what you were doing. You may have been excited at times, exasperated, concerned with your employees' feelings, angry. All of these may have caused you to miss some vital cue that would have signalled misunderstanding or a less-than-enthusiastic response.

Summarizing at the end of the meeting is a useful technique for checking understanding and commitment. The content is not of much importance. You have been continuously engaged in attempting to elicit responses. No matter what you're feeling about your success, it will take very little time and effort to verify. When you are summarizing, you are doing it for the purpose of verifying the appropriate internal states of others. This summary includes the content but it is the smallest and easiest part. The larger part and more difficult is to verify feelings about that content. When summarizing, read the agreed items and constantly look at the employee and listen to voice tone for expected signs usual to that person's states of understanding and commitment. Or, even easier, have that person read or state the summarization so you have nothing of any substance to do but watch and listen to the total communication.

How To "Do" the Model

Successful completion of the preceding steps will produce the kind of results that every manager dreams of. Yet they weren't all that startling, were they? It's the quality of the manager's performance in carrying them out which will produce exciting results. Better-than-average results will be achieved, however, even if all of the steps are completed, *in order*, without any special new behavior. What are the particular skills and abilities which a manager must possess to do a successful job of planning sesssions? Book 2 of this series deals with the "how to." Here, we want to consider what those skills are.

Just as we shouldn't expect employees to carry out tasks without an understanding of how they are to be done (we shouldn't but we do), we shouldn't expect managers to complete functions with quality unless we can tell them how it is to be accomplished. Even managers who seem to accomplish the desired results "naturally" usually still find there are particular people or situations which don't produce the expected results. Although it is common to blame the subordinate in those cases, it is much more useful to look at what the manager might do differently to influence the outcome.

The Behavorial Requirements

We all know that accessing creative resources will require the ability to establish rapport and to present the situation in a way which appeals

Managers
Set the
Tone for
Favorable
Conditions

to the interests of the individual. We all know that the desire for approval, challenge, reward for accomplishment, and similar things are motivators for people. Unfortunately, what we "all know" doesn't produce the desired results often enough. These and other general motivators are not specific enough to help us much in the actual task of motiva-

ting an individual to be creative on demand. Each individual has some or all of these needs in different combinations and different strengths. How are we to know what are the appropriate conditions to create for this particular individual's cooperation? The answer is in the response we are getting. There are certain choices of words, particular actions, voice tones, and special surrounding circumstances which will enhance the possibility of accessing creative resources. The actual result will depend on how sensitively we use them in response to each individual.

You are familiar with the person who will leap in with creative solutions at the slightest suggestion that it is appropriate. There are others

Different
Styles
Require
Different
Approaches

who will respond in a well-conducted brainstorming session only if contributions can be made anonymously. Any time that we fail to get creative action from these people when desired, it is due to our failure in establishing conditions which match their needs. A brainstorming session can be conducted in such a way that all of the technical rules

are followed and little in the way of results is accomplished. The tone of voice, non-verbal communications, and subtle choice of words can completely negate the carefully contrived conditions. Similarly, an individual who truly wants the creative resources of others can obtain imaginative results without any formal structure and with many actions which violate the supposed necessary conditions.

The ability to give acknowledgement for good ideas, to express appreciation for effort, to recognize states which aren't favorable to the current situation are often an effective contribution to the appropriate conditions. Many of us have great difficulty in doing this simple piece of communication even though we know it is useful and feels good to receive. In many of the workshops I conduct, managers have expressed their belief in the positive value of acknowledgement. These same managers can seldom remember when they last gave some and only a very few have made it an explicit practice.

We need a way of talking, different from ordinary conversation, for management purposes. The language of action is more specific than the ordinary. We often think we should be able to *Learning the* communicate effectively, verbally at least, because *Specifics of* we have done it most of our lives and we have been *the Language* moderately successful to date. The particular needs *of Action* of getting others to turn intentions into results through other people are more stringent than ordinary conversation. The language of action is sensory-grounded. It is the language that describes experience in such a way that we assure understanding. The route to this assurance is to use words in such a way that they could only describe one particular experience or limit such understanding to a specific type of experience.

This requirement goes in two directions. One is to ask questions in such a way as to direct the information source to the type of answer which is required, to those aspects of experience which will provide the appropriate shared understanding.

The second direction is when we describe things or actions, when we give instructions, when we share goals or plans. The ability to speak in sensory-grounded language is often lacking in managers and professionals. Used to dealing in the realm of ideas, concepts, and long-range goals, required to communicate broad, general principles to others at higher levels of the organization, we begin to imagine that everyone we communicate with has the same ability to understand and work with very low-quality, or general, terms.

The personnel department manager often acts as though everyone had his or her education and understanding and shares the same meaning of "a fair evaluation for every employee." The *Be Aware* general manager, who has spent many hours of *of the Limits* thought and study on the problems of return on *of Other's* investment, competitive markets, and human re- *Experience* lations, forgets that "a fair return for an honest day's work" may mean something entirely different to the laborer who is doing the day's work. The sales manager who says "make more cold calls" may have forgotten what it takes to make quality calls and that everyone doesn't know how to initiate them in an efficient manner.

An effective plan must have goals of quantity and quality and descriptions of required actions in sensory-grounded terms. With competent and mature individuals, it may not be necessary to specify such detail but it *is* necessary to be *able* to do it. In most cases, it will be a worthwhile exercise even with competent people. There are very few cases where I have done this that at least one of the parties doesn't learn something new and useful.

There is one ability which is important in all communication involving voice or visual information — that is the ability to check for congruence. At some level, we generally do this according to some expected norm; the books on body language concentrate in this area. There is another and more powerful level. Each of us has particular voice tone, expressions, body postures, and actions to go with particular emotional or mental states. As managers, we have continuous dealings with the same people and are able to accumulate information on what they look and sound like in particular states. This is the information we use to tell us whether an individual understands, is committed and enthusiastic — or not. It provides us with the warning signals, with the feedback, to suggest whether or not we can count on the results of a particular communication.

Full Awareness of Voice, Gestures, Postures Supplies Powerful Information

Most of us were brought up to accept that it is impolite or socially unacceptable to stare, to examine people too closely, even to notice anything untoward. In short, we were brought up to make ourselves selectively blind and deaf. Whatever function this might have served in our early years, it has left us with limited use of our natural resources. It has reduced the amount of readily available information which we might use. We have generally lost volitional control over whether or not we receive this information. I recommend that you reclaim the right to your senses and develop them afresh. The information which you will gain will increase the effectiveness of your communication dramatically.

Before we leave the area of the skills required to conclude a successful Planning session, let's consider the skills which will assist the employee in these sessions. If our goal is participation and cooperation, it is our legitimate concern that employees be able to look out for their own interests in the sessions. We are much more likely to get the resources we want if they are serving mutual interests rather than simply our own or the organization's. Through skillful use of communication techniques, I might elicit responses that I want. Without also considering the interests of the employee, I will likely end up with "buyer's remorse." That is, the employee will be persuaded to do something when in my presence but will be resentful later unless his or her own interests were also considered. Buyer's remorse is bad enough in sales; it is particularly harmful when the buyer is still part of the organization!

Many employees, and even managers, do not know how to bargain for resources or share goals and ideas. This is especially true when dealing with those above them in the organization. Although an individual manager can overcome much of these barriers, it is a difficult assignment for many. It can be made easier by providing encouragement and/or training to both participants in a Planning session. A concern for the employee, expressed by training in how to use the system and encouragement to do so, will produce positive new results. It is a unique thing to do but consistent with stated intentions.

The Organization as a System

The Planning procedure and the whole Performance Management System operate within a larger system. The organization is a system for achieving certain ends and the management and control systems are simply functions within that system. The form of the Performance Management System needs to be consistent with the overall system. Just as we want to achieve an alignment of intentions between individuals and the organization, we want to achieve an alignment of intentions between the organizational system and the Performance Management System. A Planning session which has creative cooperation as one of its goals will not function well or for long when the actual situation is that directives are passed down to get action plans and resources.

Let's look at how this environment of creative cooperation is set up and how it interacts with both manager and employee. The internal consistency of corporate goals is a major consideration. The context of the Planning session is determined by the corporate goals. If they don't exist, are not explicit, or contradict themselves, they provide no guidelines as to appropriate actions. There is no common ground for manager and subordinate to refer to for a check for reasonableness. A standard

Explicit Corporate Goals Provide Guidelines for Action

judgment always exists in some form. The question becomes whether it is shared, or controlled and hidden, by the manager. The hiding may not be intentional but it has the same effect as if it were. I know you have standards. If you cannot make them explicit, for whatever reason, as an employee I can guess, or retire from the game. Many people refuse to play when they don't know the ground rules.

Suppose you have to make a choice between meeting quality standards and completing production quotas when there is heavy demand for your product. Which one will you choose? This is a decision which is made frequently however formal or informal the quality-control system is. If you have come up with an answer favoring quality, look at whether your incentive system rewards people for acting in that manner. If your answer favored meeting quotas, look at the contrary message you give your people. More likely, you were unable to answer the question due to the lack of information.

Priorities exist whenever there is the possibility of choice. Those priorities form a significant part of the environment of the organization.

Understanding the Basis for Choice Is as Important as Establishing the Choices They may change from time to time, particularly if they are internal rather than published. Any set of goals can be interpreted in such a way that conflicts arise. The economics of efficient operation in relation to the long run and short run are seldom obvious. The *basis* for choice is seldom obvious either. Many of the responses which appear to be sabotage, apparent lethargy, and little obvious follow-through, are a response to the lack of clarity in the basis for establishing priorities. To the subordinate who is not informed regarding the basis for choice, there is little incentive to take the goals and directives of management seriously. The result may be just as unfortunate from the point of view of personal reward.

The apparent disregard that management has for its own announced objective is generally result of lack of clarity in stating these objectives. If you don't treat your own words seriously, if you don't carry them into action, who will? The issue, of course, is not whether you treat your own words seriously. It's whether or not you are *perceived* as doing so by others. Even though your actions are fully consistent with your understanding of all of your stated goals and intentions, if they are not seen that way, the results will be less than desired. Each individual makes meaning of the stated intentions in the context of existing beliefs, added information, and observed behavior.

Above, we posed the options of quality and production. The usual result is that, *depending on the circumstances,* the choice is made one way or the other rather than for both. We didn't present enough information to know which this particular choice would be. To those actually performing the work, this is the most common case. Although higher levels have the necessary information, it is not available to the employees carrying out the tasks. They soon come to believe the issue is simply expedience. If there is a consistent pattern, such as quality considerations becoming less important near the end of every month so that quotas can be met, then they have received an obvious communication about the relationship of quality to quantity. Choosing based on seriousness of defect, intended end-use of product, and customer preferences can all be valid criterion which don't violate the stated standards but which are invisible to the employee. If these priorities were known, even if the particular decision process was not, the employee might judge the management actions much differently and respond in a more positive manner to stated goals and intentions.

Failure To Make Choices Consistent with Stated Goals Brings Unwanted Results

The problem of representing overall plans to lower levels of the organization *and* of making operating choices sensible to them requires considerable attention. As has just been seen, failure to do so will have significant negative consequences. The problem is not, however, simply one of more skilled communication. The context of planning is provided by reality, a world largely outside of our control. The context is both uncertain and seen differently by different people. The way to make plans and related operating decisions sensible to others is to specify the assumptions — the specific plan requirements (say, sales targets) to those assumptions.

The emphasis of this system has been on planning for growth. This element becomes critical when you consider that you are operating in a world or context which is constantly changing at a rapid rate. Technology and the economy are both making major and rapid changes in direction and the social climate is likely starting to do the same. Just as planning for a new venture requires special attention due to the lack of historical experience and the requirements of creativity, so does the maintenance of an existing system within a rapidly

All Parts of the System Must Be Flexible Enough To Adapt To Change

167

changing context require special attention to planning. All parts of the system require an adaptation to these conditions. Plans and context must be made explicit. The processes to be used will replace the dependence on quantitative results. There will be a greater emphasis on quality of performance. We need to develop ways to specify and measure performance which are not based so heavily on fixed numerical data. This book is a part of that development.

Part of the environment in which we operate is the accounting system which measures our results and which provides the language for much of our accountability system. Budgets are usually primarily expressed in terms which are appropriate to the existing accounting system. (See the books *A Design For Business Intelligence* and *Basic Financial Management* by Curt Symonds for a development of a better match between accounting systems and operating requirements.) The usual budget is a single set of numbers which only make sense in relation to a static economy and a stable competitive environment. The first step towards a more useful environment is to develop flexible or variable budgets.

At the beginning of this section, we considered the idea that the assumptions behind long-term plans were more important than the specific plans. An application of this idea is to develop flexible or variable budgets which reflect the various environments which were imagined. A different set of figures is appropriate for a growing and inflationary economy than in a contracting and deflationary one. The really hard situation is in the regular occurrence of inflation with contraction. Difficult as this requirement is, it is part of the environment within which we expect goals to be achieved and rewards to be related to that achievement. When we experience that the achievements have little to do with our own efforts, we tend to focus our energies elsewhere and let the external forces do what they will. The results of systems based on single numbers are some combination of rewards and punishments based on arbitrary factors, exaggeratedly conservative estimates, and energy spent on developing evidence for blaming external non-controllable events — none of which contribute to the goals of the organization.

Sales are the dominant variable in the long-term success of a company as well as its short-term profit. Internally, in calculating return on investment, sales holds an important position. Exernally, the mark of long-term success is market position. Sales is the common significant factor. A sales manager who is producing a 50 percent increase for the year

Looking at Numbers Alone Can Never Tell the Whole Story

is apparently doing a good job. Let's assume that the budget was for a lesser amount, even that there was a variable budget which recognized the effects of various rates of inflation. Internal results such as return on investment will be good if other departments do as well. But have we gone far enough? Would you settle for these results quite happily?

It depends on other factors. You might view it differently if you also discovered that the prospect list had shrunk by 80 percent in that time period. What if the sales were based on accounted results and merely reflected a decrease in the backlog of orders? The significant factor has not yet been looked at. Although the internal numbers are important, the one for long-term significance has not been mentioned. What if the market had experienced tremendous growth and your market share dropped from 60 percent to 45 percent? All of these factors will affect your reaction to the quantitative sales performance and will affect your responses — rewards or punishment — to the sales manager. The manager and the sales force are likely to respond with more positive energy and creative contribution in a system which makes these bases for judgment known. A system which is able to provide a well-formed and useful context will produce the best results.

Summary

The goals of the organization, its intentions and plans, contain meaning only within the context of the resources it makes available to the individuals who are to achieve those results. This includes the major areas of investment in equipment, systems, time, expert advice, training, and compensation. Demands for quality from machines or processes which cannot maintain the standards will produce resentment. This is obvious, although still often demanded, at the production level. It is equally true at the higher levels of the organization. Management is often expected to produce results without adequate training and without adequate consistency or clarity of plans and goals. The consequences of asking human beings to achieve results with inadequate tools are numerous and unpleasant and apply to managers as well as direct labor.

A classic example of directives without resources is the requirement that all government agencies use merit increases and thus require formal evaluations. The timing and lack of available experience in this area indicate the futility of the ruling. A "good idea" without the resources to

169

back it up *isn't*. It will simply generate frustration and fraud. The approach which displays integrity is to make a first move in the desired direction, toward a stated goal which can be achieved by the available resources. If you develop a policy or goal, ask yourself whether or not you are willing and able to support it with the required resources before you make it public.

The reward system is a major factor in the environment of any human system. Business tends to think in terms of financial reward. While this is obviously an important factor, it is not enough. Think of your own value areas — social relations, time, challenge, a feeling of contribution, praise. Some or all of these, and others, are values which can be contributed to or detracted from by the organization you work for. The same is true for all individuals. Money is an important part but particularly with those who choose to deal with people — like managers, salespeople, and customer relations personnel — there are other significant factors. The way we are treated, the respect for our minds and individuality, are all part of the reward system. Whichever type of financial reward system you have, consider its impact on the environment of those from whom you expect something. And further, consider the message you are communicating if you think mere system as opposed to personal contact will suffice. No matter how good and flexible your system is, only face-to-face human contact is adequately flexible to meet the needs of the most complex system of all — another human being.

Our look at Planning has left out an item which is usually featured in this area. Where are the job descriptions and operating manuals, the *forms* of various kinds? We have not included the personnel department nor the other reporting needs of the various systems. The reason is twofold. One is that the techniques developed in this book will also apply to the personnel department and will assist them in determining reporting requirements. The other is that there are many reporting systems to choose from but very little in the way of making them work. Practical results from the use of these systems will result only if there is appropriate human communication to generate the action which generates the information for the reports. Reports completed as a formality will not do the job — in many cases, they will serve to restrict or sabotage performance.

One company had an employee rating system and a formal product-evaluation review system. If the product review was not completed and approved in the allotted time, the employees responsible would be rated poorly. The product review was thus rubber-stamped so that peers would not receive demerits. The result was that an important control project was sabotaged for the sake of two types of reports, both of which were regularly completed and used for assurance by higher levels of management. These actions generated cynicism and dissatisfaction without creating any useful information for management. The answer was not to design better forms or a better system. What was required was consistent goals and appropriate face-to-face communication.

Planning needs to be done with high-quality information, information that is specific enough to use for establishing control points during operations and for evaluating results at the end of the period. If adequate quality of information is attained, the review should be little more than a formality. The feedback will have been continuous and have been adequate to reach the desired outcomes. It is not a system merely for establishing accountability to place blame. It is a system with an objective — and good systems achieve their results.

Coaching

Managing is the process of getting things done through people in organizations. Planning is the part of that process which names the things to do. Evaluation is the part which summarizes what was actually done. Coaching is everything that happens in between.

Coaching *is* managing. For a system to exist, there must be a specific outcome for direction and there has to be feedback to measure results against the outcome. "Getting things done" is what happens within the system between desired outcome, or intention, and actual result. The system requires outcome and feedback but these are only the control elements for the process. Planning, feedback and evaluation all happen regularly, if discontinuously, throughout the process. Each may also be considered a part of the Coaching function when carried out at the appropriate level.

Where and when does Coaching take place? When in contact with another person, we cannot *not* influence them. We continually communicate, share information, provide stimulation to the people around us. When our role is that of manager, every interaction gives a message to our employees and often our interactions do as well.

Coaching has no beginning or end. We make distinctions between various phases or functions of the management process. This is Planning, that is Evaluation, this is decision-making, that is negotiation — each is merely a useful way of isolating particular functions for particular purposes. Problem-solving, negotiating, consulting, planning are all simply actions to be taken or functions to be completed to "get things done through people." Coaching, or managing, does not allow such convenient isolation and analysis.

172

Notice in the systems approach discussed in the previous section that most of the system is concerned with actions and the feedback they generate.

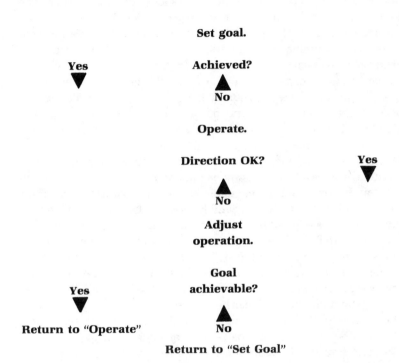

Set goal.

Yes **Achieved?**
▼   ▲
         No

Operate.

Direction OK?   **Yes**
▲   ▼
No

Adjust
operation.

           Goal
Yes   **achievable?**
▼   ▲
Return to "Operate" **No**

Return to "Set Goal"

If you apply this to your own situation, you will realize that the major involvement of time exists in those activities outside of explicit goal-setting. Most systems which have formal planning and evaluations schedule them for once a year. This acknowledges their relative importance compared to the actions required throughout the year. The assumed regular coaching contacts would make more frequent formal sessions unnecessary if competently done. (This method of scheduling is not recommended. It has little relation to the requirements of operations or to producing the results which are desired. There are some people and projects which may need less frequent formal sessions and many which demand many more frequent sessions. It is possible that with adequate high-quality coaching or managing, no such formal sessions would ever be required.)

173

Coaching—An Ongoing Activity

Coaching requires direct contact. It provides what is required for people to get things done within the organization. Let's consider for a moment the other advantages of regular, direct contact with subordinates. The best source of information is direct, sensory experience — what you can see, hear, and feel. Lacking that information source, what is the next best source? Assuming adequate skill in communicating, that is, in receiving as well as sending information, contact with a person who has the direct, sensory experience will provide the greatest potential for high-quality information. High-quality here means using words that are so specific that there can be no mistake about their meaning. The possibilities of two-way communication are far greater than any one-way system, particularly between two intelligent people.

Planning and Evaluating with no contact in between does not qualify as a system. The results of operations intended to produce desired outcomes can be expected to be minimal without regular contact for Coaching and Feedback; Planning and Evaluation themselves will tend to be sterile exercises without that contact. Planning will get little input and will be done with little shared experience or information. The Evaluation can provide praise or blame but will not have much impact on results nor, often, even be much related to the results of the past. An executive I know was given a large bonus for a year's work which he felt was well below his potential. The next year he worked hard to produce extremely good results — in his opinion — and received no bonus nor recognition. To this day, he doesn't know the reason for either result.

Effective contact will reduce the need for formal Planning and review in the management process. The organization system may require some formality for control or other informational purposes. The feedback and the high-quality information obtained from effective face-to-face communication will provide the kind of continuous adjustment mechanism where the main Planning and Evaluation requirements are simply to ensure that there is an alignment of intention, that goals and outcomes are understood.

While a system may obtain useful information and results from formal Planning and Evaluation sessions, if there is effective contact between these two points, the opposite is not true.

There Is No Substitute for Effective Contact — Formal Planning and Review sessions will not take the place of effective contact — they often won't even help. Planning and Evaluation systems which elaborately cover all necessary steps may actually produce harmful results in the absence of effective contact. The information provided will be inaccurate, employees will develop ways around the system, resentment will be generated at the insincerity, and the company will be fooled into a false sense of security. My work with one of the largest corporations in the world revealed all of these results throughout the organization even though they had mandatory Planning and Evaluation sessions.

Contact is the key. The ideal is to obtain maximum amount of sensory information available from the source of information. If direct, sensory experience of the events, actions, or situation under discussion is not possible, direct, sensory experience of the information *source* is the next best alternative. Words and reports convey only a limited amount. Individuals, through their full communication, verbal and non-verbal, convey information about the total situation.

There are three major types of information to be obtained from direct contact. One is direct experience of the context of the information source, that is, the frame of reference, the surrounding conditions, the attitude of the information source. You can readily adjust the significance of information which comes from an employee who is dissatisfied with the organization and has a general attitude that others are to blame, compared to information from an employee who demonstrates an understanding of management needs and an interest in the end-result of a department.

The second type of information is determined by the *quality* of that contact. Regular, poor-quality contact will still provide information and will be useful. *Effective* contact on a regular basis can provide the sense of security which so many managers lack, which comes from the knowledge that the information sources are intelligent and are using that intelligence in alignment with the goals of the manager.

The third type of information is the content. Most efforts at improving communication focus on giving instructions and making sure that messages are understood. This area is overrated. If you are able to elicit required information, if you are able to notice the response you are getting, if you are able to recognize the internal states of others and if you are confident of an alignment of intention, the question of giving directions becomes minor. With the above combination of personal skill and the known alignment of interest or cooperation, a manager can begin to count on one of the individuals involved in the communication, which ensures that the communication is understood and that appropriate action will result.

Sending Clear Messages Is Only a Part of Being an Effective Communicator

Much of the issues of quality control, quality circles, and employee responsibility has to do with the issue of confidence in the employees. Where is this confidence to come from? Are the employees required to improve or change in some way before it appears? If so, it isn't likely to happen. The confidence is in the ability and good will of the people we deal with. Its source is within ourselves. When we are confident in our ability to perceive other people, to receive their communications, and to make our thoughts external, we discover that our confidence in other people increases remarkably!

Coaching Contacts—Setting Up the Specifics

The amount of contact required and the type of contact are determined by each particular situation. Each individual has different requirements based on particular social and psychological needs and these are variable within the same individual. Depending on the task, depending on the environment, depending on the personal situation of the individual, a different amount and type of contact might be required. Some of this information will be a build-up of experience with that particular individual. Some will come from direct, sensory experience at each contact. Being alert to each encounter as a new experience will enable you to treat each person as a complex human being, which each person is, and increase the value of the contact for both participants.

Checkpoints, established in the Planning phase, were introduced largely to ensure some regular contact. They are the minimum requirements. I recommend that an organization build them *Checkpoints* into any formal Planning sessions as a method for *Help Guarantee* ensuring some direct contact with each employee. *Regular Contact* This will provide a recorded and scheduled basis. *and Controls* Even managers who are generally good at regular contact often will be found to have had none with one or a few employees. We tend to unconsciously avoid contacts with others which we anticipate may be unpleasant. The unpleasantness may stem from content, but will often be due to dislikes, personal difference, prejudices — any difference which we are uncomfortable dealing with.

Think of the employees working for you. How many times have you had contact with the one you like the best or is most competent compared to the opposite of that person? The results of tabulating contacts seldom are balanced. Checkpoints should include both passive and active controls. That is, some should require the employee to initiate an action whenever a certain event or time occurs and some will come from another source or require only that notation or some other non-interactive type be made. In manual systems, an active control might require that every lot weight be recorded with no consideration given to the particular lot. Another situation would require that a flange be bent after the process is completed and that the part won't fit the next step unless that flange is bent.

In manual systems, a passive control exists when the operator records only those items which are outside of certain tolerances. A similar situation exists when a specified process is complete, the operator is required to make a particular measurement and remove the assembly from the line if it is over a certain limit.

Our Planning-Coaching requirements might have an active control requiring employees to report volume of work results independent of their comparison to plan. Another would be to have employees initiate a meeting at completion of an event before the next process can be started. A passive control would be when the manager schedules regular monthly review meetings. Another example is when the manager receives all the performance reports and calls employees in when anything seems to be going wrong.

Whenever the scheduled checkpoints are likely to produce little regular contact, a manager should schedule contacts for regular intervals. These may be arranged so that they are carried through only if there has been no contact since the last scheduled one. This provides a way of ensuring adequate contact with the flexibility of adjusting for the unscheduled contacts of normal operations. It also ensures that no employee is left out of the contact part of the management process due to dislike, oversight, or unconscious avoidance.

We have provided for the contact, but what if that contact is unpleasant? What if the manager, at least with that particular employee, has ineffective "people skills"? If the contact still a benefit? Let's consider the alternatives. Without contact, the manager cannot carry out the functions of coaching and developing the employee. Without contact, the manager will not have access to the higher-quality information which the employee has. Without contact, neither will have the opportunity to give or receive feedback. Without contact, there will be no opportunity to create an environment of human response and participation which most of us value at some level.

Is negative contact, in the emotional sense, better than no contact at

all? I think it is in a large majority of cases. The question, however, is
mostly academic. If the manager is incapable of
Working Out   initiating positive contact with an employee, it is not
a Positive   likely to occur. Both manager and employee will do
Approach Is   everything in their power to avoid these encounters.
a Necessity   When we look at ourselves, we can see the lengths
we go to in avoiding unpleasant situations. Even if, in
this self-analysis, we conclude that we will still do what must be done,
it is all too apparent that most people avoid unpleasant encounters most
of the time. The solution is to be able to make them positive rather than
to anticipate the unpleasantness in a way that guarantees that it will
happen.

The Quality of Contacts

You as a manager must sense that you have significant control over the
quality of contact if Coaching is to be carried out effectively. What is
quality of contact? Who determines its level? Many of us treat this issue
as though it were not in anyone's control. Either you have it or you don't
with each individual. Some of us have it with most people and others
with only a few people with whom we come into contact. A manager is
usually chosen for a combination of technical talent and/or problem-
solving abilities and for a "natural" ability to deal with people. This "dealing with people" ability usually means to get along reasonably well with
most people and still be able to get things done.

I maintain that it is part, the major part, of a manager's job to have
control over the quality of contact with *all* employees most of the time.
I observe the opposite in the majority of cases. The
Rapport Is   higher in management I look, the worse it gets. Many
the Basis of managers seem to have the attitude that they are the
Quality   bosses — it's up to everyone else to adjust to them.
Contact   How do I know what their attitudes are? I don't.
What I can observe, however, is their behavior. The very best managers
have enough flexibility to make adjustments to their behavior, their
language, their voice tone, and their manner, to ensure that communication actually happens. The rest insist that the employee adjust to them
if any communication is going to take place.

Quality of contact has many parts. The form or process followed is
one. The end-result is another. The starting point and the critical function, however, is the ability to establish and maintain rapport. Regular
contact, with rapport, will result in positive, cooperative efforts from all

178

involved and will produce the optimum results. Without rapport, specific results may be obtained but they will not contain the rich potential and variety of those which can be achieved with the creative, unique participation of all involved.

Rapport is the most important factor in successful management and yet it is a concept virtually non-existent in management books and lectures. Sales people, therapists, interviewers, and others who depend on effective communication have some idea of the importance of rapport and how to get it. Managers have very little. What is rapport? First, what does it feel like, what state does it describe? Second, how do you know if you have it or not? Third, how do you establish and maintain it? We'll consider the first two areas below. The third will be indicated here and is covered in detail in Books 1 and 2 of this series.

Rapport is usually described as a feeling of trust or confidence in another person. We describe it as feeling comfortable in someone's presence, as feeling that we are understood, as a sense of empathy or caring. We often feel that the other person really sees and accepts us as a unique human being.

Rapport is that state where we each experience that we share significant parts of experience or existence. We sense that the other person makes sense of the world and acts in a way which *Rapport* matches our own in important respects. This may *Results from* come from acting in ways which are similar to our- *Sharing Parts* selves, from acting in expected ways in response to *of Experience* us, or by acting in ways which seem appropriate to the context. How do you know if you have it or not? We tend to assume we have it if things are proceeding in a way which matches our expectations — usually a safe assumption. The major sign is based on results. When people are in agreement and there is apparent good feeling, we can safely assume that rapport exists. Similarities of posture, voice, and gesture will also indicate a state of rapport. People in rapport tend to match each other: their bodies can be seen to match, almost a dance.

How do you establish rapport? Think of the people you have rapport with now — spouse, friends, some fellow workers, occasionally strangers. What did you do to establish rapport with them? Probably no answer comes to mind. It just seems to happen when it does. You didn't do it on purpose and probably neither did they.

Let's consider the person who you see at a party for the first time and immediately feel that you would like to know better or at least talk to. Something in a look or a manner has impressed you even before you heard the person speak. It is obvious, somehow, that he or she is responding in a similar manner. As you approach, and begin to speak, notice your attitude. You may be a little nervous or uncertain, sure, but you are already liking the other person. You expect this individual to be receptive to you and listen and be interested. You are open to listening and being interested. Whatever happens from this point on will start from a position where you are open and responsive in a positive way to that other person. If that person is, in fact, in a similar state, you can hardly miss having a pleasant experience and you will certainly experience a significant amount of rapport.

Rapport tends to exist, without thought or effort — even without intention — with some people based on their perceived similarity to us. The similarity may be an obvious one such as posture, expression, or manner. It may equally be one of appearing to meet our expectation about what is good, right, or expected from the world in a particular context. There is a strong basis for rapport in the perceived competence of another person.

But what of those times when this "natural" rapport doesn't exist. What is happening or what is missing? The lack of rapport translates into the feeling that other persons don't match the situation we are in. We experience them as looking or acting or being in some way which doesn't make sense, which doesn't match our experience, according to our understanding of the world. Our judgment is that there is something "wrong" about the way the other person is, at this particular time, at least.

These feelings and events present a particular dilemma for the manager. How are we to get the rapport we need with everyone in every situation at work when the natural condition is for *Managers Must* rapport not to exist with some people in a variety *Establish* of situations? Let's look at what usually happens *Rapport That* when rapport *doesn't* exist. This is the opposite of *Doesn't Exist* the earlier situation with the person you instantly *Naturally* liked at the party. Here you have an instant dislike or desire for avoiding the other person. Watch the way each moves to avoid the other. If they cannot avoid contact, watch the way they stand and move when talking and listen to their voices. It won't take much practice to observe when rapport is missing and when it is present.

180

Imagine the following two situations and notice the differences. The first is two old friends on a park bench on a warm summer evening. The second is a couple on the next bench who are about to break up their marriage in a bitter struggle. What do you observe, even though you can hear no dialogue? See the friends again, they are probably sitting in similar postures and positions. When one moves, the other moves in a similar manner. Now we see the couple. They are probably sitting in positions and postures which don't match. Their movements are often in direct contrast to one another. Even though there are no gestures which indicate anger, it is obvious that they are no longer getting along. Their responses to each other are either unmatched or non-existent.

We have discovered a useful signal for the existence of rapport, or its lack. This signal may also be the key to discovering a way to establish rapport. If we reverse the cause-and-effect idea and establish the signals of rapport, we might also achieve the result we are after. For our purposes here, let's consider the source of rapport. The knowledge of the attitude behind it and of the actions which create it will assist us in deciding the relevance of the issue for each of us.

The basic attitude has already been indicated. We sense that the other person experiences or makes sense of the world in ways which have important similarities to ours. We don't judge them to be wrong or bad, we accept them pretty much as they are. We understand that what the other person is doing makes sense to that person in the context of his or her experience and we can accept it easily because it matches ours in important ways.

What does this mean in terms of action? It means we will tend to respond to that other person in ways which match what he or she might expect and appreciate. We respond in ways which give the message that we understand or accept where that person is. Even in those times when we don't understand so well, we respond in ways which allow for the possibility that the other person is *acceptable* as a person. We act as though we are willing to make some adjustment in our behavior to accommodate or to attempt to understand him or her.

A manager is in an interesting position in relation to rapport. One of the standards used for establishing rapport is that there is perceived competence. To be perceived as competent as a manager, one must be able to establish rapport. Your ability to communicate, which requires rapport, and your ability to obtain organizational resources will both depend on your ability to establish rapport. You are in a circle, a vicious circle, if you have no way of establishing rapport except the "natural" basis which everyone has. The solution lies in developing the ability to establish rapport with anyone you choose to at any time you choose. When you develop this skill, it will be easier to do in more situations with more people and you will likely find that it is a choice you make much more frequently.

Rapport is created, whether consciously or unconsciously, by the adjustments you make to another person. How can you know whether

Rapport Rests in Making Adjustments to Another Person

you have rapport or not? Where does that feeling of comfort or trust come from when rapport exists? It comes from the communication to you, in word or gesture or expression or action, that the other person is responding to you in a manner which seems appropriate to you. When it happens automatically with people we like, we don't notice

the adjustment involved. The adjustments we make seem to be small ones from a common position. And the adjustment *is* small because we have already established a common base and we are aware at some level of sharing important ideas or values or ways of being in the world.

Rapport is lost or never achieved with those we fail to make adjustments to. We don't respond or we do it in a manner which doesn't match others' expectations of us. We get angry when they expect us to be sympathetic, we laugh or smile when we should be serious, we don't respond at all to something which should be significant. The adjustments we are required to make to demonstrate understanding or acceptance are too great for us to make. They often feel as though they would be threatening to our own sense of ourselves.

Here is a major challenge for managers. Can you establish rapport with everyone you work with and all others who might contribute to the success of your organization? The specific steps to assist you with that challenge are in Book 4. The basic position which can help you achieve the results you want is to realize that *the actions of others make sense to them in the context of their experience*. If you knew what in their experience made sense of their actions, you would know what to do to change their response or you would have widened your own range of possibilities. Having learned, you might change your choice. The "might" holds the threat as well as the exciting possibilities in establishing rapport with those who are different from you.

In the context of organizations, there is another aspect to the above position. As a manager, you require that certain actions be taken or certain goals reached. Making sense of another's actions doesn't necessarily

Managers Must	make them acceptable in the context of an organiza-
Separate	tion. The second major position, then, is this: *The*
Undesirable	*positive worth of each individual is recognized while*
Behavior from	*the value of any particular behavior to the organiza-*
the Innate	*tion may be questioned.* That is, the standard against
Worth of the	which a behavior is measured is the affect it has on
Individual	organization goals. This standard has nothing to do
	with the worth of an individual and no judgments of

right or wrong are called for. It also recognizes that the individual is a
being far more complex than the one or few behaviors in question can
indicate.

Feedback—The Essential Ingredient

The requirement for rapport in management is even greater than in
most communication situations. Not only is it required to facilitate the
direct communication while it is occurring. It needs to be established so
that employees will feel comfortable in initiating communication. Successful management requires a continuous process of feedback, a loop
with various points where the other person needs to be initiating contact. Some of these needs for contact will be in circumstances which
could not have been predicted and therefore cannot be formally built into the system.

The feedback loop is started by the alignment of intentions carried
out in the Planning phase. Then actions are taken towards those goals
which produce information. This information will include all of the effects of the action. The significant information will indicate whether
goals are being achieved and, if not, what direction the corrective action
needs to be taken.

Management is largely in the business of processing information. In
getting things done through people, we have an assumption that most
of the actions will take place remotely. The information is generated by
those who are acting and they are in the optimum position to get the
maximum amount of information and to assess its importance. If
previous goals are clear and adequate rapport exists, we can expect the
intelligent beings who are taking the action and obtaining the information to make the best use of it. This use will frequently include passing
the relevant parts of that information on in a meaningful form.

The exception-reporting system is a major tool of management, indeed of any control system. The exceptions which can be foreseen and

Exception-
Reporting
Plays a
Key Part in
Meaningful
Feedback

which are significant enough to be reported on relate to expected conditions. That is, in a system which is merely repeating functions in an environment which is also unchanging, exceptions to expectations can be foreseen and carefully planned. In human systems, operating for continuous growth in an unstable economy, many of the exception-reporting techniques offer only minimum controls, that is, they often indicate only major problems and seldom point to the direction of action needed for correction.

Who's in the best position to report exceptions? The people directly involved in the actions which generate information are best able to determine when exceptions are occurring and need to be reported. Creative, co-operative effort will always out-produce directed, controlled effort when intentions are adequately aligned.

This section assumes that planning has been done and that outcomes are mutually shared and committed to. We can now also make the assumption that rapport exists and information is

Sorting
Information
for the
Appropriate
Level

flowing easily in both directions in the organization. The first function of management will be to control that information flow. Even though the information is available and easily available in personal communication terms, to be useful it must be sorted and packaged for its appropriate levels. The point of view of the machine operator is different from the supervisor, mid-management, and upper management. To be considered information, data must be organized in a useful way. What is useful will depend on the purposes and point of view of the recipient. A manager's function is to convert data into useful information and transmit it, with appropriate interpretation, to those who need to act on it.

Before we consider the requirements of gathering information or the data to be converted to information, let's consider the effect of different points of view with this example: In the computer operations of a giant corporation, there are people from tape loaders to machine operators to supervisors plus three more levels of management. Supervisors set priorities and shift-loads up to 12 hours before they are to be run. There are two major problem areas common to this type of operation which we will consider. The first is a situation which has existed for as long as anyone can remember (about 3 years). Final decisions and schedules are made based on the run sheets provided by the supervisor. However, since earlier operations might have gotten ahead of schedule or run a job for which priorities have been upgraded since initial assignment, it may turn out that major jobs are not in the queue to be run. Scheduling and the ability to respond to urgent requests are often distorted unfavorably. There appears to be no simple answer to the problem and all personnel and shifts have the same problem. When this problem has been talked about in the past, the supervisor has suggested that procedures are being followed and operators need to communicate better. The information appears to be "operational" and goes no further than the supervisor.

The other situation is apparently unrelated. The computer department has an operations manual which specifies the procedures to be followed for programming, run manuals, and scheduling. The manual is out of date in many places in all three areas. Employees are held responsible for unreasonable violations, yet few jobs could be run if the procedures were followed.

The outstanding feature of these problems is the lack of data organized into useful information. The frequency of schedule changes is not known although it is stated to be almost every day, an occurence which causes considerable frustration to those involved. On weekends, special staff is regularly called in and often finds it has no time for lunch or breaks on Saturday and nothing to do on Sunday. There is no information to quantify regularly. It is claimed that all of these changes are due to violation of the procedures manual regarding approval and times.

What would constitute information for the operators? For problems which they might solve themselves, that is those where they have the time, ability, and resources, they could use the frustration levels as adequate indicators for a significant problem-solving effort. They then could discover the sources of information for originating the change and discuss the problem with other shifts. They could discover if all of the required information was recorded by each shift and required no higher authority or outside cooperation to change the situation. They could copy the previous shift's run sheet and update their own requirements.

What would be appropriate information for higher levels? The frequency of the problems, the cost of overstaffing and underutilization, and the measure of operator dissatisfaction might be significant for higher levels of management. The supervisory level would have some of the direct information of the operating people, particularly the levels of frustration and concern for what had been attempted to resolve the problem. The highest level of management might want to know simply

185

a description of the problem and its relative size and how long it had been allowed to continue. The detailed analysis required for direct problem-solving would simply be data to the highest level. The highest level needs information about the extent of re-writing needed to bring the procedures manual up to date if it is to be used for behavior guidance. The cost and effort involved in re-writing and the implications for operations and training are all significant factors at this level. Summaries of some of the regular problems, like the specific scheduling problems, would be useful information to indicate the state of the system provided for employees to operate within.

Although different data is required by different levels for their different purposes, one of the characteristics of this situation which stands out is the lack of data. Lower levels of the organization may use unquantified data for the impetus to start problem-solving. This data is adequate, based on the direct, sensory experience of the participants — adequate to start problem-solving, not to base the solution upon. For higher levels, much greater detail needs to be developed to help offset the lack of direct experience. The detail, however, is needed to support information, not for direct scrutiny. The extent of the problem is revealed by adequate information rather than *feelings* about things required. Information and time are the parameters which determine where a manager's attention is focused.

The single ability which will be the greatest asset to a manager's use of time will be eliciting information efficiently. Many of us substitute

A Manager's Greatest Asset Is the Ability To Elicit Information Efficiently written reports for direct communication because we don't know how to gather information efficiently in direct contact. Yet direct contact greatly enhances the quality of information we can receive by providing information at more than the verbal level and by allowing two-way communication or direct feedback. Direct contact also has great value in human systems as a reward in itself. Two major parts are required for efficient, direct communication (referred to as *Precision* in the book of that name). This is a language-questioning model which allows you to move from low-quality, general, information to high-quality, specific, information in a controlled manner. The components are a specific questioning model and a process for controlling the flow and direction of information.

The Specifics of Eliciting Information

Without an explicit model, many managers find that human communication has too much "noise" or interference. There is too much data, seemingly irrelevant data, important data missing and too little in the way of information. Reports have the advantage of providing the control of what is received and in what form. They have the disadvantage of predetermining the information and eliminating the valuable possibility of direct feedback.

The first requirement is to control the process of direct communication. Managers don't have enough time to allow for a random path to a goal. The process will be controlled by clearly

Setting the
Context
for the
Communication

stating what the outcome or purpose of a communication is and how it is going to be achieved. These outcomes and procedures need to be stated in such a way as to match the requirements of the manager for content and sequencing of information and allow enough flexibility to accommodate the internal processes of the information source.

Consider the preceding case study regarding the computer scheduling. Suppose the first-line manager came to you and said, "We have a serious problem with scheduling and need to do something about it." You could proceed by saying, "Tell me about it." Or you could suggest a particular procedure. You might say, "I'd like to get enough information to know whose area this problem belongs in and how to proceed further. Let me get enough information from you to understand the situation and then we'll decide how to proceed. All right?" You would then proceed to ask a series of short questions directed to the specific points you need to know more about. These questions require only short answers and take little time. Their purpose is to allow you to determine quickly whether you want to spend time on this problem or to provide simple coaching to direct the first-line manager how to proceed.

An example of the dialogue between the first-line manager (Supervisor) and you (Manager) might be useful here.

> S: We have a serious problem with scheduling and need to do something about it.
> M: (after setting procedure): Problem with scheduling what?
> S: We have a problem scheduling the computer runs and the staff requirements.
> M: What problem with scheduling the computer runs, specifically?
> S: Jobs get run in previous shifts and don't get deleted from run logs

187

and jobs get added to the queue without being approved according to the procedures.

M: And what problem with scheduling staff is that causing?

S: We have so much work at times that staff can't take their breaks and at other times we have extra help on weekends which doesn't have any work to do. This causes a lot of frustration and bad feeling.

The manager would now determine the quality of information available regarding frequency, amount of time, staff involved, and costs. In this case, upon discovering that high-quality information did not exist, you would direct the supervisor to accumulate enough data to indicate the severity of the problem and support the claim for action from higher levels of the organization if that were indicated. You would direct that the data be gathered in such a way that it would indicate a solution to the problem at the level of operations and that the summary of this data could then be used for higher levels to determine if systems needed to be changed to prevent similar situations from arising in the future. This whole transaction would take about five minutes and would provide several benefits:

- Direct contact between supervisor and manager
- Coaching in how to gather information and how to present it to the manager
- Coaching in problem-solving and organizational structure
- Adequate information for the manager to feel confident that correction would proceed in an appropriate manner
- A positive environment to ensure future information flow

In other words, it would provide a large return for a small amount of time. Notice that the purpose or desired outcome determined the appropriate questions and that the questions were *Guaranteeing that Problems Are Dealt with at the Appropriate Level* specifically directing the supervisor to the needed information. This particular problem could be and was solved by those involved. The information generated also suggested some higher level changes which needed to be made. Specifically, those were changes regarding procedures and the value of allowing employees time to solve operating problems. One of the advantages of this method of proceeding is to ensure that problems are dealt with at the appropriate level of the organization. Too many managers are simply fire-fighters, getting involved in solving other peoples' problems without developing employees so that they can solve their own problems. There is never a shortage of problems or opportunities; the question is, At what level do you want to work? With these techniques, managers have the opportunity to work at a higher level of organization questions and do longer range planning.

Being the Expert on Process

If your main function is getting things done through people, how do you accomplish it without being the expert in each area you manage? How can you coach and have contact with your people and not get involved in their problems? The key is at the level of process. As a manager you are providing the system, the framework, the process for other people to get results. You are the expert, but the expert on *process*, not content. You know how to communicate, you know how to direct a process, you know which process is appropriate for the circumstances. If you don't, you will need to be the technical expert and that will make you the one who does things directly.

The best basketball coach I ever had couldn't play as well as our worst player. He couldn't shoot with any apparent style or accuracy, he was too out of shape to run and he had never played with any team. Yet he made us all into better players and we won the area championship. He knew the process which was required to execute shots, he knew the process for getting into shape, he knew the process for building a team, and he knew the process for adjusting our style to beat opposing teams.

Being an expert on process has two advantages. The first is that you can control events to get the result you want in the most efficient way. The second is that you can teach people how to use their resources, their knowledge and creativity, to achieve results which were previously beyond their reach. You can manage people who have far more advanced technical knowledge than you do.

One of the advantages of controlling the process is that you can quickly sort out which problems are yours, and which are somebody else's. If the problem falls into the second category, you can direct the process to be followed to ensure successful completion of at least the next step, so that you aren't continuously bothered by the same problem or successive approximations of it. Gather enough information to determine the appropriate next steps for the source and in relation to your own time. What are the major goals of the Coaching phase? What needs to happen to get from Planning to actual results? These are the goals which will determine the appropriate behaviors for managers between Planning and Evaluation.

This is the action phase of the management process. It's getting things done through people. The meta-goal will be stated something like this:

Coaching —
The Action
Phase of
Achieving
Results

to achieve planned results or adjust plans in an appropriate and timely manner. Enough flexibility needs to be included so that adjustments to the uncertain future can be made to the best advantage. It is less important that fixed goals are reached than it is that individuals perform at maximum levels under existing conditions. Adjustment to external events is more important than rigid adherence to predetermined plans. Plans which were unrealistic even under assumed conditions will be evaluated as poor planning, but departments or organizations should have enough flexibility to adjust in ways most useful to the long-term growth of the organization.

Our single outcome is not enough. We require subsidiary outcomes or a greater context to adequately determine what actions and pro-

Establishing
Subsidiary
Outcomes
for Actions

cedures will be appropriate. First, let's consider what might exist in this phase for the employee. Employees also want to achieve results, particularly if they have been involved in a Planning process and have committed to certain results. Combined with that, even if not specified in the Planning, employees will want to increase their own competence if provided with a supporting environment. Other outcomes of the employees might include:

- Assistance towards achieving maximum rewards
- A desire for direct contact and feedback
- The ability to predict how they are doing
- Obtaining organizational resources to assist them in their jobs

You can add or subtract from this list on your own. Better yet, you can create this list with your own employees.

What contextual outcomes might be appropriate from the organization or management point of view? By now you should realize that the employees' point of view needs to be complementary to yours, not contradictory. Some of the management goals might be:

- Get high-quality feedback and information
- Develop employees
- Adjust resource availability
- Provide all possible assistance

- Reinforce motivation
- Utilize management resources fully

Notice that in the preceding pages the idea of flexibility and adjustment has recurred. In most organizations this is taken to mean "be prepared for less than expected." I am implying no such negative position. It is equally probable and desirable to adjust goals upward as downward, provided the system is truly responsive to actual conditions. If the goal is maximum performance rather than attempts to meet preset goals, there will be every opportunity to adjust upwards as external conditions change. The most likely event will be that the creative efforts which can be achieved will not have been adequately foreseen and the results will exceed expectations.

All of the direct employee contacts which will come under the general area of coaching occur in a variety of ways. Some should be

Keeping Track of Your Contacts for Maximum Results scheduled as feedback or checkpoints which may be initiated by the manager or the employee. Some will be unscheduled ones which may occur as a manager regularly observes the operations under his or her control. Still others will be a result of employees initiating contact for their own reasons at unscheduled

times. If you are not sure whether these events are occurring with all your employees, make a simple chart of the contacts with each individual. You may discover areas where you could significantly improve your own management performance, you may discover employees who are regularly getting into difficulty without coming to you for assistance, you may discover areas or individuals which will point the direction for improved performance.

I emphasize the value of observing operations and of talking with employees at unscheduled times. The quality of information you receive will be much higher if it involves your own sensory input and the quality of information you receive from others will be higher in the context of informal discussion at the job location. *MBO (management by objectives) cannot replace MBWA (management by walking around).*

In the worst cases, you will discover the negative employee attitudes which exist as well as the many obvious production inefficiencies of long standing. In more normal situations, inefficiencies which have become part of the accepted routine will become obvious. Simply through random observation, one manager noticed that at least one expensive machine operator was always idle. This initiated a short study which increased production 25 percent with no capital cost and minimal labor cost. In the best organizations where employees are actively engaged in improving production and have positive attitudes, the manager's physical presence still provides enough direct experience to allow him or her to participate sensibly in discussions and to compare information from other sources to sensory information.

Selecting Appropriate Intervention

The first step of Coaching (Coaching being any contact with employees more extensive than greetings and social talk) will be to gather enough information to determine appropriate interventions or next steps.

The next step in the Coaching process will be the appropriate intervention based on the information gathered. This is the place where the expert skills of the manager are put to the test. You're ready to solve the problem, provide expert advice, or do whatever is necessary to expedite matters. But wait. Remember our context, or sub-outcomes? One of our main objectives is to develop employees as well as achieve results. What is the best assistance we can give?

The first area of expertise to reach for is your knowledge and abilities regarding process. Your job is to get things done through people. That

Developing Employees' Abilities Should Be Your Goal — Not Giving Expert Advice

can usually best be accomplished by assisting them to use their own resources and by developing their abilities. Assisting an employee through the process of problem-solving will often produce better results, short- and long-term, than solving it for him or her. Negotiating a dispute will often produce greater positive results both in terms of operations and individual development than making an independent decision and giving instructions. Even offering expert advice can be done within a context of asking questions which point to the area of the information gap and demonstrate the mental processes used to arrive at the solution.

The least useful thing to do is usually to immediately offer expert advice based on content. The positive gain, which is sometimes the required one, is that of speed. The action can be taken immediately. On the negative side, the employee learns little about the process involved in arriving at the answer and will often need to return again and again with the same type of problem. In addition, the specific knowledge and experience of this particular instance in the current specific work situation will not be utilized and the creative resources of the employee will not be available to enhance the solution.

The three basic interventions most often required of managers are for problem-solving, facilitating or negotiating between individuals, and offering expert advice. At this point, we'll briefly consider problem-solving and negotiation (Book 2 pursues details of the process involved.)

Problem-solving is an activity most managers are reasonably good at on a personal level. That is, they are likely to have demonstrated an ability to come up with creative and practical solutions in an effective manner. The processes by which they do so, however, are often outside of their conscious awareness and are often of a rather random nature. This can be quite appropriate when one is engaged in problem-solving alone. It is relatively easy to keep track of internal processes or to go back to previous steps and fill in missing information.

Think of your method of solving problems for a minute. Is it an organized approach that you could explain to someone else? Could you teach it to someone else? Could you even explain it to yourself in a way that really matches what you do? This isn't an easy thing to do. We are not usually required to be so aware of our internal processes, particularly ones that work well. Like walking, driving a car, and making decisions, problem-solving has become an automatic behavior which we do well but we do it outside of our normal awareness.

The requirements for problem-solving as a coaching intervention are different from those of actively solving a problem independently. If we

Problem-Solving As An Intervention
are to develop our employees, we need to teach them how to solve problems rather than do it for them. We will gain time for other areas as well as train effective people if we do this job well. To accomplish this result, we need to be able to make the process explicit — to have a model. We don't need to teach it explicitly, necessarily. By gathering information and guiding a process with careful questions which illicit the information and resources of employees in a consistent manner, we can teach them quite rapidly how to solve a problem. After each such coaching episode, they are more likely to bring a problem to us only after they have completed more of the process on their own, until they reach the point where they can solve problems and bring solutions to us for approval if necessary.

Managers who have applied these procedures have had great success both at getting better, more creative solutions to problems, as well as in increasing significantly the ability of their employees to solve problems without management involvement.

As the number of people involved in the process of problem-solving increases, the necessity for a model or explicit process increases too. Internally, we can get results without being strictly

Having an Explicit Model Helps Focus Knowledge and Resources systematic in many cases. If there are just two of us, one can adjust the other's processes reasonably well and we can keep track of a process. As the number expands, the variety of internal processes expands and the use of mental resources becomes a random process which begins to work against itself.

Each pattern disrupts the others and resources are not focused in useful places. An explicit process will focus the knowledge and resources on the particular part of the problem so that all participants are complementing each other. Information is being gathered by everyone without the distraction of generating solutions, solutions are not criticized while they are being generated, present state information is not confused with desired state. A model helps, in training and in group processes.

Do you believe that your employees have information and creative resources which you do not and which might be relevant to a problem they bring to you or are involved in? If so, a process which involves them will likely generate better solutions. Even if you have expert advice which they don't possess, their involvement may add to your existing knowledge in useful ways. Employees are much more likely to support and enthusiastically implement solutions which include their own input. At some level, we all know this. Why is it happening so seldom?

Although we believe that there is more information and resources available and that employee involvement will produce greater motivation, we also have found that it simply takes too much time and effort. We have also discovered that even when we attempt it the results are often less than we might hope. The reason is the lack of an explicit model for problem-solving and the ability to elicit information and access creative resources in an effective manner. The value of a model is that the process required can be controlled and matched to time and resource constraints. A model can produce predictably satisfactory results in economical amounts of time without massive amounts of formal training. The change can be instituted by on-the-job application of an explicit model in the framework of the manager's function of developing people.

The second major type of intervention is some form of negotiation, bargaining, or resolving conflicts between people. This is particularly true in a matrix-style organization. Other organizations are structured so that there is regularly some of this type of activity even though it is not officially styled as a matrix organization. Scarce resources of time and money have to be allocated between projects or departments, individuals or departments have conflicting goals or wants, personalities clash and people struggle for influence or power.

The features of negotiation range from what we might call arbitration to resolving deadlock battles. The arbitration situations arise when the manager has the official power to make decisions or is the only organizational contact for getting resources from other areas of operation. In this situation, a manager will elicit information and make the best decision possible. In third-party negotiation, the manager will assist those directly involved to arrive at a mutually acceptable solution.

The requirements for all of these types of situations are similar. The central problems are the apparent conflict of interest and the high level of emotion likely to be attached to the issues. How can you deal effectively with people who have strong emotions attached to opposing points of view? How can you maintain rapport with each participant when they have animosity towards each other? Effective communication can't take place without rapport — as the people needing the negotiating assistance are demonstrating for you.

Before any solution is attempted, it is necessary to establish rapport with each participant. Even if a solution is developed or becomes obvious before that point, it should be put on hold
until rapport has been established. The desired result is for something to happen in the world of action outside of the negotiation context. If rapport has not been established, the solution may still be disagreeable to at least one of the participants and real objections may not arise until implementation is attempted. Active participation and support are part of the desired outcome of negotiating sessions.

How do you establish rapport with two opposing people when emotions are running high? The specific methods suggested earlier and in Books 1 and 2 are the basic means. They must be used with each individual in turn: Adjustments of posture, voice tone, words, and body position as each person is addressed will contribute significantly to rapport with each person. Additionally, by eliciting each representation from participants talking directly to you, acknowledging each position without agreeing or disagreeing, indicating understanding of each position and not taking sides or assuming that you know the best result will all contribute to rapport, by exhibiting behavior which participants expect from someone in the position of arbitrator.

The second major area is the content of the conflict. By the time a situation has gotten to the point where negotiation is required, the participants have often forgotten the content and are focused on the emotional aspects of the dispute. To resolve the issue and get cooperative implementation of the solution requires re-establishing rapport and finding a common base from which to proceed.

No negotiation is possible without a common base or cooperative frame. The basic negotiating position, the idea behind "win-win," is that the participants have a common higher goal than the *Establishing* positions under negotiation. If they don't, if their *a Common* goals conflict at basic levels, there is no basis for *Base Sets* negotiation. This is seldom true in an organization. *a Higher Goal* All of the employees are overtly working toward some common basic goal. The opposite positions will revolve around the best way to achieve the same goals or different interpretation of what those goals are. The assumed common base in the organization provides the basis for potential win-win solution.

How can we find this common base? It often seems that the two parties are fixed in their positions and that no common base is possible. Each position, however, is meant to accomplish some result which can be assumed to fit with the organization's overall objectives. This provides the route to establishing a common base. The question which will lead to a starting place is, "What will that (your position) accomplish for the organization? How will it help us achieve our objectives?" After this has been established for each position, it is often a fairly simple matter to combine the positions in an agreeable form for a common base.

In one instance, a company which had decided to expand through acquisition had not been able to agree on any particular one. One of the vice-presidents was violently opposed to projects which seemed too risky. Another vice-president felt that diversification made no sense except into high return areas because of the stable, regulated nature of the main operation. The vice-president who focused on safety would fight any proposal by highlighting the risk aspects of each particular acquisition. The other would retaliate by emphasizing the potential return and putting the first down as a conservative stuck in the past.

By first getting one to agree to a statement of position, such as, "Seeking a high return from business with a different nature consonant with the security of capital required by the main operation," the other saw for the first time that they might have a common interest. The "conservative" vice-president then agreed to a statement of his position as, "Ensuring that the financial health of the organization was maintained by providing safety of capital and realizing the potential returns of diversification." The two had an opportunity to experience, for the first time, that they were actually working towards the same goals and could benefit from each other's particular expertise and judgment. Restating the common goal as "A desire for increased return combined with a risk no greater than was appropriate to the nature of the main operations" gave them a common base to work from in a cooperative problem-solving mode on future potential acquisitions. This relationship was further improved when the "risk-oriented" vice-president rejected the particular acquisition under consideration due to the information provided by the "conservative" one.

Notice that agreement was obtained for the statement of the common position. It is important to the continued success of the negotiations that overt agreement be obtained along the way. It is easy to seem to agree to a position and later withdraw that agreement if it has been supplied or assumed by the negotiator.

When a subordinate comes to you with a problem, what is the first thing you are likely to do? The answer for most managers is to offer expert advice. I put this near the bottom of my list

Third
Intervention —
Offering
Expert
Advice

of interventions. Although some form of offering advice may be the final result, starting off that way is generally the least effective in the long run. Emergencies may call for this approach, but the frequent result is that there are then more and more "emergencies" to deal with. Managers are often hired to be expert consultants as well as managers, particularly at the lower levels of management. However, if a management function is really in operation, development of your people is a major consideration. If the organization wants to develop managers or if you, as a manager, want to progress in that area, then a specific process which develops employees will be the most effective.

In many situations, the employees fast become more expert than the manager at technical considerations. In others, new managers cannot be experts when they take over new departments or divisions. The optimum situation, in fact, is where all employees are more expert than the manager. If management is "getting things done through people," then

197

we *want* those people to be expert at what they do.

What then is the manager's expertise? It lies in knowing *how* to do things, in methods or process. Particularly in those processes which are largely internal — how to make decisions, gather information, solve problems, decide on priorities, and sequence activities to produce desired results efficiently. Managers are the experts on employing the resources of their people.

The last choice, whenever possible, is for the manager to offer expert advice. Even if that advice will be the end-result, talking through the appropriate process first with employees is one way to demonstrate for them how to proceed on their own.

The extra time involved in modeling the process required to gather information, solve a problem, etc. will seldom be excessive if the *Modeling the Process Helps Develop Employees* manager has explicit awareness of what he or she is doing. It may even turn out to be less time if employee understanding is required. It *will* be significant in terms of success. A great deal of time and cost is spent in many instances where understanding was incomplete initially. Knowing the process used to arrive at a decision as well as the content can contribute greatly to efficacious action.

How explicit are these processes that you're going to model? Can you sequence the required steps externally so that your subordinates can learn from you? Most managers cannot do this well. Although you have efficient internal programs to arrive at decisions, sort priorities, and so on, it is unlikely that they are well organized for external modeling. These are the first steps for making a process explicit and learnable:

1. Ask explicit questions instead of filling in assumptions.
2. Think out loud — comment on what you are doing.

If each time an employee brings you a "problem" with inadequate information you ask a consistent kind of question, that employee will soon learn to pose these questions internally and not bring the problem to you at all or at least do so at a more developed stage. It is an approach which will save a great deal of time in the longer run.

The Manager's Role In Changing Behavior

The last major area which is frequently required of managers is to obtain a behavior change in subordinates. This is frequently neglected, handled on a discipline basis, or turned into an unwarranted intrusion into another's personality.

What do you do with the employee who is constantly late, who continually makes the same kind of error, who is too often short with customers? What do you do when your suggestions and advice aren't followed, or worse, when agreed changes aren't maintained?

The most frequent comment I hear is one which attacks the personality or character of the employee who fails to change. Comments such as, "He's stupid," "He's just too stubborn," "He's a trouble-maker," reflect the manager's frustration. This kind of language does not inform us regarding the actual situation, only the manager's internal state. This way of thinking tends to allow for only one solution. The solution, of course, is termination. Equally likely is long-term suffering of the same behavior. Both are less than optimum in most cases and rely on a way of thinking and talking about a situation which doesn't allow for positive change.

Any one situation involves a specific set of circumstances which involve the actions of the employee and the actions of the manager. With another manager or a new set of actions by the same manager, the employee's behavior is in response to the external conditions that he or she experiences. By changing those conditions, say, by changing the way I communicate, I will be able to get new responses. The first area to look, then, is to our own actions. How can we change the conditions so that the employee acts in ways which we find desirable?

Changing Behavior Often Means Changing Ways of Communicating

The first area open to us is to change the communication itself. Perhaps you've been lecturing the employee or bawling them out after the first few times that ordinary instructions were not carried out. You've done it every way you know how. Try a whole new approach. Ask questions: "What do you need so what I'm asking will happen" "Do you clearly understand what I'm asking?" "What is stopping you from carrying it out?" Or, get active feedback from that person to ensure that they understand the required action or behavior and when it is supposed to happen. Have them tell it to you in his or her own words. Or demonstrate for the employee how and when it is supposed to happen. Or have the person observe one of the other employees who is acting in a way you expect and explain the steps as they are being done. Or get a specific contract from the employee that the action will be done and when or with what frequency.

Every action which anyone takes makes sense to that person at the time under the circumstances as experienced by that person. If the situation persists through the above attempts to change it, then a fuller understanding of the circumstances is in order. We continue with the assumption that the behavior makes sense to the actor. We also assume that it serves a purpose or realizes an intention for the actor. With these assumptions, we proceed as though the employee could change the behavior if it made sense — to him or her — to do so.

Intention is what makes sense of all behavior. If I know what you intend to happen, only then can I judge your behavior. Your method of

*Making Sense
Requires
Understanding
Intentions*

questioning, your manner when giving instructions, your walking out of a meeting, can be reasonably judged by me *only* if I know your purpose. We commonly make these judgments without adequate information. It is too easy to assume that we know what the intention is, that we share the same pur-

pose or view of the situation. Whenever the behavior of another person is puzzling, look to that person's intention for the explanation first.

How does this apply to the "problem" employee? If our previous flexibility of communication hasn't worked, what can we do in this area of intention? Telling, asking, contracting haven't worked. What then is preventing the result from occurring?

The basic approach is to separate intention from action and result or intention from behavior. Concentrate on the intention. If the results are the desired ones, we need not question action or intention. What is your intention from the desired action? Does the employee understand this intention? Does he or she agree with it? What is the person's intention from the unwanted behavior? Does it match yours?

During a recent airplane flight, a stewardess regularly muttered sarcastic comments, to herself and audible to others, and frequently rolled her eyes upward when passengers got in her way while she was serving. Her results did not match the airline's intention. Customers (passengers) felt put down and some were too intimidated to ask that their needs be met. The company's desired action — courteous service — was not being met, and the intention — comfortable passengers — was not being realized.

The employee presumably understood the intention and actions required and agreed with the intention. The first thing to verify is if this is so. What was the stewardess' intention? We cannot know without investigation, but it is safe to assume that she was responding to a personal, internal feeling. The intention indicated by the behavior was some version of "People are stupid, and I don't like serving those kind," which was a response to some current condition in her life — a current condition rather than permanent or else she wouldn't have gotten the job.

The airline's intention and the stewardess' intention match in general, in that the airline wants to provide good service *within the bounds of the possibility of human dignity for its employees.* This last part has either not been received by the stewardess, the appropriate behaviors have not been learned, or specific work needs to be done to keep the two operating when conditions in her life are less than optimum.

If you cannot find a match in the area of intention, you will seldom resolve the problem. If we don't agree on the outcome, through lack of understanding or difference in purpose, it can only be by chance that I will produce results which are the ones you desire. The circumstances will determine the level of intention from which to start seeking agreement. The particular actions and results being obtained will tell you whether you need to start at the mission of your organization, department, job, or of a particular action. The farther back you need to start, the more that should indicate to you the need to increase the effectiveness of your planning sessions. If an employee appears to lose her temper or be short with customers, it might be enough to review the intention behind the particular job. If the problem originates with that employee failing to turn in reports on time, the intention of that particular task may be all that needs to be reviewed. If a manager regularly fails to inform another department about products which are below specification, a review of organization intentions may be required. In any case, it will be best to err on the side of the intentions of the higher level of the organization. These intentions provide the context for making sense of the lesser intentions.

A Common Intention Is the Basis for Cooperative Action and Mutually Satisfying Results

After getting understanding and agreement on this level of intention, the next step depends on the apparent cause of the undesirable behavior. If it was due simply to a misunderstanding of the intention, nothing but a review of the desired behavior and agreement for change should be required. If it was due to understood, but not agreed to, intentions, then agreement must be obtained or termination started. The likely way to get agreement

First, Look for Understanding and Agreement

will be to move the discussion to the intentions at a higher level of the organization. These should either explain the need for changed behavior or allow room for negotiation of appropriate actions.

What if the behavior was being done even when there was agreement with and understanding of the intention? We can assume the employee doesn't know what else to do. This may mean that there is a lack of knowledge of how to act; and this is possible even when it seems obvious to us. Frequently it means that under certain circumstances the employee can't help responding in a certain way even when he or she is aware that it is detrimental to the agreed intention.

It is possible that the employee thinks that filling out a form was adequate communication, thinks that what they have been saying is clear communication, thinks that the problem is the responsibility of someone else, or is unable to hear his or her own voice tone in a communication. Here there will be agreement on the intention but disagreement on the behavior. Coaching may involve showing the correct way, training, or simply providing objective feedback about what is actually happening.

If the employee agrees on the intention and agrees on the actual behavior, the next step is discovering whether or not they agree on the results. This will usually be the easiest step. Frequently there is objective evidence of the results. You may also need to translate less objective information into sensory-grounded terms. A service representative who loses his temper with customers might not agree that he left them in a state which produced dissatisfaction. Rather than going by specific complaints, the demonstration of results might be based on the verbal content, the tonal qualities, and the visible body/facial expression of the customer. This can be done most effectively by short role-play acting out the situation.

What if all of these areas get agreement? Where will you go from there? The last area is the employee's intention. What is the outcome for the employee of the behavior? What about it makes sense to that person in that situation? The path to solution, to alignment of intention will be to find a behavior which achieves both desired outcomes. Where this is not possible, the employee needs to subvert his or her intention or find different work. The specific model for behavior change in this instance is in Book 2 of this series. It involves finding a way to change behavior from the employee's own resources, which is respectful of that person's own, personal requirements.

202

Facing Negative Situations

We've been describing the basic activities of management, of management of people, as opposed to those other tasks which managers are required to carry out. Why do these activities happen so infrequently? Why are they generally performed so inadequately? Partly because most organizations reward other behavior. Partly because there is little training given about how to accomplish these activities effectively. Frequently, the main reason, however, is that they involve direct, personal, face-to-face communication under less than optimum conditions. They threaten our sense of confidence and well-being.

Coaching and negotiation frequently involve a significant amount of negative emotion which few of us are equipped to deal with comfortably and effectively. Problem-solving involves a change in attitude and, if more than one is involved, the ability to influence the mental processes of others — frequently resulting in the possibility of more negative emotion. The most comfortable, least threatening, and quickest intervention of a manager is to offer expert advice. This includes solving problems internally for employees rather than being a "process consultant" with them.

Let's consider the requirements for dealing with negative emotion in a comfortable and effective way. The requirements of rapport continue in these situations. To maintain rapport in these situations, you must be able to respond to the emotion in an appropriate manner. Not doing so indicates an unwillingness to make an adjustment to the other's model of the world — remember, others' emotion makes sense to them — and/or the inability to deal with people as individuals. If you need to react in only one way, you can be controlled by others and you demonstrate your inability to deal with them. Adequate flexibility for control of a situation requires that you have more than one way to respond. When someone gets angry and yells at you, if you must go into quiet withdrawal or if you must become loud and aggressive in return, the scene will play itself out according to the power relationships with the minimum potential in positive results. You are in the same position as the customer service employee mentioned earlier who lost her temper with customers. What is your intention and do you have a choice?

Dealing With Negatives Relies on Rapport

Practicing the specific techniques in Book 2 will assist in increasing the number of alternate responses you have to situations with negative emotions. You will find that your effectiveness increases as well as your level of comfort in dealing with people. Most of the management tasks which are done poorly, or not at all, are the result of our internal discomfort. Most people that I know tend not to do those things which make them uncomfortable.

Another resource you have to help you respond in a more appropriate way is a technique of disassociation which most managers are quite good at. That is to keep your intention or outcome clearly in mind and to treat the emotional outburst as a challenge or a game. Deal with loud voices, strong words, abrupt gestures just as though they were simply things to respond to with no personal meaning for you. Keeping your intention in mind even when faced with strong emotion allows you to respond in ways which will help you achieve your outcome.

A requirement of management is to be able to influence the internal states of others. Let's consider the issue of negative emotions from this point of view. While angry, depressed, or even excited, many of us can't deal usefully with the requirements of the situation. Strong emotions, particularly those we call negative, tend to reduce the resources we would normally have available. The emotion focuses our attention on a few specific factors and we are unable to consider other facts or to feel differently until the original emotion is taken care of in some way. We become unable to hear, often we don't even see very well, and the content of any communication becomes the least important part. It's a problem we often insist that our people handle, say, with customers, but we often don't handle it very well ourselves. How can you respond effectively to someone in this state? The primary response must in non-verbal terms because the verbal is not heard very well. Voice tone and body posture will be the major factors in effective communication. Words which comment on the situation as experienced by the other person, without necessarily agreeing, will be the most effective content.

Summary

You have read the major communication requirements for successful Coaching encounters. Any contact or Coaching encounter may result in the necessity to change goals or plans. If this is the case, a small version of a Planning session must also take place. I have seen many companies go to significant lengths to do a good job of Planning and then fail to update the plans as the year or planning cycle proceeds. The plans get further and further from the actual situation until they are more of a hindrance than a help. They end up being ignored and then become rituals that soon disappear from the organization's management systems, in practice, if not formally.

Remember, plans are guides to action, not goals written in stone which need to be met. It is as valuable to discover that changes need to be made early as to meet the actual goals. We live in a uncertain world and Planning provides the feedback for an Early Warning System of necessary changes. If all plans were met, it suggests the Planning process was far too conservative or that those involved have figured out ways to distort results. Planning allows us to obtain the most immediate feedback and to adjust our actions at the most opportune time — in either direction.

It is equally important to reset all checkpoints if plans are changed. Review or Evaluation depends on having checkpoints. The worst failing of a subordinate is to fail to meet checkpoints. Failure to meet goals is expected, unless they are set as minimum standards only, but failure to make the adjustments which will optimize the conditions, whatever they are, is inexcusable. One company which had formal checkpoints which couldn't be adjusted, never failed to have them met — but it was done in a perfunctory manner which defeated the intended purpose. The reason was that the checkpoints were never adjusted, couldn't be adjusted, no matter how often the plan was changed by other events.

Using checkpoints also allows other departments or individuals to be informed of changes which may affect them. Sub-optimization, where one area produces the best for itself although it isn't the best for the whole organization, is less likely to occur with reviews of plans and checkpoints on a regular basis.

The final function of regular contact or Coaching sessions is to ensure that each subordinate receives necessary and useful feedback. To be effective, feedback must be timely. A year-end review, no matter how comprehensive and well-documented, will have little influence on the ability of employees to change their behavior, however motivational it might be. Regular contact provides formal opportunities to give both positive and negative feedback. Do you like to receive positive feedback? When was the last time you got some? When was the last time each of your employees got some from you? Every employee should receive it. If someone doesn't have one thing you can be positive about, why is that person still working for you?

Remember, the requirements for feedback is that it be sensory-grounded and that it include the result. The purpose of feedback at this point is for adjustment of behavior, if required, and motivation. It is not for evaluation. That is, it will indicate whether the behavior or result is good or bad, but the focus is on its expected impact on future behavior or results. It lets the employee know which behaviors are seen as positive and which as negative. The feedback is the first point of change. It gives an employee the opportunity to discover the significance of his or her own behavior and to initiate Coaching if the correction cannot be accomplished.

One of the major wishes of managers is to have a sense of control. This is frequently expressed as a desire for "no surprises." This doesn't only refer to what would be considered unpleasant surprises. Many events which might be considered pleasant surprises are much less so if they are, in fact, surprises. An unexpected increase in orders may be better than the reverse but it could cause serious problems if significant and truly unexpected.

We cannot, however, control the external conditions in which we operate and enough surprises will come from that area to last a career. Our emphasis is on reducing the significance of surprises which originate within our organization. If our system allows people to be creative, we can expect many unforseen developments. If our management system is adequate, these will be mainly on the positive side. We still want, however, current feedback to ensure that the organization adjusts in the best possible manner. The major requirement for effective management is good contact with our people in both directions.

Evaluation

Evaluation is the completion of the management process as it relates to planning, achievement, and employee development. It is the final step for meeting the needs of the individuals who make up the system. The major feedback required by the organization to meet operating objectives has been a continuing process within the framework of Coaching. The major function of this part of the process is to satisfy the human requirements and those of the organization as a whole.

Divorced from a system, from Planning and Coaching, a performance Evaluation has little value. It may still serve some useful functions, but unless it is part of a system it will have no shared base of information to start from. Evaluation is largely a summary of events with values attached. These will seem remote and unreal if no planning or regular contact has been proceeding during the year.

Evaluation Amounts to a Summary with Values

Without the required frequency of operating feedback, performance feedback at the end of the year will seem arbitrary and unrelated to anything current. It will have little meaning or motivational impact.

Planning, in a system of management of people, steps out of the regular production process and looks ahead. It sets aside normal day-to-day operating concerns, breaks up a continuous process into arbitrary time chunks, and invites a different perspective on the operations. It gives participants a chance to look at the processes and themselves in a different way and to create new paths for the future.

Coaching performs both as a regular or continuous part of the operations and as the link to the previous Planning sessions. It deals with day-to-day operating considerations and serves as a time to relate to the plans which were created. While dealing with the trees, it keeps the forest in mind.

Evaluation is similar to Planning in that it steps out of the continuous process again and invites a review from another perspective. Using the arbitrary time chunk taken for Planning, it reviews the plans, the actions which have been taken since that time, and the results obtained. It is primarily a look back and a summary of significant performance results.

Each of the steps — Planning, Coaching, Evaluation — serves two types of functions, one for the organization and the other for the individuals within it. Although the goals of each should be complementary, they are not identical. The organization may require programmed times for feedback, information regarding its human resources and their individual career goals, a basis for compensation and reward, and other employee-related information.

Project management, successfully done, has all of the same elements as required for systems, or continuous process, management. It has the added advantage of having a definite, unmistakable beginning and end. Planning is started and substantially completed at the bid or estimating stage, and Evaluation is done at the definite conclusion. Time and budget targets are either met or not. A new start is made on the next project. Nice and clean. In the continuous management of a production process, there is no such objective beginning and end. To make matters even more difficult, there is no fresh start.

Evaluation — Summarization With Value

The Evaluation process is a way to make an end to the process and a place to restart. Being an arbitrary time period related to the actual production process does not preclude using it as a place for a new start. We can recognize that the past is over and start a new process at any time. If poor work has produced many quality faults in the past, the gain from that point where the faults are known, rather than from the original plan, is the place to start. The gain will be as real and as significant as the same quantitative gain from the original plan. This implies that the Evaluation is the completion of any process of blame or penalty related to the past.

If regular contact has provided continuous feedback, what is the necessity of a formal Evaluation session for the employee? The most

*The Basis
of Evaluation
Is To Show
Employees
Where They
Stand*

common employee complaint — "I don't know where I stand" — is frequent even when there has been regular contact with a supervisor or manager. The reason is not necessarily to be found in the quality of the contacts; they may have been quite adequate. Instead it's in the nature of the generally long time period between Planning and Evaluation sessions. These are generally a year apart — much too frequently they are a year apart — and a lot has happened in between. Parts of the plan may have been forgotten. Priorities might have changed. Frequently, the original plans will have changed a number of times during the year as economic or other external conditions change.

Although these events and changes may be clear for the manager, it is unlikely that the same is true for the employee. Employees have been involved in the business of getting things done — whichever things seemed the most pressing at the time. A review of the time period is appropriate to ensure a common ground for understanding. Future actions of the employee will be based on his or her understandings about how the manager values particular behaviors and actions. The view which the employee has gained from day-to-day interaction, or lack of it, may be significantly different from the desired one.

The relative value of each goal, process, and plan may not be clearly understood by the employee. The employee may believe that although he or she failed at one particular task, overall performance has been superior. The manager may have regarded that task as so significant that exemplary performance of all other tasks does not compensate for the failed task. Although these priorities should be made clear in the Planning session, we cannot assume that they were all, in fact, made clear. Priorities and relative values of various parts of a plan — and sometimes even the omitted parts — may not be adequately clear to an employee. Dramatic feedback to that effect during the year does not necessarily make the appropriate point to the employee.

Quantitative plans and goals change and so do processes. It may not be clear to employees what relative importance is attached to the way things get done. There will be those who believe their performance to be better than average based on the quantitative results but who are valued much less than expected because of the way that the results were obtained. Others will perform according to the letter of the prescribed process, or their understanding of it, with unsatisfactory quantitative results and blame those results on factors outside of their control. These too will have personal opinions of their ratings far higher than warranted.

The standards of *how* things are done should be used with extreme caution. Controlling behavior rather than results will stifle creativity and the best use of the human knowledge and experience available. Wherever possible, a standard of *Base Your* quantity and quality should be used based on observable results. To be effective, these need to include longer term effects as well as various side effects on other parts of the organization. The need to highly specified results diminishes as the clarity of intention increases and the environment is conducive to cooperative functioning. What underlies the need for this summarization? If all of the previous Planning and Coaching action were accomplished in an exemplary manner, should the Evaluation session be little more than a rubber stamp of previous contacts? No, I don't think so. Although much of the frustration and emotional turmoil of the Evaluation session should be relieved by adequate Planning and Coaching, there is still a significant function to be played by Evaluation.

Base Your
Standards
of Quantity
and Quality
on Observable
Results

As the above discussion has indicated, there are many possible areas of confusion about the overall value of an employee's contribution. One of these is the problem of assumption. As manager, it if often obvious to you that a particular behavior is of overriding importance. This may not be obvious to the employee particularly if your behavior has not made it explicit because *you* find it obvious. It may be obvious to the employee that certain actions were the most appropriate in the circumstances even though they didn't conform to plan. The manager who may not be aware of all the circumstances may totally miss the "obvious."

There is far too much complexity in this world to assume that it can all be communicated verbally or in writing. In each job, there are always things left unsaid and information which is never shared. The first avenue to correcting this situation is obtaining an alignment of intention and ensuring adequate contact and feedback. The fact remains that there is still too much complexity to share all of the information relevant to action or decision. This is one of the reasons for having a hierarchical management structure. If it were not the case, there would be little justification for the many layers of management we commonly find.

The Evaluation session provides an opportunity to correct this problem *by exception*. What this involves is discovering which actions or

210

*Discovering
the Difference
in the
Value of
Actions*

results have produced different opinions about their value between manager and employee and identifying the differences. Most of our communication problems arise from this difference in shared information. Revealing these differences through an Evaluation process provides the basis for correction of action in a cooperative manner. If you expect creative responses to the unexpected variations encountered in actual operations, Evaluation provides one of the significant ways for an employee to learn about your ideas and priorities as a basis for that action. You are in the position of giving rewards and punishment. Employees are attempting to please you. Even those who sometimes are not needing this kind of information need to know what would please you or not — regardless of their choice in practice. They have only the information you give them to go on. Each piece that you communicate to them will allow them to achieve your goals in a manner which makes use of each of their unique talents and experience. This will provide the maximum benefit for everyone involved.

Clarifying Ideas and Priorities

We spend a great deal of time trying to please others in some form. Where the reward system is tied to authority, there is a strong incentive to want to do this. We also want to experience some control over our existence. This is frequently a paradox. I want to please you and have control. How am I to do it? The answer lies in knowing what pleases you. Then I can have a reasonable sense of control *and* please you.

Human beings and the world we live in are too complex to be covered by explicit rules. In voluntary organization, the rules serve as guidelines

*Knowing
Others' Frames
of Reference
Is Key to
Understanding*

for behavior. Even if the system states that they are the only guide to what is expected and has harsh penalties for violation, they are still interpreted and applied by human beings. Most of us have learned that if we satisfy the rule-maker, the boss, we don't have to worry much about the rules. If we stick to the rules and also antagonize or otherwise displease the boss, we won't fare so well.

As observers of other humans, we generally experience a lot of shifting and change in what seems to be appropriate. From our internal points of view, we usually see ourselves as quite consistent. What accounts for this discrepancy? What would we have to know about others,

211

or they about us, so that our views would match? The answer lies in the area of shared information and understanding. From your frame of reference, your actions and responses are quite consistent. For me to find them reasonably predictable, I need to share more of the information. In an organization, Evaluation sessions are a place for that to happen.

The requirement for an effective sharing of communication *is* effective communication. There are techniques for making this communication most effective. The starting point, however, is not technique. The starting point is the awareness of the need for communication and the desire to have it happen. With enough desire, with a firm intention for appropriate communication to take place, we can make it happen. It might be slow and painful, it might be uncomfortable, but it will happen.

The techniques presented in Books 1 and 2 are designed to make it faster, easier, less painful after the intention to communicate is established. Without that intention, the technique becomes mere manipulation. Possible, at least in the short run, but never truly effective in the long run. Manipulation is used here to mean trickery to gain advantage over another. In its more general sense, it is what we do with every attempt at communication. We try to influence the state of another person. When done for mutual benefit, I believe it is appropriate and positive behavior.

We've looked at the benefits to managers and the needs of employees which come from effective Evaluation sessions. What about the organization? What are the needs which are served *Effective* by the Evaluation function? If adequate operational *Evaluation* feedback is continually adjusting operations for *Ultimately* maximum results, what needs does a formal Evalua- *Benefits the* tion system fulfill? There are needs of formal report- *Organization* ing and others which relate to the requirements of a human system. The major factor is to fulfill the needs of the units which make up the system — individual human beings. A priority should be that the needs of individuals are satisfied within the context of the needs of the organization.

The organization needs an inventory of the human resources available for future growth, development, and succession. This should include not only the strengths, weaknesses, and rating of employees, but their desires as well. As many a study has shown, the ambition and desire of an individual often count far more than the IQ or other apparent skills which are brought to a task. The human resources, the ones

212

we talk about but do the least to utilize, are a major factor in the success of your organization. Knowing who and where they are is an important step towards effective utilization of the human potential locked up in your organization.

Development of personnel should be based on individual requirements. What is needed in the way of development is revealed directly from Coaching contacts and the review process of Evaluation. This is an appropriate time for basing development on individual ambition as well as needs perceived by a manager. To be effective and economical, both the method and content of training need to be tailored to individual requirements.

The Evaluation session provides a formal check on the feedback process. All of the goals and intentions of the Performance Management System should have been achieved by the interactions required in the system. This provides a place to verify that results have been realized. The primary source is usually a form which is completed by the manager and acknowledged in some way by the employee. I recommend that if there is not substantial agreement on the facts upon which the evaluation or rating is based or if the employee feels that inadequate planning and coaching have been done, some form of arbitration will be required. This provides a warning to higher management that the process may not be working. Another option is to review all evaluations with the next higher level of management before they take effect, for purposes of reward or formal recording.

Getting Evaluation To Work

The final requirement of the Evaluation session is to provide the basis for rewards, financial and other. This meets the needs of employees, managers, and the organization. Employees want to know the basis of their reward or lack of it. Managers need to let their values and evaluations be known in a way which has impact on the individuals affected. The organization needs to know there is some basis of fairness in the reward system and that its assets are being spent in ways consistent with their stated outcomes.

With all of these positive results expected for all concerned in the Performance Management System, why do managers find it so hard to do? What causes these systems to come and go in organization after organization? The Evaluation or appraisal sessions are the most emphasized in organizations, yet they are seldom consistently carried out and almost never effectively handled. Managers, like most people in

213

other areas of life, are uncomfortable directly evaluating another person. We will develop specific techniques to make this less troublesome later but, for now, let's recognize a fact of life: People do not do what makes them uncomfortable. Sure, if forced, they will carry out a semblance to meet the minimum requirements — sometimes. There are a few of us who will carry it out, no matter what, because we recognize the value. But most of us will find ways to avoid unpleasant duties, particularly if they involve interaction with others. One of the largest companies in the world where I discussed these ideas stated that it was of the utmost importance that each employee be evaluated at least once every year. At a later workshop with the lower levels of management, some complained bitterly that they hadn't been evaluated in two years — even after repeated requests and complaints. In smaller organizations, interaction is often more personal. But the evaluations still frequently fail to get done.

Evaluation is intended to be a part of a management system. If no system exists, and almost universally it doesn't, then Evaluation becomes a session of confrontation and surprises — or *Evaluation* nothing. That is, if no Planning was done with an *Works as* employee, if the employee was not actively involved *Part of a* in that process, then no basis of understanding or *Larger* commitment has been established. The day-to-day *Management* operations are now the responsibility of someone *System* else. Employees are simply being told what to do — or worse, flying by the seat of their pants. Failure to carry out effective planning with employees begins to take its toll. The many excuses range from not having enough time to the lack of effectiveness when attempted. This is usually followed by inadequate contact and coaching between manager and subordinate, particularly those who are a "problem" to deal with. Things get done but with very little in the way of effective or systematic contact. What is left for the Evaluation session? Everything. Too much to be handled all at once. And no basis for a mutually understood and cooperative discussion. Most will turn into ineffectual blame sessions with little positive, specific information being shared which might have a beneficial effect on the future.

The critical nature of Evaluation being part of a complete system is often overlooked because of the apparently stronger factor of the need to conduct potentially unpleasant face-to-face encounters. Remarkable skill at personal communication will be enough to overcome a significant part of the above problem. But we cannot expect this remarkable skill

214

even as a result of an intensive training program. It is necessary to implement the systems approach as well as provide enough training in the required communications skills to significantly improve them. The goal is to produce significantly improved managers, not remarkable communicators.

The importance of face-to-face contact can't be exaggerated. Done effectively, very little in the way of formal system is required. Done poorly, no formal system can be adequate compensation. If the previous contacts within the Performance Management System have been inadequate, then the Evaluation is not likely to be any different. It is primarily a summary and verification, a difficult task if little has happened previously to be summarized.

Rapport has been considered frequently in relation to Planning and Coaching. In an Evaluation session, it will be constantly needed. If rapport has not been established up to this point, it will be a difficult task to obtain it in only this setting. The techniques in Books 1 and 2 will be of considerable assistance, but your intentions and previous behavior will be crucial at this point. Although I can recommend using the communication techniques at any point, I suggest the test be saved until they can be used in Planning and Coaching.

Let's review the situation of setting the context for an employee in a Planning session. The organization has intentions for this session which include meeting the needs of the manager and the
Reviewing the employee. How can this best be communicated to the
Critical employee? How can we be sure that the employee
Components of participates usefully in the process? If the manager is
Face-to-Face aware of the organization's intentions and is an effec-
Contact tive communicator, then we can expect the desired
result. However, let us not leave this to chance, even with adequate training being given. Let's work from the worst case up to the best. Where there is little training providing or where particular managers are ineffective at face-to-face communication (how did they get to be managers?), we could provide them with a written presentation of the purpose of the session and require that it be read to the employee. We could also supply the employee with a copy for further information. The worst case will be that the employee reads it at the request of the manager. Almost as bad will be when the manager reads it to the employee. In these cases, each will escape the need for face-to-face contact and will avoid the problem of personal ownership for the ideas presented. Is a written presentation enough? Hardly, but it is a start

which will improve the results obtained. Given the appropriate wording, such a form — a management job aid — will increase the chance for positive results.

Here's an example of a written "purpose sheet":

> This company believes that all of our employees want and need to know where they stand with their managers. We believe that at least once a year this should be done as a summary to supplement the informal contacts which have been happening throughout the year. We also want to ensure that our reward system is fair and that it is fully understood by each and every employee. We also want to ensure that we have adequate information regarding each employee for purposes of training and promotion to provide the maximum benefit to you and the organization.
>
> This session is designed to provide you with any information you may need about your performance and to obtain your thoughts and feelings about your manager and the total organization. You are invited to speak up so that you can get the most satisfaction from working in this organization.
>
> The procedure which will be followed gives your manager a chance to state the basis of your evaluation, gives you a chance to respond with relevant information, and provides you with an opportunity to have your say about anything in this organization. We hope you take full advantage of this opportunity to express your views and we support you in meeting your own goals as well as those of the organization.

I'm sure none of us believe that the above sheet will take the place of effective communication. However, if the organization is serious about installing an effective system, the wording of this sheet and the policies which back it up will provide a framework which gives the employee a starting place. In this regard, we do not overlook the impact of this sheet on the reluctant manager. First, the manager is required to say or present to the employee in some way a set of words which give an explicit message. This will tend to influence the manager's behavior. Second, there is a significant group of managers who don't do these sessions well simply because they just don't know what to say. For this group, even if they read the words without any eye contact, they will mean them and their behavior will match what has been said. In this case, they soon will find comfortable words of their own and the quality of the sessions will improve.

A Purpose Sheet Sets the Policies and Helps the Manager Communicate

I find it hard to escape from a conclusion to be drawn from the above. If you or your organization is sincere about goals such as those stated in the "purpose sheet," how can you have managers who haven't been trained in communication skills appropriate to the desired results? When you have a manager who needs to read from the sheet, and in my experience many do in all organizations, the message to the employee is incongruent, unless you are also in the process of training that manager.

As we move toward the best case, the situation improves dramatically. Giving the employee the "purpose sheet," but introducing the session in your own words with some eye contact, or even reading it but adding your own comments and some eye contact, will enhance the resulting interaction and invite the employee to be more involved. This simple level will allow for the possibility of two humans interacting rather than simulate a functioning of two information machines. The demonstration of appropriate behavior by the manager will produce a quantum leap in results.

Various research has indicated that between 75 percent and 95 percent of the meaning of our communications is contained in the non-verbal portion. This includes context, physical attitude, and gesture and voice tone. The words are the least important. Most of available management training, even those that quote this figure, are primarily verbal.

Consider the above comments on the reading of the "purpose sheet" with the non-verbal message changed. In the worst case, the words are there but the situation and the method of communication and the accompanying gestures and voice tone all give another message. The response from most employees will be better only to a limited extent. The positive result from such a situation will be to provide a vehicle for discovering the actual state of affairs. Some employees, despite all of the other messages, will believe the verbal message and go to their manager or higher to obtain the stated outcomes.

The major jump in positive results that takes place when some eye contact and personal verbal input is added is not a result of the verbal content. Although it may be changed, there are few *Adding the* managers who can "say it better" in terms of the *Human Element* actual choice of words. It is better because it con- *Makes the* tains a message which is more congruent. That is, *Critical* the manager's communication will have a different *Difference* voice tone and physical content, it will have some eye contact, and it will provide a context message which

217

demonstrates that some communication is actually being attempted — that the verbal message is being carried out to the best of his or her ability.

A company policy which demands a minimum of some personal comment by the manager on the written "purpose sheet" will be a step in the right direction. The wording of that sheet can have a significant impact on the results. I recommend that a procedure sheet be given to the manager for conducting the session. It should contain specific examples of appropriate types of comments.

We want to prevent the kinds of comments which I have heard as an employee, such as, "We have to do this because the company said so. Let's get it over with as fast as possible." The procedure sheet should include the specific steps to be taken and a description of their purpose and some brief "how to."

Samples of comments might include:

> We're just starting this program and it might be a little awkward but the company is really committed to it. My manager supports it and it's part of my performance requirements. I hope we can both benefit from it.

> The procedure is already spelled out and I support the ideas in the purpose sheet. Let's see if we can relax a bit and both benefit from the session.

> I'm extremely uncomfortable doing these sessions but the company says they have to be done and I support the goals. I'll do the best I can because I want to be fair to you. Speak up with whatever you want to say even if I seem awkward.

Commenting on your own awkwardness or embarrassment is an effective technique if it is so strong that it will be obvious anyway. Communications often work better when the obvious is named. Some managers will be less comfortable than others no matter how much training is provided. If you are unable to carry out an evaluation comfortably and "smoothly," that simply shows you are human. I have found that success comes from being human much more than from trying to hide all of one's negative feelings. Most transactions between people have some rough spots. The easiest and often the most effective way to deal with them is to acknowledge them and move on.

Our goal is not to become polished communicators but to discover ways to achieve the results we want. We are trying to create the conditions for effective evaluation and two-way communication for the future benefit of everyone involved. This means affecting the mental and emotional states of employees in a positive manner when appropriate. It is management's responsibility to create these conditions even though the maximum results will be obtained when both individuals involved are attempting, with some skill, to achieve the desired results.

Influencing Internal States as Communication

All of your behavior as a manager affects the internal states of your employees. Your choice is how you affect them and whether you do it by intention or default. Stop and ask yourself, "How often do I get responses which seem inappropriate?" and recall what you might have done to generate that response. Did you do it in purpose? The answer is usually No. What happens then? Where does the interaction go astray?

The first place we tend to look is our choice of words. Phrases which imply a knowledge of intention, involve mind-reading, or attack the character of the employee will all tend to produce responses which don't lead to a desired goal. Implied intention and mind-reading is taking place whenever you state that you know the internal content of another person that "must" account for their behavior. This tends to be counter-productive because you will often be wrong; there are a limitless array of reasons for doing things. Another factor is that, even when you are right, there is no way of verifying that fact.

"You did that to get even." "You thought it would draw attention to you with other departments if it worked." "You just don't know how to handle your anger." These are all examples of speaking as though we know the contents of another person's mind or feelings. However right we may be, without high levels of rapport, these will likely lead to non-productive places. The words which will allow for the greatest cooperative effect will simply describe observable behavior and its results.

Attacking character is obvious when it uses such words as lazy, stupid, incompetent, bad, greedy, etc. Less obvious but in the same category are phrases which state that an individual is incapable of doing something. Telling people that they are unable to control themselves, that they'll never understand something, and that they have to respond the way they always have each imply that the individual is lacking in normal human resources. Again, the best way to deal with such situations is to point out the behavior and the situation which demands a different response in terms which can be recognized externally.

Although the first place we tend to look for what went wrong in a communication is words, it is seldom the most productive place to start.

The Real
Significance
Is the Non-
Verbal Aspect
of
Communication

Remember the research which indicates that only 25 percent or less of the meaning of a communication comes from words. The way that a thing is said constitutes the most significant part of its meaning. This includes the context as well as the voice tone and all non-verbal behavior. Before we consider the non-verbal components, however, let's look at the level which controls all of the rest. Intention, or desired outcome, is the controlling factor in our communication. There is simply too much going on to keep track of consciously. Most of our words and gestures are not selected consciously but are provided by our unconscious mind. By that I simply mean that they are fed to our conscious minds, as it were, from parts which are outside of our immediate awareness. When we consider that skin color, muscle tone, breathing, and facial expression are all parts of this non-verbal communication, it becomes obvious that there is simply too much to keep track of consciously. Even trying to monitor all of this communication would leave little room for the content of what we are trying to communicate.

How can we expect to communicate congruently with all of these factors? Where do these individual behaviors come from? Each is a re-

Each Message
Sent Reveals
an Internal
State and
Intention

sponse to an internal state and communicates a message which reflects that state. If all of our internal resources were being directed by a single, simple intention, then we could assume that all of our external behavior would be consistent with that intention. If we are sharply divided, say we know we should behave positively toward an employee as a

manager and we personally dislike that employee, then we can assume that some of our communication will convey one message and some of it a very different one.

Intention, in this sense, is not only our conscious intention but also the other goals and values which we hold (and are therefore trying to realize through behavior). In other words, if our conscious and unconscious intention match, we can expect our communication to be congruent. If they don't match, what can we do about it? It isn't of much use to give rules for communication when our conflicting intentions will make them impossible to carry out. Neither will it be of much use to demand that the unwanted intentions be eliminated.

In most cases, the dilemma is fairly easily resolved. We have most of these conflicting intentions because we fail to clarify, for ourselves, what our intentions really are. Particularly in situations where others (the organization) expect certain things of us, we tend to accept these without making them our own. That is, we don't clarify the desired outcomes in ways which make them full acceptable to ourselves. When we have done this and still have a major conflict, it can often be handled by simply naming it in the communication.

The value of naming what will be obvious anyway becomes clear in this situation. If one of my intentions is to ensure that you don't mistakenly believe that I like you, unconscious of course, then that message will be communicated somehow. If I comment on the fact that we don't get along too well, I can give you a clear message and then allow my other communications to be focused on the desired outcome or intention. Recognizing that this option is not the cultural norm, I still suggest it as an effective means of conducting positive evaluations. Spending a moment to clarify our own intentions will often make such statements unnecessary. Increasing our focus on the desired outcome and acknowledging internally any contrary feelings will usually suffice.

What can we do with the non-verbal components of communication if they are determined by intention? Why consider them separately at all? One reason is so that we can focus our attention on the more important ones. Another is so we can use them for signals indicating the state of the current communication. Although the components of non-verbal communication are too numerous for our conscious attention, we may selectively turn our attention to various factors as they seem important.

Returning to our problem of recalling what we might have done to generate seemingly inappropriate responses, let's consider what we did, or didn't do, in the non-verbal area. Many will draw a blank. We tend to find it much easier to recall what we said than to remember what we did with our bodies, our facial expressions, and our voice tone. If the words seem to have been all right, the other are the areas we need to consider. The major area of concern here is the use of our bodies and voice tones to establish rapport. These are also important in giving content messages and for communicating the emotional impact of what we are saying — or trying to hide. At this point our focus is on rapport because the emotion behind a statement tends to get expressed from the unconscious resources discussed earlier.

The major consideration in this area that I have observed with managers is their lack of responsiveness to their subordinates. The

221

*Flexibility
and Adjustment
Help Create
Rapport*

message which is most frequently conveyed thorugh non-verbal means is, "I am not going to change. It is up to you to adapt to me." How is this message conveyed? Primarily through a voice and posture pattern which is inflexible and contains little or no response to the vocal or physical characteristics of the other person. This applies to their apparently usual way of being and to any demonstration of emotion. A common example is the manager with a gruff manner who is short and abrupt with everyone, maintains little eye contact, and has a constantly lowered head and hunched shoulders. Another is the super-reasonable manager who never raises her voice or displays any very obvious emotion, in fact has a rather boring monotone, usually accompanied by a rather stiff and formal posture.

With the above communication considerations in mind, let's consider what will have to happen to achieve the desired outcomes suggested at the start of the Planning section. A specific procedure will outline the functions necessary to ensure satisfactory results. The particular skill with which each step is accomplished will determine the quality of the outcome. The specific procedures or model will ensure that an adequate process is followed and that it can be completed. As with all such models, as the abilities of the manager increase, the need for a strict and explicit model disappears. It then serves only as a reference point in evaluations which are not going well.

Setting the Guidelines for Evaluation

The first step of any communication is to establish rapport. This is assumed in all of my models and seldom included as an explicit step. The first step of an Evaluation model has an extension of rapport and is included explicitly. There are few evaluations which do not contain some negative feedback and many which will contain unpleasant surprises for one or both parties no matter how well the preceding steps have been done. In preparation for this occurrence, I recommend that a positive base be established which can later be regained. If a negative emotional or mental state arises before any positive states have been achieved, it is generally much more difficult to swing the situation to a positive state.

This positive state can be generated, after rapport has been established, by reference to a positive work experience or to a cooperative relationship or to a previous experience which may be assumed to contain positive elements such as the excitement of starting a new job or assignment. It requires that the manager share at least one positive experience with the employee or have the ability to access such an experience even though it isn't shared.

At this point, many managers act as though I've suggested something strange. Some have said, "You expect me to say something like *that*?!"

Accessing Experience Whether Good or Bad

But is it really so strange? Certainly we aren't used to doing such a thing as a consciously chosen behavior. Yet we do it regularly in personal relationships when they are going well and flowing freely. We say, "Hey remember when..." and we reminisce together. A manager can easily do the same with a previous work experience. Even musing out loud about an appropriate type of experience will tend to start a similar trend of thought in another person.

We want to be able to reaccess this experience and its accompanying emotional state later in the evaluation. How are we to do this? Particularly if the session has been largely unpleasant, this may seem a formidable task. It will be unless the current situation has been associated with an "anchor." This terms refers to a conscious use of a normally unconscious occurrence.

Our minds can be compared to a hologram. This three-dimensional picture is created by shining a special light source through a photographic plate which recorded an image using the same light source in a special way. The plate can be broken, yet when the light shines through one of the broken pieces the whole image appears. This analogy can be applied to the functioning of our minds. We interrelate every piece of information, whether conscious or not, and when we retrieve any one piece of that experience through memory, we tend to retrieve the whole. This means that often an apparently unrelated smell, sound, or sight will retrieve a memory and its associated feelings.

We can create this circumstance consciously. You probably have a smell — of soap, perfume, cooking or cleaning — which instantly takes you back to a childhood memory of a relative's or friend's house. The same kind of thing operates when you hear a particular tone of voice from a person with whom you have regular dealings. By speaking in a particular tone of voice and sitting in a particular position and maybe making a unique gesture as you and your subordinate recall a positive experience, you can tend to recall that same experience in the other person just by resuming that tone of voice, position, and gesture.

This is not as hard as it may seem at first glance. You can notice the

223

difference in the voice tone, posture, and words of another person when they are remembering a positive experience and when they are remembering a negative one. If you first recall a positive experience and invite your subordinate to do the same in a congruent manner, you will likely create all of the necessary "anchors" or unique environmental factors required for later access. All you need do later when you want that same experience or feeling, is to congruently recall, silently and internally, that same experience and it will produce the appropriate voice tone, body posture, etc.

One of the major reasons for using this technique, or any other, to change the mental or emotional state of another is to gain access to

Gaining Access to Internal Resources

internal resources. The extremes make the point particularly obvious. Remember trying to explain a mistake to someone who was incredibly angry. It didn't work very well, did it? The other person was so angry that he or she seemed not to be able to hear.

In fact, other normal resources seem to have been lost. When we are angry, depressed, worried, and even excited, many of our normal resources are not available to us. If I want you to start planning for the future, I should ensure that you are not in a depressed state at the beginning.

This manipulation of the internal states of others is an appropriate function of managers. The ethics of this type of communication are determined largely by the results. That is, if we both have available the maximum resources useful in a particular case, then we both will benefit. We will get the maximum mutual benefit from the particular exchange. If you do something to help me access the most appropriate internal resources, I will appreciate it even if I become aware that you used covert means. If you use the same techniques to coerce me into something, I will resent it and the effort will likely backfire.

The first formal step of an Evaluation session is to establish the basis for the final rating. How many times have you attempted this simple step and failed right here? The result is usually a lost temper or withdrawal and a summary evaluation given after some unproductive discussion. The major failing is most often that the evaluation was being given along with the "facts." It is crucial that the basis for the evaluation be given without including evaluative terms. Behavior and result need to be separated and the evaluation is another step again.

Results can be agreed to. Behavior can be agreed to — usually. Evaluations, as internal conclusions, cannot be counted on for agreement. Remember here that behavior refers to externally observable actions (including what can be heard). A "surly manner" describes an attitude, not a behavior. The words, tone, and actions which suggest the surly manner are the behaviors. Both results and behavior should have been included in the Planning sessions and the employee should have received feedback on them throughout the year. In that case, a summary of behavior and results should be a relatively easy task.

The basis for the Evaluation is the specific behaviors which did or did not happen in relation to agreed-on plans and revisions. The language used to convey these facts should be as specific as

Keep the necessary to ensure that both parties know they are
Language referring to the same thing. And agree on the inter-
Specific pretation. It is better to err on the side of being too
for Describing explicit or sensory-grounded. This is particularly
Behaviors hard to follow when it is behavior rather than results

that is being evaluated. The major points should relate to checkpoints and to results in relation to behavior. That is, the worst thing you can do to me as a manager is allow me to have unpleasant surprises. The major technique for preventing these is to establish checkpoints (see *Planning*, Book 2). If you fail to report or follow up appropriately at a checkpoint, that will be a major failing. If you respond appropriately at all checkpoints and these were set so that nothing got out of hand, then you will likely have performed well. Results must be judged in relation to behaviors, due to the uncertainty of the world we operate in. If your results were less than planned, but you performed according to standards and took reasonable action at all checkpoints, you will have performed adequately. If you exceed standards based on results, then behaviors will not likely be significant factors.

Suppose your subordinate were a salesperson who had been on the job for two years preceding this one. The first year, after sales training, he sold adequately and followed the company sales model reasonably well. The second year, he sold considerably more than quota. Most of it came in the last part of the year. This is the third year and he sold less than quota, his sales dropping off in the last half of the year. At his quarterly checkpoints he states his belief that he will make quota. You also observe that he seldom follows the company sales model, a style which he developed in the preceding year. Your coaching at that time consisted of some checking as to the reason for his belief about making quota and the request that he come to you if the situation changed. You also stated that following the company sales model was a requirement for those who weren't achieving their quota.

The first and strongest point is the fact of receiving an unpleasant surprise in not being warned about the possibility of not making quota. You requested and didn't receive advance notice — in time for action — from a third-year salesperson. There was an obvious error on your part in assuming that the salesperson was mature enough to handle the situation with the small amount of direction that was given. Although this is a signal that your own style needs to change with this person in the future, the lack of warning is a severe error. The only acceptable rationale for this is that the individual salesperson knows better and can prove it by results. "Doing your own thing" while not meeting quota is unacceptable behavior. This saves the criticism from degenerating into justifications based on the behavior of others or individual past success.

Notice that if behaviors and results and their relative importance have been made clear in Planning and Coaching sessions, the Evaluation is simply a summary of what is already known. Wouldn't the above situation be relatively easy to carry out, for an Evaluation session, if the suggested prework had been done? The selection of behavior commented upon in the Evaluation is also part of the process of indicating relative importance of performance. Setting aside the idea that we all like some positive feedback, it will be necessary to comment on positive behaviors which met standards as well. Otherwise the employee will be left with the strong impression that only the areas in which failure was discussed were important.

There is an assumption that if behavior is included in the Evaluation, either results cannot be defined adequately or the company/manager knows the one best way. The point for *Keeping* Evaluation is that a manager is not in a position to *Checkpoints* criticize task behavior too strongly unless he or she *and Giving* knows how to do it — unless that manager knows *Warning Are* how to instruct an employee how to do it. The be- *Vital Signs* havior which will be intolerable relates to missing checkpoints and not giving adequate warning of unpleasant surprises. At this stage of the Evaluation, the employee will have information to add. Particularly if it is a negative evaluation, the employee will want to offer justifications and make excuses. If this doesn't happen, you probably can take it as a sign of inadequate rapport. Being quiet while being criticized is a good indication of withdrawal.

Many managers take an evaluation to mean that at this stage the employee is to "bite the bullet" and listen to the facts. How do you handle the employee's desire to contribute facts or to make excuses?

What kind of information might you want from an employee at this point? Certainly not justification and excuses. There may, however, be relevant facts which you were not aware of. Other departments or individuals not producing as required, you as manager not meeting your own commitments, models being followed even though results were low, changes in plan which were not recorded — each a fact which may change the evaluation of an employee if included in the manager's summary. The weight of the above will relate to whether checkpoints were met or not. In any event, they are the kind of items which could affect an evaluation. You would want to hear these kinds of things so that they could properly be included in your evaluation.

But wait. You may be asking how you can allow these kind of comments without also allowing the excuses you don't want to hear. The answer is, mostly you can't. Your task is to maintain rapport and a two-way communication while preventing, to the extent possible, excuses and justification. The problem will be that the employee will interpret the nature of their facts somewhat differently than you. Pacing and leading techniques referred to earlier and covered in more detail in Book 1 and in *Planning*, Book 2 will assist in this task. The needs of the employee must be met. That will often mean that some excuses need to be listened to.

Recall the purpose of this step: Give the basis for evaluation. This might better be called *establish the basis*. Any facts which are relevant you will want to consider — whatever the source. Any which are not relevant need only be heard. That is, it will not cost much in time to hear what the employee has to say and to let him or her know that you have heard. Up to this point, little time will be wasted and the employee needs will be met.

The danger lies in dealing with the weight to be attached to each fact. Recognizing that this step is solely for information-sharing as to the basis of evaluation, it is important that any additions by the employee be treated on that basis. Their relative merits will not be discussed until the actual evaluation is given. This separation allows information, even excuses, to be heard without any need for argument. Any discussion around employee offerings should be for clarification and verification only.

The next step of the Evaluation meeting is to get agreement on the

facts. The basis for evaluation should be understood and agreed on by
both parties. The agreement we are seeking is both
Getting   overt and congruent. That is, we want an explicit
Agreement   agreement that the facts are as stated. We also want
on the   the employee to feel that all of the relevant facts
Facts   have been considered. If we have not given the
employee the opportunity to change or add to our
stated basis, we may be able to get them to agree to the facts but it will
not be congruent.

We might start this portion of the meeting by requesting that the
employee introduce more facts which might be relevant or indicate that
all of the important facts have been covered to his satisfaction. This will
tend to have the effect of collapsing into the previous step. So much the
better. Now is the time to get as much material out as possible. Having
it come up later, or not at all, will cause greater problems in the end.

You need to be particularly sensitive at this point to the power inherent in your position as manager. Many employees will feel intimidated and unable to inject facts of their own, ones which may be
relevant and which the manager would like to hear. The caution is extended at this point because of the tendency of many managers to use
leading behavior. For instance, I have frequently observed managers
who purported to be simply asking a question nod their heads as they
asked it. The obvious suggestion, which all but the manager observe, is
that they want a Yes response — no matter what the internal response
of the other actually is. Most are not aware of such behavior and do not
understand why employees don't give them "honest" answers.

It is time to move on to the evaluation proper when this agreement
has been obtained. And only after it has been obtained. If agreement at
this point cannot be reached, it is a signal that adequate coaching and
planning have not been done and that inadequate level of rapport has
been established. The manager is responsible for ensuring that adequate
previous communication has occurred so that neither party has significant unpleasant surprises at this point. If that has been done reasonably
well, agreement can be expected now. If agreement cannot be reached,
I suggest that the manager be required to review the situation, with the
employee present, with his or her own boss or with a company arbitrator or ombudsman. The manager has, after all, demonstrated a lack
of ability to deal with this particular employee in this particular
circumstance.

Although these sessions can be expected to be accomplished at one sitting, there are times when more than one will be needed. If initial agreement cannot be reached, it may be useful to break and verify the facts under dispute. The arbitration is required when even these measures won't work. The break is not to be considered a "cooling off" period, however, or used as a negotiation tactic. It is to carry out investigation into facts which will be supported by both parties.

Giving the Evaluation as a separate step allows the meaning to be attached to all of the events of the year as represented by the preceding discussion. The individual contacts during the year have each provided pieces of feedback which indicate good or bad performance. The preceding summary will have given an indication. It is not safe to assume that the employee will know from these what your overall opinion of performance is. I have met many managers who have been completely baffled by bonuses, or lack of them, even after they have been through an Evaluation session. It is often a good policy to summarize major points to check understanding — in Evaluations it is particularly important.

Even though all of the facts have been understood and agreed upon, the relative importance of each one has not necessarily been obvious.

Setting a Value On Pieces and Relaying It Clearly If the employee has contributed facts, or, what is in their mind, extenuating circumstances, they will frequently assign different values to the individual items than you. As we considered earlier, the world is too complex, there are too many variables and possibilities, there is too much variation in our internal resources and experiences to assume that we will arrive at the same conclusions. This is particularly true where we are considering the relative value of a large number of separate incidents.

I have found in workshops, in Coaching sessions with managers and in video-taped replays that the hardest thing for many to do is give an evaluation in clear, unequivocal terms. Even though they have stated it clearly to someone else beforehand, the actual face-to-face situation seems to change the words. As you may have guessed, this is particularly true if the evaluation is less than "above average." Somehow, in our culture, "average" has become a dirty word. There are two fairly simple remedies for this particular situation. The first is to use another word such as "satisfactory" for average. The second is to make clear in the Planning session what goals the employee is aiming for, what category of employee they wish to be evaluated as, and making clear what it will take to get that rating.

What is the major stumbling block to giving clear evaluations? What is likely to prevent you from getting the message across? The facts have been stated. Many times the conclusion seems obvious. So what makes it hard to name? The emotional response expected from delivering a judgment about another person or that person's worth seems to be the major block. We seldom like to make such pronouncements, no matter how clearly we feel them or how frequently we say them to ourselves. Whatever the reason, it is my experience that learning to deal with negative emotions with greater comfort and confidence makes it easier to deliver clear evaluations.

It is here that the technique of pacing and leading is particularly useful. The techniques are primarily non-verbal ones for accepting and then changing the emotional states of another. The first requirement is to notice the effects of your words on the other person. Recognizing a depressed, angry, or surprised state, the manager might simply comment on it using the appropriate voice tone and posture for a person in that state. After this has been done, the manager can gradually change voice tone and posture to a more positive state and the employee will be inclined to follow to this new state. Having had his or her state fully acknowledged, the employee will be prepared to follow the lead of the manager.

The Evaluation As Clear Summary

The evaluation itself is the overall rating which is the results of the combination of all of the employee's actions. It is based on previous agreements or plans and the intervening context. All of the important points should have been covered previously, many in Coaching sessions and summarized in the Evaluation session and some may be detailed for the first time in the Evaluation session. At this point, the major items should be summarized and their relative importance to you as a manager made clear.

The significance of each major item should be based on results and on observable behavior as opposed to beliefs about the motivation, feeling, or character of the employee. The evaluation *Keep the* is to be on the performance of the employee, not on *Focus on* them as a person. This distinction will seldom be re- *the Behavior* ceived as a clearly separate issue by the employee *Not the* and it is important to make every effort to accom- *Person's* plish it. The message is that the employee is an *Character* acceptable human being even if some of his or her behaviors are not considered useful to the organization. The particular words used will be a signal indicating success from

230

the manager's side: "You did or didn't do something" and "This or that happened" are about performance, while "You are or are not something" is about the person or the character of the person. This part of the session should end with a rating which leaves no doubt about the manager's overall evaluation of performance.

Some managers object that if they have given the details of good and bad performance, the rating is adding an arbitrary piece that takes away from the effect. Particularly if the rating is average or better but they have detailed a number of unsatisfactory areas, some feel they remove the motivation to improve. Remember, however, the goal of Evaluation process. An understood basis for reward and growth requires that the overall impact be known. The route to behavior change, even motivation, will be in the individual Coaching sessions rather than in the vagueness of an incomplete evaluation.

The most serious objection to this clear rating is that it is arbitrary and judges the person. The second issue has been addressed above. The first is more troublesome. If a formal rating system exists, it is likely to require many arbitrary distinctions to be made. It may require wordings which seem inappropriate or use a scale which is recognized to be strongly biased toward one end or the other. Worse, it will often have implications for pay or advancement which cannot be avoided.

Giving an overall rating in plain English rather than using a formal rating system will take care of much of the problem of being arbitrary. Simple phrases like "outstanding," "exceeds requirements," "barely meets requirements," and "unacceptable" will tend to get the message across quite well. If a formal rating system is required, particularly one which is numerical or uses ambiguous words, simply adding the above kind of words as well will accomplish the desired result. If they appear to conflict, then a simple explanation is in order.

When the same system is used both for pay and for advancement, a greater problem arises. These should not be based on the same standards. A totally competent worker may be unsuited for any advancement and yet deserving of rewards for performance. These kind of issues need to be discussed with the employee and made clear. I have found that most people will work in most conditions as long as they know what they are and can order their behavior accordingly. Remember the most common complaint of employees today — "I don't know where I stand." The Evaluation session is meant to address that problem. Part of the answer lies in making the system within which they are operating clear.

The surest way to avoid problems around ratings is to deal with them

231

*Establish
the Terms of
Rating in
the Planning
Session*

in the Planning session. Explain the basis that will be used and ask the employee what rating he or she would like to receive. Allowing that "average" or "acceptable" are, in fact, acceptable, you can then plan what kind of performance it will take to achieve that rating. If this is done, the rating itself will be no more of a surprise than the preceding basis. Both manager and subordinate should know the rating before the session starts. (Do not take this as removing the need to have the session and make it explicit.)

The rating needs to have some relation to the reward system. It need not happen at the same time but must be connected to accomplish the stated goal. One of the ways of ensuring a clear evaluation is to give the monetary or reward implications at evaluation time. This is also a technique which will give the maximum likelihood of employee questions if the basis is not clearly understood.

To complete this phase of the Evaluation session, the employee is encouraged to give feedback to the manager about the manager's personal style as well as about the organization. Up until this point, all of the information has related to the past. Once this is finished, we hope to turn our attention forward again. The employee, having received a lot of feedback, will often want to have his say about the past as well. This should be actively encouraged if it is not readily forthcoming.

The manager's job throughout this part will be to "bite the bullet" and listen. It is frequently difficult to elicit useful feedback and the reason is found in the behavior of the manager. One of the surest ways to prevent receiving feedback, particularly from a position of power, is to justify any complaints or challenge the facts behind them. At this stage, the appropriate verbal behaviors are limited. The first is to question if the information being given is not understood. Remember, for understanding only. The second is to indicate that the feedback was received. This is usually by giving a summary and checking whether it is substantially correct. The third will be to let the employee know that you also received any strong emotion which they may be exhibiting.

Eliciting Feedback

Simply put, these are the requirements for eliciting open, honest feedback. The Evaluation session provides the formal opportunity for the employee to give feedback. If the manager's behavior has been such to elicit feedback throughout the year, it will also happen in this session.

In the more common event where this has not been the case to any great extent, an extra effort will be required at this time. It is worth the effort. Even if there will not be another such opportunity until the next Evaluation session, an employee can get the feeling he or she at least has some chance to be heard.

We all find things wrong with our situation at times. No system I have yet run across is perfect. We all need a place and time to complain, to let others know what we think, to get things off our *You're the* our chests. If this isn't directed upwards and re- *Best One* ceived, where will it go? In too many companies it *to Receive* goes sideways, downwards, and out to the customer. *Feedback* Which would you rather have? Many managers and whole organizations choose the latter, not by their words so much as by their actions. If you indicate that you can't take or don't want to receive feedback, it will go somewhere else. But don't count on it being buried.

Congruent non-verbal behavior will greatly assist the employee in giving feedback. That is, if you can refrain from going red in the face and tensing your neck muscles, from making gestures which indicate that's enough (such as starting to fiddle with things on your desk) or from becoming elaborately casual and giving no sign that anything happening in the room interests you right now, it will be much easier for employees to tell you what you need to know — or just what they need to say. Admittedly non-verbals are much harder to control than the verbal part of the communication. Having been warned and still failing (managers are human beings too), the words suggested above and no others will go a long way towards getting the open feedback you want.

Where, you ask, is that anchor we set up earlier. Why can't I use it to change this person's mood before they dump on me? Well, you could have, but it would have indicated you really couldn't take it. And if that were true, then use the anchor. Now, however, is the time it was created for. You are done with looking backward. It is time to look into the future. You want all of the employee's positive, creative resources involved from here on in. Now it is time to go back to that voice tone, posture, and probably some related words and reaccess those resources before moving into the future.

Summary — Creating the Basis for Growth

The final step of the Evaluation is to begin to create a base for future growth. This is not a Planning session. Rather, it is simply gathering information upon which to base future plans. This part is for discovering what each party might usefully think about and do before the next Planning session. It also provides a clear statement that the past is taken care of and it is time to look to the future.

What sort of things might be of interest for future planning? The most obvious information has probably arisen from the evaluation itself. If there were specific weaknesses, if certain behaviors need to be changed, what might be done to improve them? These areas might be briefly discussed as items to consider. The solution may involve training, it may require that new procedures be set up or simply that some more specific agreements be reached. The specifics are not to be decided at this meeting.

Another area will be a consideration of the opportunities open to the employee. What do you have in mind for employees? What might they consider for themselves? Maybe the organization has growth plans which offer potential that the employee is unaware of. Or maybe the reverse. What are your ideas about potential career paths?

Finally, what are employees' goals and plans? What are their likes and dislikes? It is my belief that people need to do very little that they don't like and that, within the realm of their working world, someone can be found to do almost any task willingly. And these people usually do it much better. Spending some time exploring employees' personal preferences and goals and assisting them in working along those lines will pay major dividends over a period of time. Just listening and considering personal preferences will likely improve the relations and productivity of most employees.

The circle is finally closed. The plans have been achieved or not, the actions have been performed, and the results have been evaluated. The circle of course does not end. From the perspective of a system, it appears to be complete. From the perspective of a human being engaged in the business of living, it continues. From the point of view of the actors, managers and employees, it is more like a spiral. Done well, it is a spiral that moves continually upward producing rewards for everyone.

234

4.

The Basis for the System

Managing For Performance

Management is neither a science nor an art. It is a process which uses various sciences and is greatly enhanced by individual artistry. Excitement, drama, and elegance are added by the personal style of individual managers. In isolation, as a separate field, though, management is merely a technology.

Merely a technology? In the domain of business, technology has all the glory. Technology is applied science or art. In business, where achieving outcomes is so highly valued, science and art are valued only where they contribute to those outcomes. In this domain, artistry is admired only where it contributes to achieving results. This work presents the technology of management with the framework whereby it can be performed with artistry.

Management in its simplest terms is getting things done through people. Certainly managers are often required to perform other actions such as inventing new processes or designing systems. For purposes of this book, we will separate the management process from the technical expertise which a manager is usually expected to possess.

The primary sciences which provide the foundation of the technology of management are psychology, communication theory, systems theory, and praxeology. Psychology studies internal events
The Technology that result or can result in definite actions: it pro-
of Management vides the basis for specific ways to plan for humans
Depends on in systems. Communication theory, which studies
Knowledge of how humans can influence the internal states of
Psychology, others, provides us with ways to speak and act which
Communica- will produce desired actions in others. Systems
tions, Systems, theory, which studies processes of interaction aimed
and Praxeology at a definite goal, provides the minimum elements
necessary for achieving specified outcomes through

237

other complex systems. Praxeology, which studies human action in its most general forms, provides the means for combining outcomes, systems, and complex human beings. This last science, praxeology, requires some explanation.

Human action is purposeful behavior. Acting people choose and try to achieve ends or goals. We continually attempt to move from a less satisfactory state of affairs to a more satisfactory state. Action, in this sense, means the employment of means for the attainment of ends. The action may be simply a word or a smile. Wherever the conditions for human interference are present, we act no matter whether we interfere or refrain from interfering. He who endures what he could change acts no less than he who interferes to attain another result.

The condition necessary for choice is that we recognize a more desirable state than the existing one. But to make us act, another condition is required. We must have an expectation that purposeful behavior has the power to move toward the more desired state.

The ultimate goal of human action is always the satisfaction of the acting person's desire. We are not dealing in vague terms with human action in general, but with the concrete action which a definite person has performed at a definite date and at a definite place. Human life is an unceasing sequence of single actions. But the single action is by no means isolated. It is part of a whole with links to other actions and goals. In its simplest form this would be a link in a chain which has two functions— one is to connect the adjacent links and the other is to lift a load off the ground. I write this to satisfy my own desire to share some information and also to put that information in such a form that will be useful to you. You work to provide for your own needs and also to provide a useful service to your organization.

The Possibility of Improvement and Satisfying Desires Influences Behavior

A successful organization is the outcome of the conscious and purposeful behavior of individuals. Each individual is acting in the interest of the organization only because and to the extent that the interests of the organization are complementary to the personal outcomes of the acting individuals. In larger terms, we become social beings not in sacrificing our concerns but in aiming at an improvement of our own condition.

Let us emphasize at the outset, *action* necessarily aims at future and therefore uncertain conditions. A system or organization which fails to

238

take into account the element of speculation in all action or in the planned outcomes which initiated it will fail to utilize the potential inherent in human action. Absolute safety or surety cannot be attained. What can be achieved is continuous improvement with the finest, most responsive feedback system in existence — the individual human being.

We are dealing with the real actions of real people with real weaknesses and limitations. The technological models we are creating are neither for the ideal nor the average. With all our weaknesses and limitations, every person as he or she lives and acts is the subject matter of this book. The models have been shaped on the presumption that the great measure of success will be in developing the potential of each individual.

The working definition of management in this book is this: Management is the process of getting things done through people in organizations. We define management as a *process* rather

Management —
An Ongoing
Process of
Getting Things
Done Through
People

than a function or a fixed ordering of specific tasks. The major activities of management are all continuous and all influence each other. The continuing nature of organizations, the uncertainty of action and the "choosing nature" of human action demand we approach management as a process and the individual manager as an element of a larger system, the organization. We will use a systems approach to achieve the complex outcomes involved in this interaction of systems.

Human action is outcome-oriented and nowhere is this more explicit than in business. Each organization is a system for achieving certain outcomes. The organizational goals are generally independent of the individuals who are to achieve them. And the goals must be realized whether the particular people doing the individual tasks remain the same or not. The organization outcomes will be achieved only by creating an environment which allows individuals to satisfy their *own* outcomes at the same time. The organization creates the conditions for maximum cooperative action not for reasons of charity but to best achieve its own outcomes. The challenge is not to create common goals but to create complementary ones. The success of organizations depends on the ability to create this harmony of interests.

Business organizations are complex systems and it is management's role to successfully bring the actions of individuals into harmony toward the desired outcome. Again, our emphasis is on process. The goals of in-

239

dividuals and the organization must be interwoven in such a way that appropriate feedback controls exist while allowing enough freedom to take advantage of the creative potential of human beings.

Information and Systems

If management's role is to get things done through people, then the raw material of management is information. The operation and control of any system depend on the information generated by the actions or processes which make up that system. Management requires that information be received and organized so that it is useful to the many different individuals who are engaged in "getting things done."

Every action involves change and that change is the source of information. All information is a result of action. Experiments in sensory deprivation demonstrate the connection between action and information. If there are no actions, or changes, in our visual field, we receive no information. We soon cannot see anything even though the physical world is unchanging — in fact, *because* the physical world is unchanging.

An organization of individuals, a system of human action, will generate more information than any single person can be aware of or handle. The multitude of actions is generating vast amounts of information. To turn that information into useful order and communicate it also requires action — and the use of time and resources. In a very small organization, we could easily spend as much time communicating information as we did in productive work.

The remedy lies in creating a system which makes use of the information-processing abilities of those actually doing the work. The first level where information can be handled is right where it is created. In fact, it must be handled to

Using Information- Processing Abilities Helps Us To Communicate Effectively

some degree at this level. A system which ignores this fact will get far less productivity from its work force *and* will miss many effective information-processing opportunities. Making full use of the work force in this way requires an assumption that each individual will make reasonable decisions with that information. But what is reasonable? *Reasonable* means "based on logic," which means based on a set of understood premises. Given full understanding of the premises, which includes the desired outcomes, we could all make judgments and possibly even agree on what is reasonable. In fact, though, we can never fully share our

240

premises and desired outcomes. They are the sum of our personal experiences and many of these are below our conscious awareness.

For individuals to be reasonable, in our opinion rather than theirs, their actions must make sense to us within *our* context. Their behavior is always reasonable to them because it is in their own context, their own understanding of the environment. The solution to this situation, then, is to create a shared understanding rather than look for "more reasonable" employees.

The first step to a shared understanding of the environment, is to make explicit — with examples — the desired outcomes within a cooperative framework. Examples provide the kind of *Specifying* explanation which can be related to the personal *Outcomes* experience of each individual. Outcomes which can *Creates a Shared* be clearly understood provide the basis for each *Understanding* individual to organize his or her own behavior without explicit direction. When this framework is well established, employees will become more reasonable in your view.

In a computer system using intelligent terminals, these terminals organize, verify, check, and pass on information based on the explicitly programmed purpose or outcome of the system. Your employees are much more sophisticated than mere terminals. They can carry out a great deal of selection and processing. All they need is the same starting point as the terminal system — clearly stated outcomes for the system as a whole.

We are moving toward the development of a system for change and growth which utilizes the creativity of the human beings involved. Before we develop this system further, let's look at the basic reporting methods which involve some form of exception-reporting. Here, the information required is a report of deviations from expected results, often based on past performance. This system can be relied on to the extent that processes are familiar and operate within a fairly predictable environment.

Despite the fact that this principle of exception-reporting has been the standard for many years, it is violated continuously. In my years as a systems analyst and financial manager, I have never seen it consistently applied. Every manager still gets reports that are *not* exceptions to the expected. Computer systems are still spewing out reports which are too voluminous to even be scanned by those who receive them. The exceptions to exception-reporting are so prevalent that, if we examine them, they might point to a basic unsatisfied need of managers for information.

A manager needs to feel that he or she is in control and can comfortably be held accountable for operations for which the manager is responsible. The basic need is for information to be communicated because the manager cannot have direct, sensory experience of the operations and their results. No matter what the organization, managers are managing in uncertainty and know that they require more than the results of exception-reporting. Before we leave this aspect of exception-reporting, apply this test to your own organization. Does information in the same form get reported to more than one level of the organization? If so, you are probably producing reports to satisfy feelings of security rather than for the information they contain.

Using Exception-Reporting Adds to Feelings of Control

The feeling of control will come from understanding of systems and recognition of the source and use of information. The old "numbers game" provided little in the way of real control and prevented a great deal of growth and creativity. The intention of this work is to show you how you can have control *and* creative growth while using the maximum potential of your employees. The requirement is for a system which starts right at the source of information — the actual work being done and the employee doing it.

The highest-quality information is that which contains the most detail. It is information with the least ambiguity and is the kind which can be most confidently acted upon. It is the information created by original action. Therefore, those who must act on the information should have it. If they do have it, no one else will need it. This information is provided at the point of action. What is often lacking is the translation into a useful form and the authority to act on it. One company reported rejects to supervisors in total only once a month but in weekly detail to their managers. This violates two reporting system requirements. The first is that the highest-quality information, that is, the most specific, goes to the lowest level of the organization. The second is the application of the Pareto Principle to information. Simply stated, this is a recognition that events can usually be divided between the vital few and the trivial many. There are many exceptions to what we anticipate but only a few of enough significance to attract attention or energy. Lumping all of the individual items together will not allow for

High Quality Means the Most Detail and the Least Ambiguity

the selection of significant items and, for purposes of action, makes the information too low-quality.

We all recognize that it is certainly uneconomic and probably impossible to document all of the items needed to control a system of human action. Whether or not we recognize it, all of our systems acknowledge this circumstance. We expect our employees to "act reasonably," to exercise good judgment.

In doing this, we assume that others in the system share approximately the same information about the system's goals and expectations as we do. Otherwise, how could we expect them to act reasonably? We act, based on our assumption that we share information about the world and that we process it similarly.

We are here developing a system which acknowledges this assumption and builds it into the system. It will be capable of growth and creative action from all individuals. It will be built to meet all of the requirements for a functional system. Growth means that we will be attempting to achieve states never before reached. We will not share information about these states from experience but can only create shared expectations. The old control systems will not work. A totally new approach is required. Creativity, individual initiative, and timely responsiveness will be possible only if different management processes are employed. We will succeed only with a full systems approach.

The first requirement will be that a system is created where the outcomes of individuals doing the work are complementary to the outcomes of the organization. One of the difficult requirements

Alignment of Goals Requires Communicating Them Clearly
for this to happen with any assurance is the ability to communicate goals and actions effectively, especially if they have not been achieved before. Arriving at a confident feeling about shared information, without yet having direct, sensory experience of the acts which would constitute that experience, requires far more skill than for events with actual shared experience. Even if we share what we think is specific, we can arrive at different conclusions.

Often a new process or project will be proposed with numbers which back it to the hilt showing that it's likely to be profitable and a reasonable approach. Often these same projects never get into actuality. What stops them? Not the realization that the future is uncertain; the future is uncertain for every project and action. The missing information will

243

often be the realization that there is no shared experience to provide the required sense of security and no system for dealing with such uncertainty.

A system for dealing with growth, breakthroughs, or new products or technology requires far more than a simple control system. Increases in numbers and frequency of checkpoints, more immediate and effective feedback, flexibility in dealing with new knowledge and situations, the ability to accept cultural changes and make them acceptable to others, are all part of the specific requirements for creative systems.

Managers are often required to be technical experts. Whether or not this is an actual requirement of the job or merely the result of higher management's beliefs, it is useful to distinguish between this element and the managerial element of the job. The fast growth and changing technology of our world makes it almost impossible to be a manager and maintain technical expertise. Lawrence and Davis in their book *Matrix* make the point that conflict resolution must be accomplished at a level other than that of technical knowledge.

To give them access to the technical expertise that exists at the lower levels of an organization, managers will need the ability to ask questions and to be skilled observers. These abilities of questioning and observation will be valuable aids to any manager, whatever his or her level of the organization is. Even if a manager has been promoted from the ranks of those he or she is managing, the work will change enough over time so that the possible edge of being a technical expert will be lost. The best managers will insist that the edge be lost as quickly as possible. Continuous growth of employees is both possible and necessary.

It's easy for managers to focus efforts on doing, rather than getting things done, or managing. Having come from the ranks of "doers," managers often feel more comfortable in that role. Valuing the technical expertise will frequently lead them to use that expertise rather than manage. This behavior will lead to the opposite of the goal of management — getting things done through people. The system should encourage the appropriate behaviors for whatever level. One way to do this is to create career paths which are equally respected and well paying for technical experts as are the paths available to managers, so that those with technical expertise do not have to subvert their best abilities in taking on a new role as manager.

If managers are expected to manage and are paid for managing, then the technical expertise required of them is the expertise of managers.

244

The Expertise Required of Managers Is the Technology of Management

What is the technology they should be experts at? Few seem to know. Most managers are hatched, that is, "You're now a manager because I said so." They are usually chosen because of technical expertise, demonstration of problem-solving ability, likeability, seniority, etc. The assumption is that they already have the required skills from natural experience in the company or, worse, on the assumption that we *all* have such skills.

The technology of management is a rapidly growing area which is unknown to most managers. Sure they know what they are supposed to accomplish. Specifically, *how* are these things to be done? Which behaviors will work and which will not? Managers need to be aware of theories and their practice, but there is very little in the way of this technology that is readily available.

One reason for this void is that the technology required is behavioral. Books can impart theory but it is very difficult to present behavioral techniques adequately in writing. I cannot stress too strongly the need for practice, which is often best carried out in the safe and structured environment of a workshop. I suggest that you attempt to experiment with the techniques suggested here in situations where there is no fear of drastic consequences if they don't work comfortably on the first try. If practice is not done with successful results, the specific behaviors practiced are not likely to become part of your normal functioning. If successful, you will automatically start to use them. Change is what we're after, and if you fail to change your behavior as a result of this book, it will have been a waste of both of our efforts.

The Work Of A Manager Is Communication

The behavioral competence required of managers rests particularly in the area of communication, or *influence.* The link between the internal states of others and their coordinated action in an organization is the communication which influences those internal states to generate appropriate action.

The first requirement of communication for a manager is the ability to translate organizational goals into specific plans which can be acted upon with the confidence that the goals will be achieved. In doing so, managers must be bilingual. That is, they must be able to speak the language of planners and the language of doers. This is no mean task in

245

itself. Frequently the planners believe that they have expressed their goals in clear and unambiguous terms. As often, those who are to achieve the goals misunderstand or carry out their work and achieve goals which are a great surprise to the planners.

Let's take a look at planning. Planning is an activity carried out in what we call low-quality terms, that is, the language could refer to a great variety of activities or circumstances. We *Find the* are not using low quality as a pejorative term. There *Right Place for* is a place for extremely low-quality information — *Low-Quality* such as in the early planning stages — and anything *and High-Quality* else would be inappropriate. An example of such *Language* low-quality language is the statement of Hewlett-Packard that they are to be leaders in the field of employee compensation as part of their corporate policy. This later caused a problem for them when certain managers and employees believed it meant that if *any* company had a better benefit in *any* area Hewlett-Packard should incorporate it. Needless to say, this interpretation would have led to uneconomic employee compensation costs for the company and was not the intended meaning.

What was intended was that the total package at Hewlett-Packard be equal to anyone else's or better. Bringing this policy into practice required some skilled translation. Particularly noteworthy in the situation was that without such skilled translation, the employees might easily have come to believe that the statement was just so much propaganda in the usual corporate game. However sincere its intention, the way it was translated caused some bad employee relations.

By contrast, operating people require high-quality language. By this, we mean words which can refer to only one situation or action or at least only a relevant grouping from which there can be no mistake about intent. It is frustrating at best for operating people to carry out actions towards goals they think they understand only to find that they are not heading in an appropriate direction. One woman reported to me that she had been doing a medical job for two years and believed she was doing it well when suddenly she was discharged for incompetence. The "we/they" feelings of labor and management often stem from such missed communication. These same feelings are often felt by different levels of management in an organization.

Managers must be able to recognize the appropriateness of high- and low-quality language at all levels of activity. They must be able to select

the quality which is adequately precise for the task at
Managers   hand. Language which is too low-quality will in-
Must Select   troduce ambiguity, uncertainty, and misdirection.
Language That   Language which is too high-quality will produce frus-
Matches Need   tration and reduce the potential for creativity. The
needs will be different depending on the goals and
circumstances. In a "brainstorming" session, for instance, low quality
will often be the most appropriate language. In establishing controls or
giving orders, high quality will be appropriate.

The translation function is important for all of the people in an
organization. Many top managers can only function comfortably and
effectively in low-quality terms and many operating people can only
function in high-quality terms. They create antagonism and ill will when
attempting to communicate to each other. Notice whether you are comfortable or uncomfortable when talking to people a few levels above or
below you in the organization. When the president and the janitor talk,
it is often the president who feels most ill at ease.

Trust and confidence come about when people are able to speak the
same language. Being given messages or instructions which are unclear
creates an immediate feeling of insecurity and often leads to results
which produce dissatisfaction on both sides. Part of the solution to this
situation is the ability to speak in the appropriate language and the other
is the awareness of the responses being given as feedback — however
subtle they may be.

The part of management called "getting things done" is the part of
turning plans into action. This requires a series of translations from the
broadest goals of the organization down to the
Managers   specifics needed for instructing the individuals who
Must Be   must carry out a myriad of tasks. It is the sum of
Translators   these individual actions which will produce the re-
To Turn Plans   sults desired. The coordination of these multitude of
Into Action   actions will determine their success in achieving the
larger goals of the organization. What about getting
the job done? Motivation is seldom a problem. The goals and rewards are
clear. Many incentive systems have been set up which have produced
unexpected and undesirable results because the task and rewards were
clear but the immediate goals were not integrated into the overall goals
of the company. This is referred to as *sub-optimization*; that is, a part
optimizes its own performance without regard to the requirements of

the whole. For example, a company which paid a bonus for the number of plastic articles extruded from machines forgot to include the required product mix, and ended up with a warehouse full of the most easily produced items and none of the other necessary parts.

Motivation is not something we can manufacture. It is an internal response to external conditions or internal goals. The desired motivation will appear if we can create the conditions which produce the appropriate internal response. These conditions are partially the organization system, the physical environment, and the amount of self-control within congruent goals. (The planning of congruent goals will be covered throughout this book. The issue of self-control will be discussed shortly.)

Creating the Conditions—Communication

The major element in creating the conditions for motivation is communication. However fine a system, however congruent the stated goals, without effective communication the system will not work. The key elements in any system — feedback and adjustment — are accomplished through communication in human systems. The complexity of individuals and organizations; the differences between people, times, and places; the differences in people from time to time — all place demands on communication greater than any formal system can handle. And so this immensely rich and varied world requires that we remain flexible or perish. And the information that indicates what degree of flexibility is appropriate comes through communication.

Communication includes actions as well as words. The actions include any response which is discernable to an external listener/observer. Beckoning with your finger, nodding your head, *Only a Small* smiling or remaining serious, blushing, moving your *Part Of Our* eyes, all are actions which are part of your com- *Communication* munication. Various studies indicate that only a small *Depends on* fraction of our communication is contained in the *Words* words we use. Much can be accomplished in total silence. Whatever the significant amount of communication contained in words, there is certainly an important part independent of the words we use. Try arriving home and yelling at your spouse in an aggressive or angry tone of voice, "Hi. I'm home and I love you" and notice what kind of response you get. It will most likely match your tone and not the words you used.

The impact of the words you use has already been considered when we spoke of high-quality, or specific, words, and low-quality, or general,

248

words. Your choice of words should be determined by the response you want to achieve in the other person. Using low-quality words when issuing instructions might be effective if the result you want is a creative implementation of a general approach and the individual you are talking to is relatively mature related to the task assigned. For example, the department manager might instruct the senior analyst to "develop a solution for the sales department and review it with me in two weeks' time." If you want the task done in a particular way or if the individual is unsure in the particular role, then high-quality language is much more likely to achieve the desired response: The senior analyst might instruct a junior programmer to "talk to the sales manager to determine the department needs, then develop a decision table and flow chart of a potential solution which will need to include information from existing files, and review progress with me every Monday at 9:00 AM."

We select the particular words we use out of a large vocabulary. There are numerous ways to say any particular thing, to impart any

Our Words Are Based on our Intention — Whether Conscious or Not

single piece of information. The specific words we choose are selected unconsciously within the normal flow of speech. It would be too slow and cumbersome to select each word consciously from all of the possible alternatives. Words will be chosen based on the intention of our communication. However, the choice will also be made based on unconscious intention which may not be congruent

with our conscious intention. An executive of a large corporation could not communicate verbally or in writing in a way which could be clearly understood. Yet his conscious intent was not to generate the confusion which was constantly around him. His choice of words was determined by various unconscious intentions which produced contrary results. A college graduate, this executive needed to become aware of both his intentions and the actual results before he could bring the two together and become much more effective at his job.

Another factor in this vocabulary selection process is more subtle still. The particular words we choose all have meanings or implications beyond their pure definitions. The very fact that we have a choice of words to say the "same" thing indicates that one is better than the other, for the "non-essential" things it implies. We cannot communicate without making various assumptions about the receiver of the communication, about reality, and about the extent of our shared experience. Each of these assumptions is reflected in our words and conveys implications to the listener. The appropriate use of implication can work powerfully for us — or against us — but work it will.

If the study of the use of language is not at an advanced stage, the use of the action or non-verbal part is even less. Although much of the actions which I will refer to operate mainly as part of communication, many people tend to treat them as though they were a particularly sacred part to us, that if we change these actions to communicate *more* effectively, we would somehow become different people — or phony.

The main areas of non-verbal communication are fairly easily recognizable — posture changes, gestures, facial expressions, voice tonality, voice volume, skin color, muscle tension, and touch. *Non-Verbals* All of these and more register on our senses and *Affect* become part of the communication we receive from *Us Whether* others even though they often remain outside of our *We Know* awareness. It is possible to have control over all of *It or Not* these as messages which we send, but for most of us they are a mixture of conscious and unconscious control. We can dramatically improve our effectiveness as communicators by becoming aware of each element and experimenting with its use. Many people do not hear their own voices when they speak and have no idea of the flatness of their tone. Be hearing their voice, and consciously practicing introducing variation, they can increase the interest and attention that their words receive. The idea is not so much to make all of these elements conscious as to develop them as tools for natural or "out-of-awareness" uses — as resources which will be automatically available.

As with the selection of words, there is too much detail, too many items, for our conscious minds to attend to. We cannot control the nonverbal elements by conscious means. They can, nevertheless, be under our control. Congruence in communication is the coordination of all verbal and non-verbal signals to the end of sending the same message. Congruence in our intention will tend to produce congruence in our communication. Incongruence is the sending of conflicting signals simultaneously. An example of this is asking someone in a group whether he understood what was just explained. Not understanding and not wanting to admit it, the person responds with a Yes and with a shaking of the head (indicating No). I have seen this response many times, yet if you try it right now, you will find it very difficult to perform. Many people who do it naturally in such a situation cannot perform it as a conscious act.

Your intention serves as an organizing principle for all of your unconscious communication. Your conscious intention, if in conflict with other goals or beliefs, will be able to control only your conscious behavior. Since it has been stated that we can be aware of only seven bits of information at any one time, some part of the remaining behavior will likely send a conflicting message.

As a manager, communication is your major tool. The ability to gather information, to gain creative and cooperative resources, to give instructions that are understood, to access appropriate or relevant experiences in others is your major influence within the human system of your company. Effective communication is required, even for the most mundane tasks. If you want to find out what physical environment might be best for the individuals who work for you, a questionnaire will produce much more limited and less effective results than would an interactive communication approach—talking to employees face to face.

A manager, primarily, is a professional communicator at least on a one-to-one basis. In any contact between a manager and non-management people, I expect the manager to have *Flexibility Is the Mark of an Effective Manager* the most flexibility. In fact, the single most important attribute I would select for a manager is flexibility. And yet, I frequently find the reverse to be true and that the manager has structured the interaction in a way that demands the other be more flexible. It takes real ability to act differently in different situations to get the same results as well as to get different results from the same behavior, each one depending on the circumstances. Each person a manager must deal with may require a different approach. The same person will require different approaches at different times. The ability to make the appropriate shifts is the mark of an effective manager.

The need for flexibility becomes apparent when we look at the broad picture. The manager is a part of a system. He or she is generally thought to be, or at least expected to be, the controlling part. Systems theory states that the controlling element of a system is the one with the most flexibility. The organization is a human system and the major element in feedback — and control — is communication. Therefore, the manager requires the most flexibility in communication to control the system. I have seen whole offices controlled by a clerk when she was the one with the greatest variety of communication techniques and those around her had a severely limited number of responses.

Again, we communicate for the purpose of influencing the internal

states of others. When I use communication in this book, I will be implying at least one of two conditions. The first is that there *is* some intent
to influence, whether fully conscious or outside of conscious awareness.
The second is that the sensory recipient of the behavior, the receiver,
is in a context where he or she believes communication is appropriate
or actually taking place. In any kind of sensory contact with others —
visual, auditory, or kinesthetic — we cannot *not* influence them. The
issue is not did we influence someone but did we have the *desired*
influence.

An example of "out-of-awareness" communication with intent is a
situation where a manager turns her back to an employee each time that
employee comes into a group situation and the
manager is totally unaware of her behavior. It can,
however, only be explained as a direct response to
the employee and thus a communication by the
manager. An example of the second situation focusing on the receiver is where an employee reports to
a manager and expects a response. By not looking pleased, as appropriate (according to the employee), or not acting when it is called for
(as far as the employee is concerned), the manager is making a direct
communication. We cannot be nothing. If we are not smiling, we are
doing something else. Each contains a message. Whether or not it is
intended, the employee receives the message.

*Communication
Is Influencing
the Internal
States of Others*

Being alive and conscious, we are responsive. A large part of communication is in response — to what we see, hear, or feel. In most situations, we are aware of wanting responses from
others and of the possibility of our having an impact
on them. An overt response is our signal that we
have influenced the internal state of another. To
not respond to another implies that the sensory
messages that are sent out are not being received:
that somehow the other person is not there. At times
we focus inward so intently that we are not aware
of the signals of others; for us, at that time, they are *not* there. When
the context demands a response, however, and none is forthcoming, the
lack of response is a communication.

*The Internal
State of the
Receiver Defines
the Meaning
of the
Communication*

The *meaning* of our communication is the response it elicits, not the
overt behavioral reaction but the internal response in the receiver. To
influence your internal states in specific ways, I must access some experience, some meaning, in you. The meaning you attach to my action

will depend on your expectations, beliefs, previous experience and understanding. Words obtain their meaning through this same kind of process. It is not the dictionary which determines the meaning of words. Meaning comes from experience, which is personal. The dictionary, at best, suggests which kinds of experience are relevant for a particular word. Each word you say triggers off a search through my past experiences which will influence my internal states. As I recall similar instances, I will experience some fractional portion of the original content and emotion. The combination of words chosen will create a new experience for me, the receiver.

Since I want to be sure that the meaning I want you to get is the one you actually *do* get, I will first direct your attention to relevant parts of your personal experiences. This is the first step of

Setting the powerful communication — to set a context for the
Context Is receiver. The context is a major factor in deter-
a Major Step mining meaning; it should not be left to chance. We
refer to this as *framing,* that is, setting the framework around a particular communication which will access the appropriate past experiences or mental resources for the coming task.

The purpose might be to access previous creative experiences, to create more useful emotional states, or to recall previously unrelated or unassociated information. If I were meeting with you, the simple way to do this would be to tell you whether we are going to "brainstorm" or make a decision about "a new production process." I've started to set the context for you. Knowing the purpose of the meeting before it begins will allow you to adjust your internal state so that you can participate most productively.

Many managers I teach are initially repulsed by the idea that they are expected to influence or change people's internal states. Theirs is the field of results, of external action. Manipulation is a dirty word. You have seen by now that we influence people all the time. The question then becomes, "Do you want to influence people purposefully, or not?" The alternative to a Yes answer is that we choose to influence people without being aware of what we are doing. This kind of influence will sometimes work for you and sometimes against you. It will sometimes be beneficial to the other people involved and sometimes not. In learning to become more aware in this area, most managers discover that they are influencing people, some of the time, in ways that are not beneficial to either party.

The issue is often expressed as one involving integrity. Integrity and congruence are two sides of the same coin. It is difficult to maintain your

*Integrity
and Congruence
Go Hand in
Hand with
Getting Desired
Results*

integrity if you refuse to acknowledge the effect of your actions or words. Being aware that you influence others will allow you to make choices. Integrity is not simply a state for the external world where your actions match your beliefs. It is also an internal state where mismatches, internal or external, can cause direct physical problems. The material presented here is intended to allow you to achieve your desired outcomes and to protect the healthy functioning of your being.

The system you are in is one which *expects* you to influence the internal states of others. This is generally recognized for good or evil by both labor and management. Even those who recognize explicitly only that a manager's appropriate function is to get overt action realize at some level that this will not be accomplished satisfactorily without various cooperative internal states being created or maintained in some way. Any talk of incentive pay systems, enhancing the physical work environment, instituting penalty systems for disobedience are predicated on an understanding that these might influence internal states so that overt actions are more likely to take place.

The internal states which can be influenced are numerous. We are talking about emotions, memories, physical sensations, alertness, creativity, ideas, intellectual facts, understanding. Some current writers on productivity are suggesting that it costs no more to use the minds of the people who come to work — they bring them anyway. The facts are even more promising than that. It profits you and your employees to use the full human resources available to each of them — and you — individually.

The goal is to improve an internal state which is less than optimal in order to achieve the desired result. Total change is not to be expected. You may find that it begins to happen in positive ways but the desired outcome is a change in the desired direction. An employee who is discouraged about her performance or afraid for his job is not likely to bring the fullest of their resources to the task at hand. It would be better for all concerned if a manager could get them to access the missing resources by recalling for them (with them) a time when the employee worked on a successful project. The result will be a better performance from an employee with increased self-esteem and, maybe, a significant change for the better.

Meeting the needs of employees, as *they* see them, will be the most powerful way of creating the conditions for productivity and growth. As

*Meet
Employees'
Needs As
They Define
Them*

has been demonstrated in the more recent past, giving employees what they "should" need or want is not cost-efficient. The major need of employees will be discovered by communication and often a major need *is* communication. Response, contact, appreciation, trust, guidance are all important to employees and are all basic communications. Providing appropriate education is also a major function of managers. Education related to the organization goals, the job performance, and to an employee's goals for the future are within a manager's ability to define. This is an area where it is relatively easy to match the goals of the organization and the individual employee in a complementary manner.

When we talk about influencing the internal state of another, we are talking about specific changes in specific circumstances — creating the conditions for others to act in certain ways, according to the needs of the job. People, with all their strengths and weaknesses, are what a manager has to work with. We are developing a system which will take people as they are, not as we would like them to be. Managers are not there to "fix" people or provide therapy for them. Any influence should work for the mutual benefit of employee and organization. An employee can be expected to change only enough to accomplish the job or to choose to leave rather than change. Either choice should be acceptable to the company. Any influence intended to create change in another person should be cautiously considered and agreed to explicitly by that person.

Moving Toward Empowering Employees

Empowering is a current word which describes the intent of much of what we've been discussing. Most managers complain that they don't have time to do adequate jobs of Planning, Coaching, and Evaluation with employees. If they gave more power to their employees, they would have more time for the very functions of managing they are being paid for. Yet to do this effectively and confidently they need more time for the very activities they don't have time for. A radical change is required.

The element which is missing is the ability to communicate so effectively that there is adequate feedback about actual performance and potential problems, and there is adequate training and coaching to ensure that employees can do their jobs. This will leave time for the

255

possibility of employee participation in creative problem-solving and planning, an activity which requires more training and even more effective communication skills.

So let's take a look at the mechanics of effective communication. The first requirement for effective communication is the ability to establish rapport. (The Concise Oxford English Dictionary defines *rapport* as "communication." While this fails to make adequate distinctions, it indicates an important connection.) We will return again and again to this issue of rapport. It is a word and concept missing from management texts, yet it is crucial to the development of effective communication and therefore of management skills. Rapport is the state or feeling which exists between people when they experience that they share a common view of the world in some important way. It is commonly labelled as trust, harmony, good will, comfort, etc.

We establish rapport with one another by demonstrating that we share some significant part of another's view, experience, or model of the world. Often the most powerful demonstration is that we are willing to make an adjustment to others so that we share even more of their experience. Most teaching around this area concentrates on the verbal or content level, especially in the field of sales where its power and necessity are recognized. In these cases, we are required to agree with another person whether or not we do in fact. I will suggest other more effective and respectful verbal means, but first suggest another, much more powerful, area for your attention.

Our experience of the world is powerfully manifest in our bodies. We experience through our bodies and reflect our experience in our bodies.

Establishing Rapport Can Begin with Our Bodies The most powerful area for establishing rapport quickly is through adjustments of our bodies to those of the other person. Posture, breathing rate, and gesture are three areas which are easily accessible to observation and to use for establishing rapport.

The general technique for getting rapport is called *pacing.* Pacing is a matching of the other person's experience in some consistent way. Two simple examples will help. The first is the common picture of two old friends on a park bench. They both sit in mirror image of each other. When one moves, the other makes a similar shift. Arms along the back of the bench, bodies turned slightly toward one another, legs crossed toward each other; they look as though there were a mirror between them. This is a natural result of the rapport existing between them.

The second is less obvious but easily verifiable. A "laid back" California beach bum and an armed services officer are requested to communicate to each other about a current situation. The beach bum slouches down in his chair, stretches, and slurs out a greeting. The officer sits ramrod straight, adjusts his pants leg, and gives a crisp greeting. The only place this "conversation" is going is towards a fight. Each refuses to make any adjustment to the other, made obvious by their physical postures and voice tone and rate of speech. If these two were each to make some shift toward the physical state of the other, there would be a much better chance of some content being shared or communicated.

The direction or method for establishing rapport has been indicated. The basic question is, "Are you willing to make an adjustment to the other person?" If the answer is No, then the process of communication will be ineffective and the sharing of content can be expected to be minimal.

One of the participants at a workshop teaching these techniques said of the people he was managing, "You can't be serious! You expect me to act like *them!*" My answer is that if you don't act "like them" or *with* them in some way, you can't communicate with them. The situation reflects our example of the beach bum and the officer. If you expect to manage successfully, then you will have to find a way to make some of the necessary adjustments to your own behavior.

Let us return to the verbal-content method of establishing rapport. This suggests that we have to find an area of agreement with the other person at the level of content. In social gatherings, this is something we tend to do regularly. However, in business situations where we are required to establish rapport, it can put us in the position of feeling that we have to agree with others whether we actually do or not. There are two basic alternatives to this approach. The first is that we need not agree on content but simply acknowledge that the other person's belief or feeling is real. That is, we can comment on the content without agreeing that we also believe it. When another person is angry, for instance, a comment such as, "I can see you're really angry at what your local government did" will acknowledge that person's reality without the necessity of agreeing with it. Rephrasing a belief, or asking questions which ask for the experiences causing that belief, will also tend to acknowledge that experience without having to agree with the content.

Establishing Rapport Through Verbal Content

These verbal responses will have much greater positive impact for rapport if they are accompanied by the appropriate non-verbal behavior. Commenting on "being really angry" will have a more beneficial result if your voice tone rises and gets louder and your muscles tense a little as you say it. This is an issue of the congruence we talked about earlier: The most powerful communication is when all of the messages sent by the various parts match each other. Your integrity can be maintained while you establish rapport in this way. You are not required to indicate agreement on anything which violates your beliefs, simply to acknowledge that the other person's experience of the world is a fact of existence. Which of course it is.

The effectiveness of using these techniques, for others and your own integrity, depends on your intention and beliefs. If your intent is to use them to manipulate others for your advantage alone, they will tend not to work. If you believe that it is wrong to influence others and fail to recognize that you cannot *not* influence them, you won't use them. If your intent is to influence others in ways which are positive for both of you, if you believe that is appropriate for your position, and if you, in fact, are willing to make some adjustment to the other person, these techniques will come naturally and make you a far more effective manager and communicator.

You have all had the experience of meeting someone who agreed with everything you said and you still didn't like the individual. And you probably know someone who disagrees with almost everything you say and yet you look forward to meeting that person again. The difference is in the integrity or congruence with which they present their ideas and their willingness to actually make an adjustment of some kind — they communicate that your experience is a reality which is interesting rather than threatening.

There is another source of rapport, one which is extremely powerful in the long run. That is the rapport of competence. No matter how well you are liked, if you are considered to be incompetent, you will not maintain rapport in the context where you competence matters. For a manager, we begin to go around in circles. The competence of a manager is based on communication skills which are based on the ability to maintain rapport. Other competencies are related to communication abilities as well. For instance, one of the requirements for being viewed as competent is the ability to gain access to the necessary resources of the

Being Perceived as Competent Contributes to Maintaining Rapport

258

organization. The ability to establish and maintain rapport at specific times in response to specific situations is a highly valued behavior especially when the rapport of competence is present. It will often help to smooth the way and make it much more likely to achieve mutually satisfactory outcomes. Synergy is the combination of all the necessary and named ingredients along with other contributing and unnamed factors—such as the maintenance of rapport.

Your continuing effectiveness as a manager depends on your ability to maintain rapport with your people and those from whom you must obtain resources. It is possible to operate without rapport in some situations which require limited contact or are "one shot" in nature, such as contact with waiters, where you don't plan to return.

It is possible to use rapport techniques in short-term relations simply as tricks to get what you want but where doing so will later leave a bad feeling, such as a "fly by night" sales situation. Managers cannot operate successfully with such tactics. The continuing nature of their relationships demands that effective rapport be maintained, not simply used periodically for short-term goals. The apparently effective manager who comes in and "cleans up" distressed operations often does it without any concern for rapport. This person, while often more effective than the predecessor, usually leaves behind an equally large set of new problems in the area of employee relations, which reduces the possibility of gaining creative, cooperative resources for continuing operations.

The upward mobility of a manager is directly related to his or her ability to communicate and particularly to the ability to establish rapport. Another way of saying the same thing is that the manager with the greatest flexibility, the greatest ability to adjust to others in a positive manner will be of the maximum benefit to the organization. Being technically competent, such as being sharp with numbers or adept at marketing, will cause a manager to stand out at the lower levels of an organization. The ability to communicate effectively will make this expertise more available and useful to the organization and will be the determining factor for promotion to higher levels.

The Components of Control

A major issue for managers is control. A manager who is going to be held accountable for results needs to feel in control. What are the requirements for control and how might they be attained? The answer lies in the basic elements required of any system.

These are —   An outcome or goal
                    Feedback
                    A mechanism for adjustment

These elements apply equally to human systems and all are carried out through communications. The outcome must be a specific, recognizable target. Goals must be set in clear, unambiguous terms. The feedback requires enough sensitivity to indicate the direction of change in time for adjustment so that the original goal can be achieved. It combines technical information and external results with direct communication at lower levels. At higher levels, all feedback comes through various remote communication channels. And there must be adequate knowledge of what to do differently if the feedback indicates a change is required. The adjustments required are often in communications themselves and must at any rate be communicated effectively.

These elements are often not simple in mechanical processes. In human systems, content of the specific elements are far more complex. However, each element is an absolute necessity. Some cultures and some American companies are discovering how to apply the principles of general systems to human systems and are gaining rapidly in productivity.

Both feedback and the related adjustment must be immediate for them to be considered elements of control. The problem of the steam engine in our earlier example was that by the time *Feedback* the regulator got the message of a need for change *and* and the change was made, the conditions were no *Adjustment* longer the same. Sometimes they are even directly *Must Be* opposite. This is not unusual. Managers are often *Immediate* basing decisions on reports which are indicating conditions that no longer exist. Financial reports are usually received much later than the events they report. There is, however, a control element available at every action point — the actor. The requirements of the system, then, are to move that information the shortest possible distance in the most useful form for corrective action as required. *Control will come from the speed and reliability of the system, not from direct access to information or pre-determined reports.*

Managers can give employees decision-making and action power with confidence by meeting the requirements of the system we've discussed above. The level at which information can be allowed to stop will be determined by the beliefs of the managers involved and the security of the system which they are responsible for. Adequate training of the people below them will be required for the necessary degree of self-control. The competence of the manager will be judged by the effectiveness of a system he or she operates. The measure will be in achieving agreed results and in what the manager spends time doing.

The manager will be giving feedback directly to employees, whether formal evaluations or simple ongoing comments which provide useful information for positive change. The major activity of a manager will be carried out through people. There is a need for continuous contact with all of the direct reports and all operations in the manager's area of responsibility. The contact will provide the best means of communication and the sensory-based information needed for "reality checks." There is no substitute in this world for information which we receive through our own senses — it is the highest-quality information available to us.

Managers feel a decrease in their control when results are not as they should be, when they are unpleasantly surprised, when they sense employee dissatisfaction; their response is usually to increase the formal system of controls. More and faster reports are requested, more accuracy is demanded, managers are instructed to "get tough" or spend more time giving closer supervision.

The solution to a problem, however, is never to do more of the same. In the case of control, this is certainly true. The problem is not one of too few controls but the wrong ones at the wrong *Increasing* level of the system. The lack of control will be a *Communication* result of the lack of communication, not of too little *Will Produce* system. The appropriate response is to increase the *Feelings* communication and decrease the system. *If* the *of Control* ability to communicate is present. If not, there is no solution which will replace communication effectively. However, a decrease in the formal controls will usually force an increase in communication.

What about control by numbers? If the financial reports regularly meet budget, it is often assumed that everything is all right. But look below those numbers. If everything is always achieved, it must have been predictable. But change and growth are not predictable. Even if the corporation isn't growing, the economy is changing rapidly in different ways and the results are not predictable to such a level of certainty by anyone. A manager who treats numbers as all-important will usually get the numbers — but they will be much lower numbers than are otherwise possible. Adequate control of human systems, which must include growth and change, requires attention to the processes involved and to qualitative issues, not only quantifiable results.

Summary

Managers are paid to get things done through people. They are the professional communicators in the organization. A major part of their function is to make the necessary adjustments to those hired for their labor or technical expertise to create the most beneficial conditions for productivity and motivation. The individual who can make these kind of adjustments and maintain direction toward desired outcomes is one with a significant amount of self-esteem. We usually find there are those who operate only by making adjustment to others and don't seem to get things done and those who are solely intent on the results but don't know how to get the best out of people.

The issue is, How do you make the necessary adjustments to others and still maintain your own goal-directedness? The approach of this book is that the missing ingredient for most managers is an appropriate technology of communication. An increase in self-esteem will help many managers to become more flexible. An increase in communication skills will help all managers become significantly more effective — and increase self-esteem as a by-product.

Managers are dealing with human systems which generate more information than the system can handle without utilizing the intelligence at the point of action. The most immediate way for the manager to handle his or her responsibility for getting results can only come about through a system of exception-reporting. The information which a manager obtains must pertain to the vital few operations, actions, or processes which require attention. The rest must be handled by those below the manager. This confidence in the ability of others to make appropriate decisions and take necessary actions will be directly related to the ability of the manager to create the conditions for self-control; namely, to specify goals clearly and in a non-contradictory manner and to ensure that those people have the goals necessary to make appropriate responses to give accurate feedback.

An effective manager will be translating the goals of higher management into smaller goals appropriate for the level of the organization for which he or she is responsible. The manager will then utilize people to achieve, or better, these plans and continuously improve his or her part of the operation. The manager will also consolidate high-quality information into lower-quality information for the next higher levels of the organization in ways which will provide them with the best planning information. The manager will determine what training is needed for his or her people and provide the means for it to happen.

Again, when we come in contact with others, we cannot *not* influence them. We can only choose the direction of influence. This is particularly true for managers. The nature of the system, the ability to give or withhold rewards, the assumed authority, will cause most people to be even more strongly influenced by the response — or lack of it — from a manager. A manager who doesn't accept this position will be influencing people in many ways which are contradictory to his or her objectives and confusing to the people working for that manager. The position of management carries with it the responsibility to influence others. Awareness allows this responsibility to be carried out with integrity.

A basic requirement of a manager is the ability to establish and maintain rapport with *all* the people who work with, and particularly *for*, that manager. We all maintain rapport easily with those we like and appreciate. The challenge is to maintain rapport with those who are different in ways which we don't appreciate. The easiest way is to find a way to appreciate those people. The method requires that we acknowledge and respond to reality — that is, to what we are actually experiencing externally — without violating our own integrity.

Awareness of the elements of control will assist a manager greatly in fulfilling his or her responsibility. They apply to every system, person, and task. To have confidence in the ability of employees to exercise adequate control, they must have clear understanding of the desired outcome, accurate and timely feedback related to the progress and the final result, and the ability to make any required adjustments. These elements relate to machining a part, running a computer, dealing with a customer, providing training, completing employee evaluations or directing the operations of a whole factory. To perform this function, the manager needs to take into account the specifics of each particular situation. There is no set answer except that revealed through effective communication. Each person for each task may require a different degree of specificity related to goals, feedback, and potential adjustments.

Control is in the hands of management. Responsibility is placed there because management owns the bat and ball and sets the rules of the game. The control expected is not that of direct, hands-on experience. Control comes from creating an appropriate system which will allow for growth and at the same time ensure that the processes which will produce the desired results are followed. Those who create the system and monitor its functioning are held accountable for its results. Creating the conditions for each person to have self-control will provide both the maximum in control and the greatest use of the most underutilized resource in America — the brains, energy, and creativity of the workforce.

264

Outcomes

Human action is outcome-oriented. Business organizes human action specifically for achieving outcomes. It is a system designed to coordinate the outcome-seeking of each individual person with the outcome-seeking of a different group—the owners of the corporation. The power of this form of organization is amazing when we consider that management is generally unable to define its outcomes in precise and unambiguous terms. The benefits of the division of labor, specialization, and concentration of capital are so great that we profit in spite of the lack of clear goals and adequate communications. The proof of the power of these benefits *combined* with effective communication is being demonstrated by the Japanese and various smaller American companies, notably in the computer field.

In a system, each element has a specific function, process, or job to do. That job is determined by the function or desired outcome of the system. In performing its specific function, each

Each Function element is operating on at least two levels. One is
Is Defined By that each part is a conduit, or, as Arthur Koestler
the Desired would say, it is Janus-like, two-faced. Each element
Outcome of receives information and gives back information.
the System Each element also transforms that information in some way by acting on it. The other level is that each element in the system has its own defined outcome or purpose. If it is a complex part, and in living systems it is incredibly complex, it will have parts of its own. Each will be two-faced and will be operating on the same levels.

In microbiology there is communication between cells. Each cell has its function to maintain a body part, which has a function to maintain the body. Each cell also has a myriad of functions which are required for the existence of that cell. In looking after itself, it looks after the

265

whole. The functions, in a healthy body, are in harmony. If they are out of harmony for any period, the cell dies and then the body part dies, and then the body dies. The communication is carried on between the cells by a membrane which connects them. The membrane, of course, has its own functions to perform besides that of communication.

Every living system is this complex. These cells carry on two kinds of functions *and* information-processing. One is passive and the other active. Some materials pass in and others pass out without work being done. Others are pulled in or pushed out by more complex processes and an expenditure of energy.

The major difference between human organizations and living organisms is that in the latter the outcomes and communication required, the information needed, and the corrective actions necessary have already been coordinated and programmed into the system. For human organizations we need to create the necessary relationships and to maintain them in harmony with a changing world.

In a human system where the parts are individuals with their own desired outcomes, it is seldom obvious what the organization's goals are. Yet converting those goals into action, into practical terms, will be based on many individual understandings of what the final results will look like. A goal like, "We want to be the best retail brokerage firm in the country" certainly could be interpreted differently by every person who heard it. To each of us, that end-result would look different.

When I ask managers to be more specific about their outcomes, they frequently answer, in essence, "I'll know when we get there." One of the problems with this approach iş that that is not, in fact, an end-result. It is a guiding principle or control element for the system. The organization will never get there because "there" keeps changing. To set goals for a process and more specifically for stages within that is simply a way of breaking down events or experience to provide control in a changing environment. Goals are themselves ways to accomplish something else, so goals are set to carry out the overall purpose of business to produce profits of certain degree, a return on investment, with the maximum possible return over the life of the investment.

Being Specific About Desired Outcomes Creates the Stages for Control and Accomplishment

Another factor which makes this process of specifying outcomes important is that we all have complex value systems and goals. Our organizations do not escape this limitation. Many managers think it is absolutely clear when they state an outcome in quantified terms. "Your job is to produce 150m units per month at a cost of $5 per unit." Absolutely clear? No. There are many other conditions which are also to be achieved or maintained. There are certain quality and reliability standards to be met. There are times when more units are required and times for less. The external cost conditions may vary to such a degree to make $5 too high or too low. Various personnel policies must also be achieved so that there will be a continuous supply of labor in the future. The list goes on and on from the major and fairly obvious to the minor and obscure. The major and fairly obvious become much less obvious when a conflict between two of these items appears. We have enough difficulty ordering our own values. When the hierarchy of values belongs to someone else and is only sketchily specified, the task seems impossible.

The parts in biological systems have two major advantages over human organizations. The first is that the total outcomes appear to be programmed in; the issue of being specific is taken care of. The second is that the communication takes place through channels which are innate; the parts do not have to learn how or what to communicate. As humans, we have to learn what is appropriate to communicate and how to do it. We have to do this not only for the control of actions necessary to achieve goals. We have to do it to establish the system goals themselves in useful terms so that the parts can be coordinated. Neither the ends nor the means are given. The system must provide both. Quantification of results alone will provide only the ends, and these ends will be inadequately specified.

Learning What Is Appropriate Communication Is Part of Reaching Goals

We organize our experience and obtain meaning from context. And the information that offers meaning comes through definition of terms: Low-quality language would say, "This is the class of thing we are talking about," and high-quality would say, "This is the particular thing within that class." It is the first element that supplies the context. In the same way, we define the outcomes of our organizations by first stating the context within which goals, statements, and actions are to be evaluated. The goal of "providing low-cost housing at a profit" uses low-quality language to indicate the general area of appropriate activity; it's a general outcome statement. Using high-quality terms to quantify "low cost" in relation to total dollars, the competitive market, or within a particular area would be required before the goal would be useful for

267

deciding on specific plans or proposals. Quantification of "profit" in terms of how it is measured, market rates of interest, or alternative uses would be required before decisions could be made on which projects to assume and which include the performance of employees or contractors. Other issues such as minimum quality are not even indicated in a general outcome statement.

The language requirements are becoming obvious. Adequate specification requires continuous work and awareness of the possible conflicts between unclear goals. The saving factor is experience. What we have done and what we are doing will specify what we will do. The meaning or context for understanding the low-quality or general goals is the previous actions of the organization. Based on what was done before, we can guess what is to be done next, unless we receive a change in overall goals. This explains the conservatism of business. If what we were doing was acceptable up until now, it will be safer to continue than to attempt a change, which will *have to be* inadequately specified through the limitations of language. The previous experience alone will not be a guide to the future. We will have to depend on communication, the intelligence of the functioning parts, and our own direct experiential information. In a changing world, however, the experience base becomes progressively more out of date. The choice, then, is to respond creatively with an active system, or passively wait until unsatisfactory results force us to change.

Specifying Goals Clearly Is Helped by Awareness of What Has Gone Before

Again, an organization is a system and we emphasize that it should be approached as such. That means that all parts interact towards a specific outcome. This book is written for those organizations who could state as a major objective something like, "To manage people for continuously improved results" in whatever area of production or service is appropriate to their more specific goals. This statement will create the context for understanding and converting into action all of the more specific goals and objectives. It will be the standard against which any sub-system is measured, any plan is compared, any action is evaluated. The models or systems presented throughout this series of books will all be judged against this standard.

The requirements for "managing people" were dealt with extensively in the preceding section, *Creating the Conditions.* The nature of human action, choice, motivation was related to the requirements of communication and systems. The functions and abilities of a manager were indicated. The addition of "continuous improvement" adds a new requirement to the functioning of the system. Since a system for human action is so complex, I believe that you might as well build one for growth as for maintenance. And the effort is much more rewarding.

Here, we are concerned with the issues which determine the system rather than the creation or operation of that system. The first management task is to establish the objectives and requirements of the system — the goal or goals which determine all the elements and their purposes. It is activity which starts before the system exists and always stands outside of it. It is the level which takes the owners' or managers' world views, beliefs about the economy and people, reasons for being in business, and translates them into meta-goals which determine the nature of the system. (This level is "meta," that is, outside of the system under consideration.) The meta-goal will create its own system: a planning system which will have elements for gathering information, sorting it usefully, creating organizational goals and providing for feedback relating to the original assumptions and any indicated revisions. The Performance Management System starts after these higher levels of planning have established organizational goals and the goals of the system.

This Level Considers All Issues Which Determine the System

The Challenge of Continuous Improvement

The continuous improvement we are considering is not simply a question of more of the same, of doing this faster or working harder. We are considering new ways of *looking* at things, new ways of *doing* things, dramatic breakthroughs and creative solutions to problems which were searched out. We are talking about an active approach to change rather than a reactive approach to external conditions.

Continuous improvement is an issue of the economy, new technology, and, especially, people. The economy is growing or has the potential to do so. Technology is growing at a rapid pace, possibly more rapid than the economic, political, and business systems are equipped to handle. (The approach recommended in this book may help to change that.) The real challenge and the force which require a system for change are the people.

Underutilized resources are the major area to look to for improvement of return on investment. The people in your organization, their knowledge, experience, and creativity are the major underutilized resource you have. It is just good business sense to expend energy on

*People Are
the Force
Behind Change
and a Resource
Waiting To
Be Developed*
the better utilization of that resource. But it is much more than that. Your other resources which are underutilized are merely wasted; they sit idle without much direct drain on energy. By contrast, the human resource, when underutilized, has a much more negative potential. These people can, and regularly do, spend their unused energy in ways detrimental to the organization. These range from gleeful compliance with mistaken orders to negligence with long-term negative results to personal unpleasantness to outright sabotage. The personal and social effects of those who submit to being underutilized resources are also significant. Using our bodies, our energies, our lives in counterproductive ways is detrimental to our very beings.

The first step towards a Peformance Management System which operates under conditions of continuous improvement is the decision to commit to positive, controlled change. This isn't a decision to be made lightly. It's easy to say, "Of course we want that kind of a system." Unfortunately, management frequently does just that kind of thing on many positive-sounding issues and then fails to put them into practice. Commitment means that some knowledge of what is involved exists and that energy and resources will be used to achieve the results. Let's look at the decision more closely.

What will be needed? What is missing from your organization right now that it isn't already operating under these assumptions? Chronic problems remain unsolved, acceptable levels of performance are far below the possible, there is too little information about the nature of problems, the responsibility for this kind of change is not clear, there is no room in the budget for creative use of resources. The existing structure does not support the commitment of time and resources nor do the required skills exist to the necessary degree.

A culture is the sum of the beliefs and learned behaviors to which those involved have become attached. The culture of the organization is one which matches the existing system. A significant change in goals and system requires attention to the cultural changes which must also occur. What will be required, then, is to commit to the goal, create the system, and provide the training.

*Changes in
the System
Also Affect
the Culture*

The system required to implement such a change will be the same basic system as that required of the managers who will operate within it.

270

The system required for managing continuous growth must contain provision for the following:

1. A method of identifying the projects to be attempted or the areas of most likely application
2. Organizing resources, time, money, and people on a project basis as well as developing an approach to the problem
3. Analyzing data for causes and potential solutions
4. Developing the solutions in a way which will deal with "cultural" resistance
5. Taking action and verifying the efficacy of the solution
6. Instituting controls to ensure continuation of the benefits

Let's look at each of these in a little more detail.

1. *Identifying the projects to be undertaken* cannot be done intelligently without the use of the Pareto Principle. Pareto discovered that a small percent of the population accounts for a large percent of any particular attribute of that population. For instance, 20 percent of your customers will account for 80 percent of your delinquent problems. As a systems analyst, I was involved in designing many programs whose major result turned out to be rediscovery of the Pareto Principle. The simplest and most useful way of describing the application of this principle is that it separates the vital few from the trivial many.

In any situation with limited resources, the most effective use of those resources must be found. Which application will have the most significant effect? The significance of this division between the few and the many is that the few items which will provide the greatest return get the major attention individually and the other items get treated as a group. If such an analysis produces no "significant few" items, it indicates that the level of analysis has been inadequate. Either it is not an area which will likely yield significant benefits relative to others or the problem is being looked at from the wrong point of view: not enough detail has been found or too much is given.

An example would be when a study of the errors of individual workers reveals no particular pattern or concentration. The study should be moved to another area, such as the production processes, or the whole project dropped as beyond the level of existing technology. The major important issues or problems are mainly found at the interdepartmental level. This reflects the relative advance of mechanical technology compared to communications technology. Most problems

271

reside in the system. The largest return for an organization will likely be to develop an appropriate system.

2. *Organizing resources on a project basis* is necessary to provide the appropriate system, to allocate responsibility, to consolidate information, and to provide that each improvement is integrated with the regular operating system. The task of solving problems is separate from monitoring ongoing operations; this is true, though, only for purposes of analysis. The same people, particularly managers, who are involved in the control system should be involved in and have responsibilities related to the continuous improvement system on a project basis. The resources required will include the allocation of management time for continuous participation in breakthrough projects.

The people involved in this effort should include everyone in the organization, or at least all those who would like to be involved at non-management levels. The extent of involvement may be from information sources all the way to full-project team members. Other professional resources which may be required at some point in the process include technical experts and someone who is familiar with the culture which will be affected.

3. *The analysis of data for causes* is seldom adequately done. To the problem-solving procedure outlined in *Precision: A New Approach to Communication* should be added various techniques for defining the problem, particularly the present state. These include the Pareto Principle, statistical analysis with tools such as histograms and break-even calculations, and cause-and-effect diagrams. Cause-and-effect diagrams, or Ishikawa diagrams,* are a device for gathering information about the present state of a problem or condition in sufficient detail to do adequate prediction and apply the Pareto Principle. It is a device which will assist in going beyond the existing prejudices and understandings to a level of detail which will produce the kind of information required for direct action.

There are always multiple causes for a problem. A thorough analysis with that in mind will allow us to discover which is the most likely to produce the "vital few" results. In an operation for painting automobile parts, the major problem was in "damaged finish." A study revealed that there were about ten different causes as well as six different damage types. Of these, three causes and two damage types accounted for 80 percent of the total damage. It was found that all three causes could have

*See J.M. Juran, *Quality Control Handbook*

been influenced, if not eliminated, by changes in equipment, work methods, or operator attention.

Applied at another level, top management may decide to expand market share by a significant percentage. The questions to answer will then be, "What major factors limit growth right now?" and "What elements in these areas can be effectively changed?" The cause-and-effect diagram will include the major elements which influence growth and then sub-categories for each of those areas. A Pareto analysis on the result will indicate the potentially most effect method for expansion.

4. *Consideration of the culture of the organization* or the parts affected is usually left out in American business. Part of our more general culture seems to dictate that management has the right to make whatever decision it deems appropriate. The culture does not, however, appear to include enthusiastic acceptance.

The culture of an organization is comprised of the learned beliefs, understandings, and experience of the workforce. It is a social system which exists in every organization and within particular areas. Management has been instrumental in creating this culture and to effect changes, management must take the existing culture into account.*

One of the cultures which is generally ignored is that of the various levels of the management structure itself. The strongest resistance to change is often contained in these levels. Managers and professionals are reluctant to delegate to the workforce authority and responsibility which for years have defined their position. ICI spent a great deal of money on planning for major revisions to its way of working and finally succeeded in convincing its workforce to give it a try. The union provided almost insurmountable resistance, as was expected. The program later failed in many plants because it undermined the management culture and the support of individual managers was not forthcoming.

Remember that rapport was earlier defined as the ability to see the other person's model of the world. At a general level this is a basic necessity for considering culture in an appropriate manner. This will include such things as making a member of that culture a part of the project team, ensuring that there are no major surprises to the people affected, providing information or education before the change occurs, and, probably most important, making the change the minimum required for the immediate needs of the circumstances.

Cultures do not change instantly — except with what we call revolutions (and surprisingly little even then). Even a dramatic change in policy

*J.M. Juran, *Quality Control Handbook*

273

will affect the culture only a bit at a time. A concentration of resources on the change effort will speed it up but the change affects too many parts of too many people's internal and external worlds for it all to take place on a particular day.

5. *Taking action and verifying the efficacy of the solution* is the most familiar area to most managers. Finally, we are in familiar and comfortable ground. Implementing solutions is our strong suit. But is it? How many times has an implementation decision been delayed while various committees and staff departments evaluate it and develop it? How many computer systems do you know of that took years past the expected date to be running successfully? And how many never quite made it? It gets worse. Of those organizations which implement changes reasonably quickly, how many have effective procedures for verifying the efficacy of the solution? There are few companies which devote adequate resources or attention to this area. Establishing success criteria on a test basis and performing the tests are seldom done in any formal manner. Although many companies employ some form of breakeven and/or probability analysis before attempting major projects, very few check the results against the assumptions or conclusions used in decision-making. More testing and experimentation at implementation will frequently pay large dividends over the operating life of equipment and systems.

One company using an extremely narrow-tolerance manufacturing process required a special measuring tool which was calibrated quarterly by the quality department. While this was being done, the operations were shut down for a day. After much complaint, a study was done which discovered that the tools were all recalibrated on the same day due to interpretation of the wording of a company quality policy and the convenience of the quality department rather than for manufacturing considerations. The solution of rotating the calibration task was employed to everyone's satisfaction. It was later discovered that this problem had occurred and been solved in the same manner three times in the past ten years. Part of the successful system of managing for continuous improvement is the provision for continuation of the benefits!

This type of management is on a project basis and its results must be integrated into the ongoing system. The control mechanisms of an effective feedback loop are part of the task of the project team. The integration of people and functions into project and regular control management provide the necessary elements for a system of management which can achieve continuous improvement. A special project department or staff improvement team will remain outside of the operating culture and be likely to produce minimal results with maximum expenditure of resources.

Which system would you rather work in? One created for continuously improved results or one for maintenance of the status quo? If your answer is the latter, the techniques to come will be useful. If your answer is the former, they will be imperative. Managing for control can be done with an emphasis on forms, reports, and a minimum of face-to-face contact. Managing for continuously improved results requires contact, confrontation, and effective personal communication skills. It's also the most fun.

Setting the Framework of the System

Every successful complex system has developed from a successful simple system. Even the computer was originally just a series of Yes/No answers strung together on cards. Living organisms developed from single-celled entities. All started with simple systems. The simplicity was also related to a single overriding goal: a machine which could use repetitive calculations faster than any other and store the results. The most complex system was even simpler: maintain the life of the organism. Each piece of the system and each behavior was judged against this standard. As the complexity of the system increased, each function could be measured against whether or not it made the goal easier to reach.

Think of the companies that work, that is, the companies which have growth in sales and profits well above the average for significant periods of time. IBM in its growth period. Avis with Robert Townsend. What did they have in common? Most had a leader who was adept at communication. Most had particular personnel policies which made a difference. All had a strong unifying principle or direction. Usually in writing, a clear goal by which every activity could be judged was always consistently pursued by the leader. The question asked for purposes of comparison was not, "Will this help or will it hinder us?" It was simply, "Will it lead to or support the goal?" If the answer was No, the function, action, or product was rejected. The principle was applied throughout the organization. A producer of high-quality animal feed refused to put anything into their product in the way of binder or color which didn't contribute to the nutritional value. It made their product more expensive and harder to make — it also made it the best on the market and made them a highly profitable company.

Each organization should have one boldly stated objective. Alfred

Sloan, while CEO of General Motors Corporation, stated their overriding objective as "Quality competition below a certain price/price competition above that price." Why only one organizing goal? *Each System* Because each organization is a system and each *Needs a Clear,* system can be organized around only one goal. *Organizing Goal* This goal needs to be capable of consistent interpretation. It also must be capable of encompassing many alternatives and variations in the ways of reaching it. One of the most frequent conflicts between goals in business organizations is that between profits and quality. Notice that Sloan's major objective takes care of the conflict. Being the best at something is a goal which can be used effectively. Being the cheapest can also be used. Being both or somewhere in the middle cannot be used without more definition. Remember our earlier reference to the requirements of a definition: the category within which the specifics make sense must first be established. Something having four legs could be tables or animals, depending on whether it was animate or not. The implications for action are enormous.

Each sub-system will also have its own goal. That could be anything which supports the primary organizational goal. Whether or not it actually provides support will be determined by its *Goals of the* effectiveness when put into action. When accepted *Sub-System* as a policy, its fit, or lack of it, will be determined *Must Support* by the beliefs of those in authority. The personnel *the Primary* department may have this as its policy: "Continuous *Goal* development of personnel to ensure an internal supply of qualified people for each new position." It might choose as its policy: "Maintenance of superior employee compensation and benefits so that good people will be attracted to the company." Both of these will support most overall organizational objectives. Each of these goals or outcomes are to be measured against those which are higher. If there is a positive fit, the next lower or more specific level can be formulated.

Each of the general goals will spread into more detailed goals until they finally reach the highest quality possible, or desired. That is, what are the specific activities, resources, and systems re- *Each Level* quired to get the desired outcomes in the real world? *Has Its Goals —* What things are people to do, specifically, to make *Organized from* the desired something happen? The process can be *the Top Down* seen as a cascade. The overriding goal has a series of qualifications; the requirements for sub-systems

276

which are generated develop overriding goals which are further qualified; each of these require sub-systems with goals and qualifications. The final result is that the original goal has been translated into a high-quality plan which can be made specific for the individuals, each of whom has individual goals — to put them into action. The process, to be successful, must develop as a cascade. Top down is the only way that works. The context must be specified before the details are filled in.

Our minds are capable of imagining more than we can ever complete in practice. The individual goals which might be generated from each person in an organization without reference to a specific set of outcomes is a chaotic jumble. Those who suggest that they do planning from the bottom up are fooling themselves. They must have ways, subtle or overt, to establish a context and to set the goals. One of these ways, of course, is simply the history of the organization and the experience of the people in it. However it is accomplished, the level of planning which we are considering here is done from the top down.

Remember, we are considering issues prior to and outside of the Performance Management System itself. We are establishing the framework for the system, its organizing principles. The planning required to turn them into action will often involve the active participation of lower levels. Appropriate participation will be determined by the goals and systems previously established. The information which comes back up will be a factor in revising this level of outcome, planning, and systems. The original system must have provision and encouragement for feedback from the lower levels of the organization if it is not to become a dinosaur, unable to adapt to a changing environment. Action generates information. The first action will be stating the outcomes and systems. The second occurs as people attempt to put them into practice.

The dilemma of the managers of smaller companies which are growing into large ones is, "How do I keep control of all the things I need to?"

Moving from an Idea to a System Often "keep control" means "do the things" that I used to do myself. These manager/owners often were successful because they had a vision, a reasonably coherent outcome or organizing principle. They also were usually not very explicit about this vision in the outcome terms we have been talking about. The success of the vision depended on their personal example, their involvement, and the accumulated experience of the people who worked with them. The principle was shaped by the sum of the individual decisions and actions of the CEO.

Although this method has drawbacks, it can work well up to a limited

277

size. At the point where a more explicit cascade of outcomes is required, where the system has become too large and complex for the previous direct observation, the system breaks down. And too often it is not replaced, or is replaced with a control system violently opposed to the original culture of the organization — the culture that made it the success it is.

In the development of a system based on an explicit cascade of outcomes, the inconsistencies will become apparent as the low-quality or general goals become higher quality or more specific. They will begin to generate conflict. The inevitability of this conflict is due to the fact of time. Quality can be quantified, as can profits, prices, and volumes. The uncertain future and the fact that an organization is meant to be a continuing entity, however, introduce an element which cannot be handled so easily. The economics of the situation, the considerations of cost, uncertainty and future value, present a multitude of choices in the real world. Quality emphasis at a "prohibitive" cost today may provide the base for long-term leadership in sales and profits — it may also spell short-term disaster and bankruptcy.

How are we to resolve this dilemma? We can develop rigid control systems. We can insist that everything of possible importance is seen or heard personally. We can hope that people will make the right choices. We can, in short, pretend that the situation is otherwise, that the world is not like it is. Or we can create a system which recognizes the nature of the world, which accepts its uncertainty, and which uses the information provided by action. The latter is a system which meets the systems requirements for successful operation in the real world. That is, it has a specific goal, it has feedback, and it has mechanisms for adjustment.

Resolution of conflict or contradiction can be built into the system. In fact, a system may be considered to be an organism or organization that does that very thing — the resolution will come *Systems Should* from the process itself. With enough feedback and *Acknowledge* flexibility, a system will adapt and change according *the Nature of* to external environment to reach its goal in an *the World,* effective manner. Congruence within itself, con- *Including* gruence of lesser goals, and congruence with the *Conflict* external world will ensure success. The system must be designed to work continually toward this congruence. The system has no interest in any goals except the organizing one. All others, all functions, all actions, all outcomes are simply means to the end.

To utilize information at its source, employees must be capable of self-control. J.M. Juran* defines the requirements for operator self-control in this way:

- specific definition of an end-result which will be a product sample, a written specification, or other quantifiable "objective" measure
- a specific method or process to be followed to arrive at that end-result, the means to the end
- a clear definition of responsibility regarding actions and any decisions to be made

Managers require the same standards as operators. Although the above was developed for machine or physical type operations, the same standards are required for salespeople, customer contact, and even managers. For a system such as we are developing, the route to ensuring that goals are consistent with the overall outcomes is to specify them clearly enough for the next lower level and then work them out with the people involved. This will have the desired impact and result only if the people doing the work have adequate conditions for self-control. The situation is that we know how to define machine controlled and labor (muscle) controlled operations quite well. We have known very little about how to make similar specifications for communication-controlled operations.

You already know how to set quantified goals for all levels of your organization. You probably set, or at least know how to set, process methods for machine and physical operations. Most of your communication-controlled operations that you have tried to control come under the area of sales and your quantified goals seem to work quite well for them. Or do they? Could you be getting far greater productivity from your sales force if they had training in behavioral processes and had performance measures based on them? Think of some of your personnel involved in other communication-controlled operations — customer service, switchboard operator, public relations. Chances are, you have poorly defined outcomes and no process definitions. Your solution has been to hire someone who had a nice personality and hope that the individual would already know how to do a good job. And maybe she does. However, any control you exercise over such a person must be on an arbitrary basis. Have you ever had an argument with these personnel about a difference in perceived courtesy? Did you have a way to resolve it? I worked with a telephone company who did not know how to

*J.M. Juran, *Quality Control Handbook*.

define courtesy, yet it is the single most important element in the customer perception of effective service *and all operators are rated on it.*

Management is a communication-controlled function which produces no direct results — quality, volume, profits, the very existence of a product are all a direct result of the efforts of others.

Measuring Managers get things done through others. Managers
Results are responsible for the system. But how do we know
Accurately whether a system is working except through the
and with results which others produce? We quantify the end-
Enough Time results of a manager based on the external results of
for Change a long chain of events. Although these goals are
treated as objectives and are often all that is taken into account — officially at least — they seldom measure the correct thing and almost never are reported soon enough to meet the requirements of effective feedback in a system.

The quantified end-results are the first part of control with all their difficulties. And the quantified results represent the easy part of the problem for most organizations. The second part, the hard part, is how to specify the processes, the *means* to the ends, which a manager is to follow.

Let's take an example related to the overall topic of this book. Suppose you want to install a Performance Management System in your company. You agree on a system and explain it to your managers, maybe even give them some training. Now you tell them to go out and do it. How are you going to measure the results? In terms of end-results? In terms of the processes followed? The standard approach is that the results aren't measured and the "system" soon quietly fades away with only lip service for a while, and then, "We tried that here and it didn't work very well." With those few who try to measure results, the solution is to go for quantifiable results. The number and frequency of education sessions are recorded or completed forms are checked. In a sophisticated system, maybe the number of Planning sessions is checked in the same way. But what happened in those sessions? Were they effective and did they contribute to the objectives of the company? If you don't know the answer to that, the effort spent on monitoring the system was wasted. It might be better to have no Evaluation sessions if they are conducted in such a way as to be detrimental to the employee-relations goals of the organization.

The second part of proper control, then, consists of being able to specify which processes or activities are appropriate as means to the end. If an organization is unable to make these specifications, the managers are on their own. The organization must then either turn a blind eye to its own stated goals or system or it must terminate managers. If the second choice were taken with regularity, managers would move around the country more than baseball players.

Let's look at the development of our Performance Management System. What is it to accomplish? The major statement of outcome we agreed to earlier was to manage people for continuously improved results. We have also agreed that a systems approach is required. The system will support the stated outcome. Within the context of an organization seeking to continuously improve results, the specific purpose of a Performance Management System will be "to convert the organizational goals into coordinated action with maximum utilization of the organization's resources."

Such statements are frequently written off by executives as mere platitudes, like "motherhood and apple pie." The difference between a platitude and a powerful operating statement,
A High-Quality however, is frequently the vigor with which support-
Statement ing goals and systems are pursued. Ideals become
of Goals, With platitudes when not followed by appropriate
Congruent specification, commitment, and action. The first and
Action, Bring organizing goal sounds like something anybody
Results could — and should — go for. The specific words are
important; they indicate differences which are often
meaningful. The first statement in defining a desired outcome should be of this quality. It is only a first statement, a broad classification. The attributes, the sub-parts, of that classification will make the difference. The meaning of your stated goals comes from what else you say and, equally important in the long run, what you do. The original statement followed by words which don't match will create confusion. When followed by actions which are not congruent, the original statement of purpose is meaningless. The system generated from that will be based on some other goal than the stated one. It is not likely that the result will be worthy of being called a system.

Let's pursue the "cascade of outcomes" which might develop from the overriding purpose "To manage people for continuously improved results." Some of the supporting goals or outcomes might be:

- To keep cost increases below the rate of inflation

- For each manager to undertake at least one major project each year which will be an improvement over the preceding year, while maintaining performance in all other areas
- For employees to be developed at the fastest rate possible
- For our market share to increase each year and each department is expected to contribute to the sales effort
- For employees to be rewarded fairly for their contribution
- For new positions to be filled from the inside wherever possible

Developing such a list of outcomes will provide a framework — the details of the definition — to develop specific systems and sub-systems required to meet the organization's outcome. All sub-systems form necessary parts of that outcome. A well-formed outcome, one which is complete, provides a statement about each element which is a part of that outcome. The parameters to be included in the business will generally be profit, costs, sales, investment, personnel, technology, and industry position. Sub-categories may be considered so important as to be included in this main statement of what our outcome will look like. Part of that statement will include specifics related to the industry in most cases. Robert Townsend's stated outcome for Avis is a good example: "We want to become the fastest-growing company with the highest profit margins in the business of renting and leasing vehicles without drivers."

List of Outcomes Sets Framework for Systems and Sub-Systems

The external forms of business which fit the Avis statement of outcome are quite well-defined. What types of business are appropriate can be readily determined. Other questions, however, such as what investment is required, what personnel policies to pursue, and which expenditures are most appropriate are less obvious until further policy statements have been made. Instituting profit-sharing, developing piece-work standards, eliminating hourly pay are all alternatives which might lead toward the overall outcome.

A system develops by establishing an outcome or goal, determining what will have to happen, and then specifying precisely how it will be accomplished. In engineering design, the middle step is referred to as a black box; that is, we assume it can be done even though we don't yet know how. We then proceed with designing and return to the *how* later. We are now at the black-box stage. We know the outcome desired. The questions to ask are, "What functions will have to be performed to accomplish that result? What will have to happen?" The *who* and *how* come later. This order allows the complete system to be developed in such a way that interdependent parts will become obvious and the most elegant use of system elements or sub-systems can be accomplished.

What will have to happen for the system to be effective at our meta-level? That is, what are the requirements from outside the system. The purposes for setting it up require certain functions for fulfillment. First, we require a system of planning and converting those plans into goals specific enough to be guides for behavior and measurements of success — to meet the action and information or feedback requirements. Second, we need a system for translating those goals into action which will require a number of sub-systems. Third, the operating system must provide us with adequate feedback information for evaluation of the system and for adjustment of plans if necessary. These functions will provide the control of the system and will meet the basic systems requirements — establishing a goal, providing a mechanism for adjustment, and providing feedback.

Providing the Control of the System

We talked about a systems approach being employed at all levels of the organization to achieve the desired outcomes — at the level of planning and implementing a system, as well as later at the level of the operational system. If no Performance Management System exists, the first step will be to set the "outcome cascade" mentioned earlier and the outline of the systems functions above and then have the organization go through a process of translating those goals, determining what actions are necessary, and providing feedback on the results. This procedure is designed to highlight potential conflicts between interpretation of outcomes in an effective manner. The information provided will be of two types. One will be that generated by the lower levels in terms of opinions about goals or implementation. The other will be that the procedure will be a test of the processes to be used. The basic systems approach will be used to gather information about a basic systems approach.

The paradox experienced by most managers is that there must be a choice between creativity or control. How can there be control of creativity in an uncertain world? Creativity means that you don't know what will happen, doesn't it? The solution has just been presented. If the outcome and its subsidiary elements are clearly known and the functions or processes are specified, then the means of control have been developed. Anything which satisfies the outcomes and performs the necessary functions is within the bounds established. The maximum flexibility for finding creative ways to accomplish ends has been established within the boundaries necessary for control. The feeling of lack of control, which is shared by all levels of the organization from board of directors to direct labor, occurs when the first two elements aren't specified. To repeat — the outcome and its subsidiary elements must be clearly known, with functions and processes specified. Without this type of control, the top of the organization knows it can't get enough control information, let alone creativity. The bottom of the organization knows that it can't know what is appropriate behavior, what will be rewarded and what will not. With outcomes and functions clearly specified, each can have a reasonable feeling of certainty in an uncertain world. Can you expect to do better?

The above conditions apply to any system. A system for organizing human action has all of the same requirements and it has additional ones. People bring their own values and meaning to

Human Systems Have the Same Requirements — And More
the system. They introduce elements of choice and creativity which don't exist in other systems. They have purposes of their own. If this is so, it would appear, on the face of it, that a different system is required. How can the requirements of trust, fairness, and cooperation be combined with the requirements for an inanimate system? What needs to be different?

The answer is that there *is* no basic difference in systems terms. The requirements are the same. The way they are carried out will be different, according to the nature of the entities involved. Chemical or mechanical systems carry on their communication in pre-programmed terms which have no emotional requirements — but the *communication between them* is what binds them into a system.

Communication in the Human System

Human systems require much more complexity in the communication area. The communication channels are noisier and values or meaning are involved. The problem of values has been dealt with in the method for establishing an outcome cascade which can be used to coordinate the values of those involved. The problem of "noise" has not yet been considered. The "noise" in the communication channels means that much more is being communicated than is required by the system, as a system, and that the need-to-know information must be sorted from the rest. The other information must still be dealt with. The humans in the system have needs which must be taken care of if the system is to function. There is an analogy to the mechanical parts of a production system which must be oiled and otherwise treated appropriately if the machine is to continue functioning. Human requirements are needs of the subsystems which make up the higher system.

Value-laden words such as trust are related to the requirements of the system. Each individual is voluntarily part of the system and

The Value of the System Rests on Expectations Being Met

therefore hopes or expects that there can be a complementary benefit from the association. Trust is a result of expectations met. The expectations mainly consist of communicated plans, goals, and beliefs which the individual uses to predict actions. If these are communicated in good faith, but are poorly expressed, the subsequent actions will often seem

incongruent and generate mistrust. If they are communicated clearly, and in good faith, they will generate appropriate expectations and subsequent trust.

Commitment, cooperation, fairness are all equally dependent on good communication—assuming integrity. Commitment and cooperation are

One of the Needs of the System Is To Satisfy the Individuals in It

more obviously related to clear statements of goals and consistent actions than is fairness. Although individuals will bring various cultural values relating to fairness to the workplace, the overriding condition is that they are there voluntarily to perform a function for an organization. The determinant of what is "fair" will be in relation to the stated goals and implied terms of the contract. The first step in

gaining an employee is representing to them something about your organization which attracts them. Although the most obvious condition is money, it is seldom only that. Each individual received an impression about your organization and his or her place in it which suggested a relatively attractive match to that individual's situation. If goals are stated clearly at the start, then consistent action later will tend to be perceived as fair. The communication requirements are for creating the conditions which will produce the value alignment required for complementary functioning.

You will evaluate the proposed Performance Management System concepts based on how they fit your own beliefs, experience, and desired outcomes. How will others evaluate it? The same way. The system is being proposed for purposes of the organization, for the organization to achieve its goals. However, its acceptance will depend on how it satisfies the goals of the individuals involved. Its ultimate functioning depends on how it satisfies the goals of *all* affected individuals. Others suggest that a Performance Management System is the *only* kind of system where the values of the parts must be taken into account. I hope by now you disagree with that last statement. The nature of the parts, their values or needs, must be taken into account in *any* system. The only difference is the nature of the parts and their values and needs. Let's consider some of the different values of the different people involved before we proceed to more detailed consideration of the system.

The organizational needs are almost universal. Sales, profits, and growth have been mentioned. One of the unique outcomes which must be considered is that the organization is intended to outlast any of its parts. The system created is intended to be self-generative, in that it doesn't require the continued input of its creator, yet it is expected to continue its growth. Although any owner may liquidate it, it is not organized for that purpose. The enterprise will tend to bring less than its operating value on liquidation for this reason. Its organization was for continuous operation, not for building liquidation value.

The organization also must deal with the reality that individuals functioning in it have their own goals, which, for them, are overriding. All of these individuals will use their creative resources to achieve their own ends which may be contradictory to those of the organization. The basic choices confronting the organization are to develop controls which will ensure there are no harmful results or to create a system which utilizes this aspect of human nature.

Now, let's consider the desired outcomes of managers as a group. Their interests are to promote and maintain the values or outcomes of the organization by getting results through other *Looking at* people. They want to advance the outcomes of the *Managers'* organization and thereby advance their own careers. *Common and* They also have a normal complement of human *Uncommon* values such as integrity, desire for acknowledge- *Goals and* ment, wanting to be liked. Their values appear to *Values* be one with the organization. But are they? How varied might those "normal human values" be? Some exhibit a strong desire to be liked, while others don't seem to care much. The same is true for all the other values. Any one of them may override the organization's outcomes unless the context is appropriately and congruently defined. If a higher level manager is getting the overt results required by the organization but is playing off favorites with those under him, it may be more to a subordinate's benefit to meet personal goals than organizational ones.

Managers also require a feeling of control. In an organization where outcomes are clearly specified, their needs will complement each other. Where these outcomes are less clearly specified, many different reactions to the resultant insecurity will surface. Some will attempt to clarify the goals with those above them; some will guess and/or hide information. The list is as long as the individuals involved.

A major error in taking managers as a group is that they may have vastly different values depending on their level in the organization. I have been in many companies where the top management group ate in exclusive cafeterias and generally set themselves very much apart from the rest of the management group. It was not at all apparent that the "we/they" line was drawn between management and labor.

There are often many such lines in large organizations. Lower levels of management require different skills and will often exhibit different values, as a group, than higher levels. Some lower-

Values Differ According to Level

level managers would like to remain at the level they are at with direct contact with the non-management levels. There may also be a feeling that the upper management can or will install policies which will

affect the lives of lower levels without changing their own lives — sometimes to the extent of removing their jobs. The value of job security and its relative existence in the organization may cause managers to feel that their interests are antagonistic.

A manager is held responsible for events which happen outside of his or her direct control. Besides requiring clear outcomes and an adequate system, most managers could readily use some process information for themselves. How are they to carry out their functions? If results are inadequate, what adjustments are required to their own behavior? The activities expected of managers are often left to their own invention. And when there is not help forthcoming, the only solution which most managers have is more detailed information and controls and longer hours of work. A model for more effective communication would benefit many managers. With appropriate goals, systems, and training in process skills, the goals of most managers will be complementary to those of the organization. After all, the job a manager accepted was to realize the organizational goals through people.

Finally, what might motivate managers to actively implement and participate in a Performance Management System? Directives may get compliance but it takes more than that to create the conditions for cooperative effort. The requirements from the top management level will be using and involving these people in the system, providing training and active support, and building performance with the system into the planning and evaluation of each manager. A major source of motivation will be the system itself. A system which actually helps a manager accomplish his or her own objectives will soon be actively used if it can be done reasonably comfortably. As use of the system becomes more familiar, as contact with employees becomes easier and more effective, and as subordinate cooperation becomes obvious, managers will pursue the system with their own energy. If the system is just an exercise to conform to requirements or is too unfamiliar and uncomfortable to perform as it is supposed to be done, managers will soon drop it or convert it into a formality which will ease their own discomfort and not accomplish any useful objectives.

Acceptance of Performance Management Systems

When was the last time you seriously considered the benefits of your organizational system to the non-management people who work in it? Really put time and effort into that exercise? In my experience, the non-management people are seldom seriously considered until all decisions have been made. Only then, in the better organizations, is thought given to the people who are to do the work. By this time, the thought is, "How can we make this acceptable to the labor force?" Creating the conditions for active cooperation requires that the non-managers be considered in the design stages of a system. Right at the beginning ask, "How might this system benefit the non-management individuals in this organization?" I believe that there is no reason that an effective system can't benefit all concerned. Remember the earlier reference to alignment of interests? My assumption is that if the alignment doesn't take place, if there are not complementary benefits, then the system is not likely to be implemented effectively.

Let's consider the desired outcomes of the non-management people. Like the managers, they are a group with "normal human values" which vary widely from individual to individual. Like the managers, they have widely varying goals within their organizational roles. Some want to become managers and are attempting to make the goals of the organization important to them. Some want to be managers and are looking to other ways to accomplish that. Many don't want to be managers — ever.

Some of these people take pride in their work and just want to do a good job. Some want to do different work than they are presently doing. Some just don't seem to care about anything. If most of the people in your organization are at the end of this list, look to the conditions you are creating.

There are some important common elements which all of these individuals tend to value. One of the important ones is knowing what is expected of them. They are in a system which takes a significant part of their lives and provides rewards and punishment in the nature of pay and social approval. There are few of us who don't care about what is expected. Most of us want to know even if we choose not to conform. Notice I say "most of us."

Knowing What Is Expected and Where We Stand Are Basic Needs

The non-managers are people who, in their basic needs and desires, are not very different from anyone else. We each have unique ways of responding and of realizing our values, and our basic values are similar.

The other side of knowing what is expected is knowing where we stand. Another strongly and frequently expressed need is for information from managers about their opinions about subordinates. There are many cases of employees being surprised that they were fired. There are countless more where the evaluation, pay raise or lack of it, promotion or lack of it are complete surprises to the employee. It is a common desire to know how our own evaluation of how we are doing in relation to organization goals matches the manager's who has some power over us. Specific information about how we are evaluated will assist in changing our performance in positive ways. We like to have choice and we like to have control.

Non-management people need more than this if they are to experience those feelings of choice and control. They need assistance in reaching the expectations set for them. Knowing which areas need change or improvement leads to the "how." Many times all that is needed is to be able to be more specific about the goal and its relative value. Often, however, some coaching, training, guidance, negotiation, counseling, or problem-solving is required which takes active management support. A basic premise which I operate from is that *people — all of them — are doing the best job they know how under the conditions I have created.* What they are doing makes sense to them. If it doesn't make sense to me, I know that I am not aware of at least one of the important conditions within which the person is operating. If a job is being

289

done inadequately, what are the conditions which I have control over that might be changed for improvement? It may turn out to be outside of my control in individual cases but *the place I start to look is the conditions that I control.*

There is one other major value which should be considered. In a human system, one of the major elements is communication. It is valued for the direct information it carries to make the

Communication Means Information Supplied — and Contact

system function. It is also valued for the direct contact which it supplies. We all value social contact to some degree and a system which provides it will likely be more effective than one which doesn't. Remember the last time you got a recorded message rather than the live human you were expecting? The experience was less pleasant than if you had spoken to a living person, wasn't it? Even though the words might have been identical.

Any human system has built-in rewards and punishments, whether intended or not. The humans who are functioning parts of the system bring meaning and values with them and attach meaning to the actions required and to the system itself. A system which fails to take into account the needs of the individuals who carry it out conveys a meaning to those individuals. Any such system which requires communication will provide a set of positive motivators for rewarding appropriate communication and various devices to prevent incorrect or inadequate communication. Without awareness of this issue, many systems have built-in motivators for the wrong behaviors.

Human action is outcome-oriented. People will find ways to achieve their own outcomes within the system provided. Usually this is translated into "beating the system" and assumes antagonistic interests. An alignment of interests, a system which creates the conditions for complementary outcomes, will not require the effort at controls for compliance which the above assumption creates. Make it easier to *use* the system to achieve individual values than to beat the system for those values.

The System

The following material, and the other books in the series, will present a model for a Performance Management System which is flexible enough to accommodate the individual values of an organization. A model is not a theory, it is not the truth, it is merely the minimum number of elements required to accomplish an outcome. My models are behavioral

290

and provide for flexible and creative application. Based on the above, our Performance Management System will have three elements, Planning, Coaching, and Evaluation. *Planning* is the activity of translating the goals of the organization into continually higher quality as they move down through the organization, so that each individual knows what is expected. The process includes the creative resources of all involved to determine the best way to achieve the objectives. It requires a shared understanding of the tasks to be completed. Finally, it provides the information necessary to know whether plans can actually be accomplished and whether there are any contradictory parts which need to be changed.

Evaluation is the activity of closing the circle started by the planning of completion. Specific goals were set and relative importance was established. Evaluation is a formal feedback point but its use for feedback within the original objectives is limited by its lack of timeliness. Rather, it is intended to provide a summary to the employee of the results of his or her actions during the planning cycle under review. It will be more a formal confirmation of shared information generated during the planning cycle and its overall meaning. This part will also provide a formal place for information from the employee to be fed back up the organization, whether to the immediate boss or more generally for the organization. Finally, it will provide information to the system about the qualities and goals of the people in the system — the resources of the company.

Coaching is everything that needs to happen in between Planning and Evaluation. Here is the continuous contact and communication required to provide feedback and adjustment in real time. Without this part being done effectively, the *The Essential* Planning and Evaluation will serve little purpose and *Parts of* may even have a negative impact on the organi- *the System* zation. No system can be said to exist without a *Are Planning,* mechanism for adequately timed feedback and ad- *Coaching, and* justment. The tools involved include problem- *Evaluation* solving, fact-finding, negotiation, training, expert advice and, above all, regular, effective direct communication. Here is the sensory experience upon which managers base their "reality checks," the information which tells whether actions and information are reasonable or not. If the activities which come under the name Coaching have been done well, the Evaluation is little more than a formality, usually pleasant. The emphasis placed on evaluation skills is generally to reduce the discomfort which an untenable situation creates. It takes great skill to conduct an Evaluation in a reasonably cooperative manner when the Planning and Coaching prerequisites have not been performed first.

Let's turn our approach around and work from the desired outcome. Knowing the outcome we want, how will we know if we are going to achieve it? The first response is to know our outcome clearly and to know what functions will have to be performed or what events will have to take place for us to reach that outcome. From this, we develop a system which has been designed to achieve these results. The first assurance then is provided by the development of the system. The second is provided by feedback, checks, and controls, which tell us whether the system is functioning as intended.

The third requirement will be adequate information relating to the progress of the system toward the goals it was intended to achieve. In an uncertain world, any of the assumptions which went into development of the plans or the system may be changing. Information concerning progress will indicate any deviations which have not been met with adequate adjustment. The assumptions behind a plan are often more important than the plan itself. (Frank Hulswit of Arthur D. Little, Inc. has suggested that when planning is complete, the plan be thrown away and the assumptions retained.) In a complex world and with a complex system, each event will have many causes. The environment is changing in many directions at the same time. There are multiple points at which change can be made to respond to external events. Each part of a system is a sub-system which can be influenced by a variety of means. Continuous gathering of information is required.

The system of an organization is an ongoing process. It is like a living organism whose goal is survival and growth. The final result is never to be reached: it is a life intended to extend into infinity. *The Life of a System Is Always Developing, Changing* All Planning and all Evaluation are also ongoing processes. We divide them into convenient time periods to meet our own requirements of time and understanding. The processes are continuous at all levels and we formalize them periodically. What is there about reality that suggests we plan and evaluate annually? Generally, only requirements from some other system like the social/governmental one, which constitutes part of our environment. Our own way of understanding the world usually requires that we have some definite, if arbitrary, time divisions.

292

Within these time divisions we have definite goals to be reached. The nature of a system requires that we receive feedback in time to make adjustments to achieve the desired outcome. Although the final result in these terms is going to be reached — at least that is hoped and expected — the end-result is not feedback. The end-result *is*. Once you have reached the end of the time period, you have either achieved what you intended or not. It is too late to use that information for corrective behavior.

Let's return to the original question: How will you know if you are going to achieve your desired outcome? The answers need to be known before you can design the system. Before you can feed content into that system, they need to be known even more precisely. What functions need to be performed? What will the results be if they are? And if they are not? What will be happening along the way to indicate whether it is time to do something different? What does that "something different" need to be? Despite the outcome-oriented nature of business, my experience is that the answers to these questions are lacking to a significant degree. They are lacking from the level of the technical machine operator to the level of the president and board of directors.

The process has already been indicated for gathering the information needed for this level of planning and systems creation. Let's review it
Reviewing with some examples and specific questions. The
How To Gather starting point is a broad statement of the purpose or
Information desired outcome of the organization. This will likely
for Planning include an approach, an essence, the spirit of the
and Creating enterprise, as well as some more objective represen-
the System tations. An example from Newport News Ship-
building: "We will build good ships — at a profit if we can, at a loss if we must — but always good ships." The business and the spirit of the organization are indicated by that statement. Another example from the Sherwin-Williams Company: "To construct and operate a safe, clean, efficient plant in Richmond, Kentucky, which will produce the highest-quality automotive refinish paint in the world and keep itself ahead of the industry in competitiveness and profitability." These statements are close to concepts of "motherhood" unless they are supported by further specification and action. They may also lead to bankruptcy if not more precisely translated.

This first low-quality statement will be expanded by a set of outcomes for each of the major components of the business. (In this context, remember, *low quality* simply means that the word or phrase could refer to many different things or actions in reality. It refers to variety and allows for potentially different understandings.) Each of these will be higher quality than the previous one in that they will refer individually to different components of the system. The major areas may include people, profit, quality, competitive position, technology and investment.

Each of these statements will be developed to higher and higher quality until each unit or function of the system has clear goals. The first, low-quality statement at each level is the function it

Always Focus on Higher- Level Goals

will serve towards the higher level goals. The test of validity is the answer to the question, "How does this contribute to the higher level goals?" In the Sherwin-Williams example, the statement for "jobs" was, "We will develop a safe, clean and healthful working climate that provides challenging and meaningful work with the opportunity for personal growth and development." This contributes to the goals for that particular operation by defining a "safe, clean environment" and providing a type of working conditions which will encourage quality and profitability by creating the conditions for individual motivation.

The next higher-quality statements will come from answering the question, "What would be happening if we were providing that type of environment?" or "What will it require to create those conditions?" Some of the next level of outcomes generated from this type of questioning in the Sherwin-Williams example include:

Plant Management: Manner that demonstrates good communications, respect for people, honesty.

Compensation: A fair and equitable compensation system that will reward all plant personnel on the basis of job knowledge, performance against goals/objective, and training skills.

Training: A day-to-day activity in which each plant employee participates as a learner and as a teacher.

Work Groups: The plant will be operated by teams and all team members are required to learn all the jobs in that team's department.

Each level of higher quality specifies how that outcome will be reached within the context of the previously specified outcomes. Notice that we are not yet to an operational level. Although far more specific than our original statement of desired outcome, we are still at fairly low-quality statements. The test is, "Can there be more than one meaning for this goal?" Some are getting close. The statements under Training and Work

Working
Toward
High-Quality
Specification
Groups are possibly ready for quantification, time constraints, resource allocations, and the operational details for implementation. Others, such as Plant Management and Compensation, are not. If the statements contain adjectives or value states, they need further clarification. These words need to be put into operational or behavioral terms. Respect for people and honesty can be interpreted in many ways; they can cover a multitude of behaviors. Even lower quality is in the phrase "fair and equitable." Wars have been fought over the meaning or interpretation of such words. The interpretation of Sherwin-Williams was a combination of annual merit increase, "earn-and-learn," and a modified Scanlon Plan.

Each level must be able to answer the question, What will I need to do to achieve those results? And this has to happen before each level can be satisfied that the outcome is stated in high-enough-quality terms— high-enough quality for appropriate action and feedback to get results, high-enough quality to meet the needs of the system.

The outcomes must not contain negatives. We don't want outcomes which are not adequately specific. You can't *not* do something. Each negative statement contains a minimum of informa-
State the
Outcomes
in Positive
Terms
tion. The world is infinitely varied, and eliminating one of the options leaves a great deal to be specified. There are a few occasions when we want people not to do a certain thing — when anything else would be preferable — to such an extent that we need to specify it. Usually, we want people to do a particular thing or achieve a particular result. By telling you what I *don't* want, I leave a variety of choices open to you which will include many which I also don't want. By telling you what I do want, you will have the most exact definition appropriate to the circumstances.

Negatives should seldom be used as measures of outcomes either, certainly not the only measures. They can be useful indicators. A lack of complaints seems a desirable goal. But wait. There are many ways to achieve this goal, at least some of which will be prohibitively expensive or otherwise defeat the purpose intended. The desired outcome is more appropriately stated in a positive way such as, "We want our product to be the highest quality on the market based on failure rates and to maintain that leadership." Lack of complaints may indicate success or it may reflect a loss of customers or hide a trend. As an outcome, it is inadequate; as a measure, it is limited.

295

The highest-quality information is sensory-grounded, that is, direct experience — what can be seen, heard, felt, tasted, or smelled. The vast majority of business experience falls into the first three sense categories. Our goals and outcomes should be capable of being stated in sensory-grounded terms. Whether or not they need to be so highly specified depends on the level of the organization and the use to which they will be put. Try these alternate ways of explaining what you want to a subordinate.

First, in your own words, say something to the first individual such as:

> I want you to conduct employee evaluations which are fair and encourage two-way communication.

Second, say the following to a second individual of comparable ability:

> When you conduct employee evaluations, I want you to read this memo before the session and say something like this to the employee before you start the session: "We're here to do the annual performance evaluation as I mentioned to you last week. There's a procedure that we'll follow which I'll outline for you in a minute. The purpose of the evaluation is to review what's happened over the past year, to get your opinions about what we can do better next year, to find out what the company can do to make your job easier, and to find out what goals you have for your future here. We'll use the standard company procedure to make sure that we accomplish all of that and to assure you that you have ample opportunity to have your say." If you start your interview with this kind of introduction, I think it'll help you to have better two-way communication with your people.

The second way, while not requiring a word-for-word reading of an introduction, indicates to your subordinate how to conduct a "fair evaluation with good two-way communication." It is an example of providing some sensory-grounded information and demonstrates that it applies to everyone, not just to first-line supervisors or the labor force. Done effectively with lower levels of management, this should develop promotable people with high-level skills.

Returning to outcomes, what are the experiences, in sensory-grounded terms, which would let you know that the outcome had been successfully achieved? This question needs to be

Learning How To Recognize Achieving Your Outcome answered before we can establish, in the same terms, how we would know if we were heading in the right direction at the appropriate speed. If you get stuck on this question, as many people I meet at the heads of businesses do, here is another ap-

296

proach: How do you know that employees are not reaching their outcomes now? How do you know their performance is unsatisfactory? How do you know that the training I have to offer might change the situation? The answers to these questions begin to produce higher-quality representations of the desired state.

Any low-quality starting place will do. Say the answer is, "My managers could motivate their people better." I then ask them how they would know if it was happening. Often I lead them to some sensory-grounded information by asking something like, "What would it look like if the managers could motivate their people better? What would be happening that was different?" I continue with this line until I have a clear understanding of what they would see, until I know what activities would be taking place and what kind of things were being said. The final piece will be information about the internal state of the manager making the request and the events which he or she will hear, see, or feel which produce that state.

Let's get higher quality about some of the things which would be included in each category. First, what kind of things might you see to know that your outcome had been achieved? Well, you might look at a financial report and see that the numbers matched or bettered your expectations (budget). You would remember that you had observed body postures and interactions between people that reflected a feeling of good will. You could look around as you toured the facilities and notice that they were bright, neat, and efficient-looking. You could see that your employees were moving actively and remember that you saw groups of employees helping each other out. Or, in the categories mentioned, you saw other things which suggest problems to you. *You would know they had been solved when what you saw matched what you wanted.*

The Signs of Success Are What You See and Hear

What you can expect to see is a mixture of good and bad in each category, varying by individual. Some of the reports aren't so good; some of the individuals don't appear to be cooperating; some places are dirty, and the people in them don't seem to be motivated. Let's return to the managers who can't motivate their people. How do you know? Maybe they have been heads of sales of various branches and each time sales in their areas has dropped and then picked up as they were replaced. Maybe you see that various people are leaving the organization when these particular managers arrive on the scene. Maybe you observe their posture and manner when they deal with their staff and are aware that no one could operate effectively from that position.

What kind of things might you *hear* for you to know that your outcome has been achieved? Reports again. The content of verbal reports will provide many indicators. These reports are the obvious source of information but they are seldom adequate sources. A report never includes the context and is limited to particular time spans. What else might you hear? You will hear, including *overhear*, complaints or compliments. You will hear ways of speaking which indicate taking responsibility or placing blame. You will hear greeting and pleasantries or no human sound where some should be, or abusive language. All verbal communications will carry meaning in the tones and volume that are used. There will be ways of responding which are helpful, or questioning sessions that sound like information being extracted from a spy. The clatter of machinery and other activity will be a signal of the state of things. The manager who is failing to motivate people may be inflexible and directive and give direction in an unpleasant voice. The words he or she chooses may be strictly factual and fail to create the conditions necessary for commitment and motivation.

Summary

This same kind of information described above relates to the outcomes in terms of the processes being used. You can see and hear whether the actions and communication are of a style which you believe will produce the results you desire. Remember, the results are the total of what is happening in your organization, not just the numbers which signify quantitative output. Managers who can maintain rapport with their people and get cooperative effort and produce results look, sound, and act much differently from the authoritarian managers who get prompt but uncreative results with very little growth or employee involvement.

In most businesses, at most levels of organization, what one might feel externally is not a significant part of the information to be used. What is significant and is generally not overtly talked about are your internal feelings. The motivator for action and change is your internal states. Right now, as you remember what your organization is like—as you review the sights and activities and recall the sounds—what is the feeling you get? If the feelings are positive, your organization is healthy. You will provide training and make change as part of a continuing program of satisfactory growth. If you get a knot in your stomach or just sense a feeling of unease, you will also feel that you want to make a change without necessarily knowing what that change should be. If part of your outcome is to have an organization with people who are vibrant, energetic, and productive, you need to know what that would look like, what conditions are required for that to happen, and then to go out and create those conditions. They all arise from the actions and communications of people which are observable in action—which can be experienced.

We all seek a feeling of control. We seek it in different ways but the positive cultural value of such words as confidence, satisfaction, self-esteem indicate the general desire for control or positive influence. The final way to a sensory-grounded description of desired outcomes is through these feelings. When the answer I get to the earlier questions is, "I would know when we got there. It would feel right," I respond by asking, "What would you see or hear around you right now to have that feeling?"

The exciting challenge facing executives today is to develop systems and the communication skills to match to convert their ideals into reality. We all know, at some level, that our organizations and the people in them are operating at a fraction of their potential. We all have dreams and goals. Systems theory and communication technology are combining to provide the means to realize values. The ultimate requirement is to recognize our commitment and evoke it in others.

Recommended Reading List

Bandler, Richard and John Grinder. *The Structure of Magic I & II*. Palo Alto, CA: Science and Behavior, Inc., 1975.
An outline of the linguistic base for effective information gathering which is easy to read. Also covers various non-verbal communication techniques and other verbal patterns. This book was written for therapists but its application to business is apparent with a little work.

Bandler, Richard and John Grinder. *Frogs Into Princes*. Moab, UT: Real People Press, 1979.
Excerpts from various workshops which give a clear picture of their work in an entertaining manner. Easy to read. Mostly examples from therapy.

Cornuelle, Richard. *Demanaging America*. New York, NY: Random House, Inc., 1976.
A well-written book which points to the weaknesses of our current management approaches and suggests a route out. Provocative reading.

Dilts, Robert. *Neuro Linguistic Programming*. Cupertino, CA: Meta Publications, 1980.
A detailed presentation of all of the basic material of Neuro Linguistic Programming. It is difficult to write effectively about the complexity of face-to-face communication. This book succeeds although there are places where it is difficult to grasp the application. Contains business examples.

Erickson, Milton. *My Voice Will Go With You*. New York, NY: W. W. Norton, Co., 1982.
A collection of "teaching tales" from the master of communication and metaphor. The stories support the ideas of respectful personal change through coaching.

——. *The Collected Papers*. New York, NY: Irvington Publishers, 1982.
Fascinating study of how to recognize the world of others and communicate with them in an appropriate way for change. These are technical works designed for therapists and any serious student of communication should read them.

Gilbert, Thomas F. *Human Competence*. New York, NY: McGraw-Hill Book Co., 1978.
Presents a clear and easily used way for determining excellent performance and providing the material for coaching. A systematic way of discovering what needs to be done.

301

Juran, J. M. *Quality Planning and Analysis.* New York, NY: McGraw-Hill Book Co., 1964.
All you need to know to begin the serious challenge of introducing quality. Supports the needs for different performance systems, ways of managing and communications. Shows the place of those that do the work within the system.

Peters, Thomas J. and Robert H. Watterman, Jr. *In Search of Excellence.* New York, NY: Harper & Row, Inc., 1982.
The basic values of continuously successful companies presented in a readable style. The basic outcomes to be controlled could be arrived at from this book and supported by the Performance Management System.

Symonds, Curt. *Basic Financial Management.* New York, NY: American Management Assoc., Inc., 1970.
A simple outline of the basics of financial management. The simplicity is deceptive. It tends to hide the power of the material which is presented.

———. *A Design for Business Intelligence.* New York, NY: American Management Assoc., Inc., 1971.

Townsend, Robert. *Up the Organization.* New York, NY: Fawcett Books Group, 1978.
An irreverant look at management. Highly entertaining and thought-provoking. He would probably throw out this system along with everything else he discards.

Other Sources

Productivity. A monthly newsletter. P.O. Box 3457, Stamford, CT 06905.
The latest in techniques, systems, production equipment, and culture which supports productivity. About equally balanced between studying the Japanese and learning of current American companies.

Werner Erhard & Assoc. Workshops. 765 California St., San Francisco, CA 94108.
Consulting for the transformation of organizations and communications training for business. I also highly recommend the EST Training.

Related Resources from
Metamorphous Press

■ Books

The Challenge of Excellence
Learning The Ropes of Change
Scout Lee, Ed.D. & Jan Summers, Ed.D.
ISBN 1-55552-004-9 PB

Magic of NLP Demystified
A Pragmatic Guide To Communication And Change
Byron Lewis & Frank Pucelik
ISBN 1-55552-017-0 PB

The Phone Book
Breakthrough Neurolinguistic Phone Skills For Profit And Enlightenment
Richard Zarro & Peter Blum
ISBN 1-55552-011-1 PB

The Professional A.C.T.: Acting Communication Technique
Public Speaking Know-How For Presenting The Confident, Relaxed
Image You Need
Mary Stark
ISBN 1-55552-033-2 PB

Sales: The Mind's Side
James Robertson
ISBN 1-55552-006-5 PB

Sales On The Line
Meeting The Business Needs of the 90's Through Phone Partnering
Sharon Drew Morgen
ISBN 1-55552-047-2 PB

■ **Audio Tapes**

NLP Made Easy Series
Tape 1—How To Build Rapport
Tim Hallbom & Suzi Smith
ISBN 0-943920-10-8
Tape 2—Understanding Communication Styles
Byron Lewis
ISBN 0-943920-05-1

Exclusively Distributed by Metamorphous Press:

Making The Message Clear
How To Master The Business Communication Tools That Direct Productivity, Excellence and Power
James Eicher
ISBN 1-55552-048-0 PB

Precision
A New Approach To Communication
Michael McMaster & John Grinder
ISBN 1-55552-049-9 PB

These are only a few of the titles we offer, and new resources are added regularly. Prices and availability may change without notice. Call or write us for a current catalog, information, prices, and shipping and handling charges.

Metamorphous Press

P.O. Box 10616   Portland, OR 97210-0616
TEL (503) 228-4972
FAX (503) 223-9117

Call TOLL FREE
when ordering products or catalogs
1-800-937-7771

Metamorphous Press

P.O. Box 10616 Portland, OR 97210
(503) 228-4972 FAX (503) 223-9117

Metamorphous Press is a publisher of books and other media providing resources for personal growth and positive change. MP publishes leading-edge ideas that help people strengthen their unique talents and discover that we are responsible for our own outcomes.

Many of our titles center around Neurolinguistic Programming (NLP). NLP is an exciting, practical, and powerful communication model that has been able to connect observable patterns of behavior and communication and the processes that underlie them.

Metamorphous Press provides selections in many useful subject areas such as communication, health and fitness, education, business and sales, therapy, selections for young persons, and other subjects of general and specific interest. Our products are available in fine bookstores around the world.

Our distributors for North America are:

Baker & Taylor	M.A.P.S.	Pacific Pipeline
Bookpeople	Moving Books	Sage Book Distributors
Ingram	New Leaf	the distributors
Inland Book Co.		

For those of you overseas, we are distributed by:

Airlift (UK, Western Europe)
Specialist Publications (Australia)

New selections are added regularly and availability and prices change, so call for a current catalog or to be put on our mailing list. If you have difficulty finding our products in your favorite bookstore, or if you prefer to order by mail, we will be happy to make our books and other products available to you directly. Please call or write us at:

Metamorphous Press
P.O. Box 10616 Portland, OR 97210-0616
TEL (503) 228-4972
FAX (503) 223-9117

TOLL FREE ORDERING
1-800-937-7771

METAMORPhOUS
AdvANCEd
PRoducT
SERViCEs

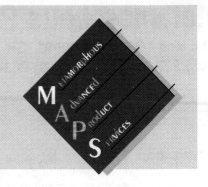

METAMORPhOUS AdvANCEd PRoducT SERViCEs (M.A.P.S.) is the master distributor for Metamorphous Press and other fine publishers.

M.A.P.S. offers books, cassettes, videos, software, and miscellaneous products in the following subjects; Bodywork & Fitness (including Alexander Technique and Rolfing), Business & Sales; Children; Education; Enneagram; General Interest; Health & Wellness; Hypnosis; Music/Arts; Personal Development; Psychology (including Neurolinguistics); Relationships/Sexuality; and the work of Virginia Satir.

If you cannot find our books at your favorite bookstore, you can order directly from **M.A.P.S.**

TO ORDER OR REQUEST A FREE CATALOG:

MAIL   M.A.P.S.
P.O. Box 10616
Portland, OR 97210-0616

FAX   (503) 223-9117

CALL   Toll free 1-800-233-MAPS
(6277)

ALL OTHER BUSINESS:

CALL   (503) 228-4972